CPCU 520

Insurance Operations

Review Notes

About This Study Aid

This guide was developed to help you study the course material and prepare for the examination. Each assignment is outlined according to the Educational Objectives (EOs). As a study aid, this material is not intended to present all of the information found in the textbook(s), course guide, or online modules published by The Institutes. Instead, we strongly encourage you to use this study aid to supplement the course materials.

Some EOs involve the application of skills in a case study or situation. The material presented provides information to help you acquire the skill, but cases or scenario situations are not provided within this material. You may find such cases and scenarios within the textbook(s), course guide, or online modules.

1st Edition • 1st Printing • December 2010

ISBN: 978-0-89463-435-2

Dependent people need others to get what they want. Independent people can get what they want through their own efforts. **Interdependent** *people combine their own efforts with the efforts of others to achieve their greatest success.*

—Stephen Covey

...and Achieve
Your Greatest
Success.

The Institutes ™

Proven Knowledge. Powerful Results.

Time Savers

We know your life is busy, and that's why we've developed some tips to help you make the most of your study time. By following these tips, you'll study more effectively—and couldn't we all use a little more free time?

To be time-efficient, we recommend that you:

Order your copy of *How to Prepare for Institutes Exams* or download it free from our Web site. This booklet will give you helpful study and exam-taking tips.

Create a plan for study time. A study schedule will help you identify up front the time you will need to study the course and the dates when you plan to study. Simply use the worksheet that follows to enter this information and, when you're finished, block out those dates on your calendar. This is an investment in yourself!

Start studying right away. If you wait to start studying, you create a time crunch near exam time. Getting a strong start on your studying keeps you on track for the exam date and may allow you a week or two to review all the assignments together.

Decide how you learn best. The Institutes offer a variety of study materials to help you learn in the way that you feel most comfortable. Read the textbook or complete the modules for the full course content. Practice what you're learning with the course guide or Knowledge Check questions. Use the flash cards to remember Key Words and Phrases. Or, use the SMART Online Practice Exam product, if available for this course, to test your knowledge. Use the best combination of study tools for your learning style to help you retain your new knowledge.

Consider joining a class. Some people learn best with the structure and interaction of a formal class. We offer both online classes and public classes. The online classes combine the flexibility of self-study with the support of a knowledgeable instructor. Public classes are in-person classes offered by third-party vendors in your area. If structure helps you maximize your use of time, choose a class today. See our Web site for more information about either of these class options.

Call us if you need assistance. We believe in helping you achieve powerful results. This means supplying prompt answers to your questions, online counseling, and telephone and e-mail Customer Service. Call us with any questions at (800) 644-2101, or send an email to customerservice@TheInstitutes.org.

Good luck with your course!

Study Timetable

To help you make the best use of your time, keep the following suggestions in mind as you create your study timetable:

- **Allocate study time conservatively; give yourself ample time to digest the material.**
- **Limit your study time to two hours or less on a given day.**
- **Vary the types of study tools you use, for maximum retention.**
- **Study when you have unexpected free time.**
- **Keep to your study timetable to avoid last-minute "cramming."**
- **Enter this study timetable into your daily calendar.**
- **Evaluate your timetable periodically, and make adjustments as necessary.**

The Sample Study Timetable below shows what one student's study plan might look like using the textbook and course guide. A student taking online courses will be able to allocate study time based on the length of each module. Take 15 minutes to fill out your own Study Timetable. Doing this will ensure that you have carefully considered the dates and amounts of time you will need for each assignment. Make the most of your study time by making it efficient!

Assignment # and Title (From Course Guide)	Assignment Notes	Study Time	Study Dates	Activities	Assignment End Date
Assignment 1, Risk	Important foundation concepts. Will read carefully.	45 min. / 45 min. / 30 min.	5/9 / 5/10 / 5/11	Read Text / Complete Course Guide / Practice Exam CD-ROM	5/12
Assignment 2, Ethics	I am familiar with some of this content from prior ethics training.	30 min. / 1 hour	5/15 / 5/17	Read Review Notes / Complete Course Guide	5/19
Assignment 3, Managing Risk	A number of key words in this assignment	1 hour / 1 hour	5/23 / 5/24	Read Text / Practice Flash Cards	5/26
Assignment 15, Allocating Costs		1 hour	8/15		8/17

Exam Date: Sept. 9, 2011

Study Timetable

Exam Date: _____

Assignment # and Title (From Course Guide)	Assignment Notes	Study Time	Study Dates	Activities	Assignment End Date

Overview of Insurance Operations

1

Educational Objective 1

Explain how insurers have organized to provide property-casualty insurance.

Key Points:

Property-casualty insurers can be classified in these four ways:

- Legal form of ownership
- Place of incorporation
- Licensing status
- Insurance distribution systems and channels

Study Tips

Have you contacted The Institutes to schedule an exam?

A. Legal Form of Ownership

  1. Proprietary insurers

    These include stock insurers, Lloyd's of London and American Lloyds, and insurance exchanges.

    a. Stock insurers

      Stock insurers are the most prevalent type of proprietary insurer in the United States. These insurers are owned by their stockholders.

- By purchasing stock in a for-profit insurer, stockholders supply the capital needed to form the insurer or the additional capital the insurer needs to expand its operations.
- Stockholders expect to receive a return on their investment in the form of stock dividends, increased stock value, or both.
- Stockholders have the right to elect the board of directors, which has the authority to control the insurer's activities.
- The board of directors creates and oversees corporate goals and objectives and appoints a chief executive officer (CEO) to carry out the insurer's operations and implement the programs necessary to operate the company.

b. Lloyd's of London (Lloyd's)
- Lloyd's is technically not an insurer. However, it does provide the physical and procedural facilities for its members to write insurance.
- It is a marketplace, similar to a stock exchange. The members are investors who hope to earn a profit from the insurance operations.
- Today, a declining proportion of Lloyd's accounts are underwritten and secured by individuals.
- A larger portion of Lloyd's members today are corporations, and the liability of each of these members is limited to the amount that the member agrees to write.
- Lloyd's provides coverage for many unusual or difficult loss exposures and underwrites much of the global marine and aviation insurance.

c. American Lloyds
- These associations are smaller than Lloyd's of London, and most are domiciled in Texas because of the favorable regulatory climate.
- Members (called underwriters) of American Lloyds are not liable beyond their investment in the association.

d. Insurance exchanges

An insurance exchange is a proprietary insurer similar to Lloyd's because it acts as an insurance marketplace.
- Exchange members underwrite any insurance or reinsurance purchased on the exchange.
- Members can be individuals, partnerships, or corporations, and they have limited liability.
- Members belong to syndicates and delegate day-to-day operations to the syndicate manager.
- Member syndicates operate as separate businesses that focus on a particular group of loss exposures.

2. Cooperative insurers

This type of insurer is owned by its policyholders and is usually formed to provide insurance protection to its policyholders at minimum cost.

a. Mutual insurers

Mutual insurers constitute the largest number of cooperative insurers and provide low-cost insurance to their policyholders, who are the owners of the insurer.
- Because a traditional mutual insurer issues no common stock, it has no stockholders.

- Its policyholders have voting rights similar to those of a stock company's stockholders, and, like stockholders, they elect the insurer's board of directors that appoints officers to manage the company.
- Some profit is retained to increase surplus, and excess profit is usually returned to policyholders as dividends.
- Mutual insurers include some large national insurers and many regional insurers.

b. Reciprocal insurance exchanges

A reciprocal insurance exchange, also simply called a reciprocal, consists of a series of private contracts in which subscribers, or members of the group, agree to insure each other.

- The term "reciprocal" comes from the reciprocity of responsibility of all subscribers to each other.
- Each member of the reciprocal is both an insured and an insurer. Because the subscribers are not experts in running an insurance operation, they contract with an individual or organization to operate the reciprocal.
- This manager is called an attorney-in-fact. The subscribers empower the attorney-in-fact to handle all the duties necessary to manage the reciprocal.

c. Fraternal organizations

Fraternal organizations resemble mutual companies, but they combine a lodge or social function with their insurance function. They write primarily life and health insurance.

d. Other cooperatives

Cooperative insurers include captive insurers, risk retention groups, and purchasing groups.

- When a business organization or a group of affiliated organizations forms a subsidiary company to provide all or part of its insurance, the subsidiary is known as a captive insurer, or captive. This arrangement is sometimes referred to as "formalized self-insurance."
- Captive insurers can take several forms, and their ultimate purpose is to fund the losses of their owners.
- Some states have enacted legislation to facilitate the formation and operation of captive insurers within their jurisdictions, while others do not permit the formation of captives.

- Legislation has also allowed risk retention groups and purchasing groups to form. These cooperatives can be stock companies, mutuals, or reciprocal exchanges. They are usually organized so that a limited group or type of insured is eligible to purchase insurance from them.

3. Other insurers

Other insurers are the third type of insurer in the legal form of ownership classification.

  a. Pools

Pools consists of several insurers, not otherwise related, that join together to insure loss exposures that individual insurers are unwilling to insure.

- These loss exposures present the potential for losses that either occur too frequently or are too severe (catastrophic) for individual insurers to accept the risk.
- Pools can be formed either voluntarily or to meet statutory requirements.
- A syndicate pool issues a joint (or syndicate) policy to the insured, listing all pool members and specifying the part of the insurance for which each member is responsible.
- Under a reinsurance pool, one member of the pool issues the policy to the insured, and the other pool members reinsure an agreed proportion of the policy's insured loss exposures.
- Many pools are required by law. Most states have pooling arrangements to provide auto liability insurance and workers compensation coverage.

  b. Government insurers

Private insurers do not provide some types of insurance. Some loss exposures, such as catastrophic flooding, do not possess the characteristics that make them commercially insurable, but a significant need for protection against the potential losses still exists. Both the federal government and state governments have developed insurance programs to meet specific insurance needs of the public.

- One of the largest property insurance programs the federal government offers is the National Flood Insurance Program (NFIP), which is administered by the Federal Insurance Administration under the Federal Emergency Management Agency (FEMA).

- The federal government provides a government "back-stop" insurance program through the original Terrorism Risk Insurance Act (TRIA) of 2002. TRIA ensures that commercial property owners can obtain reasonable and predictably priced terrorism coverage by specifying that the federal government will share the risk of loss from foreign terrorist acts.
- To make liability insurance available to almost all licensed drivers, all states have implemented automobile insurance plans through a residual market.
- In most states, Fair Access to Insurance Requirements (FAIR) plans make property insurance more readily available to property owners who have exposures to loss over which they have no control.

B. Place of Incorporation

1. Insurance is regulated at the state level. Therefore, a domestic insurer is incorporated within a specific state or, if not incorporated, is formed under the laws of that state.
2. Reciprocal insurance exchanges are the only unincorporated insurers permitted in most states. Insurance exchanges and Lloyds organizations are permitted under law in only a few states.
3. A foreign insurer is a domestic insurer that is licensed to do business in states other than its domiciled state.
4. Alien insurers are incorporated or formed in another country.

C. Licensing Status

1. An insurer's state license authorizes it to sell insurance in the state.
2. A license indicates that the insurer has met the state's minimum standards for financial strength, competence, and integrity.
3. A licensed insurer (admitted insurer) is an insurer that has been granted a license to operate in a particular state.
4. An unlicensed insurer (nonadmitted insurer) has not been granted a license to operate in a given state.
5. Producers for primary insurance (except surplus lines brokers) are licensed to place business only with admitted insurers. Licensing status is also important for purposes of reinsurance.

D. Insurance Distribution Systems and Channels

   1. Insurers use many types of distribution systems and channels, designed to meet their particular marketing objectives. Most insurers use one or more of these insurance distribution systems:

      a. Independent agency and brokerage marketing system

      b. Direct writer marketing system

      c. Exclusive agency marketing system

   2. Insurers also use these common distribution channels to promote products and services as well as to communicate with existing and prospective insureds:

      a. The Internet

      b. Call centers

      c. Direct response

      d. Group marketing

      e. Financial institutions

Educational Objective 2

Describe the major goals of an insurer.

Key Points:

Senior managers of insurers seek to meet the goals established by the insurer's owners. However, insurers' goals pose some challenges that other organizations do not face in meeting their goals. Insurers have five major goals:

A. Earn a Profit

1. The profit goal is most commonly associated with proprietary, or for-profit, insurers.

2. Insurers earn money by charging insureds a "premium" for the insurance contract (policy).

3. To be able to meet the contract terms through the payment of covered losses and to meet regulatory requirements, insurers invest the portion of premiums that is not needed to pay their operating expenses (called surplus).

4. The return on investments generates additional income to be further invested to pay future covered losses, to expand the insurer's operations, or to be returned to the insurer's investors.

5. A proprietary insurer must earn a profit to provide a return on the investment made by the individuals and institutions that purchased the insurer's stock (stockholders).

6. Funds from policyholders (usually premiums) are one source of capital for cooperative insurers. Growth of surplus derived from underwriting operations is another.

7. Under certain circumstances, a cooperative insurer can obtain additional capital by borrowing funds using surplus notes.

8. Increased premium volume through marketing and underwriting performance provides greater profits for an insurer.

B. Meet Customer Needs

Attaining this goal involves determining what customers need and what price is competitive and then finding the best way to satisfy those needs.

1. Insurance customers expect prompt service and timely responses to inquiries.

2. The insurer must provide quick and professional assistance, which requires well-trained, customer-focused personnel and automated support systems.

3. Meeting customers' needs can often conflict with the profit goal.

4. In some cases, offering high-quality insurance at a price that the customer can afford may not generate the profit that the insurer needs to attract and retain capital.

5. Providing training, operating automated call centers, and maintaining current information technology can also become costly and can conflict with achieving the profit goal in the near term.

C. Comply With Legal Requirements

    1. Being a responsible corporate citizen dictates legal compliance.

    2. Lack of compliance can lead to fines and penalties.

    3. One of an insurer's greatest responsibilities is compliance with state regulations.

    4. The insurance industry is highly regulated, and the expenses associated with compliance can be substantial.

D. Diversify Risk

    1. Diversifying risk is an emerging goal for property-casualty insurers because of the increased catastrophe losses that have occurred over the past decade.

    2. A high concentration of losses in a geographic area highlights individual insurers' need to spread risk over a wider geographic area and over multiple types of insurance business, such as property-casualty insurance.

E. Fulfill Their Duty to Society

    1. All corporations are obligated to promote the well-being of society.

    2. Many insurers contribute funds, and sometimes they volunteer employees' time to medical, educational, and other public service organizations.

    3. Many insurers establish employee benefit plans that provide for the current and future well-being of their employees.

    4. Benefits such as medical insurance, disability insurance, retirement plans, employee assistance programs, and numerous other benefits help employees and retirees to use their personal resources to meet their needs and help to minimize the use of public resources.

    5. While fulfilling their duty to society through philanthropic activities and employee benefit programs, insurers maintain a well-qualified, knowledgeable staff, which promotes the profit and customer needs goals.

Educational Objective 3

Describe the internal and external constraints that impede insurers from achieving their major goals.

Key Points:

In achieving their major goals, insurers face numerous constraints.

A. Internal Constraints

Several internal constraints might prevent an insurer from meeting all of its goals. Some of these constraints are imposed only in certain circumstances or only on certain types of insurers:

1. Efficiency

   a. An insurer's lack of efficiency may be caused by poor management, insufficient capital, lack of information technology, an inability to adapt to change, or other causes.

   b. Inefficient insurers are at a disadvantage when competing with efficient ones.

   c. Inefficiency, particularly in information technology and customer service, can prevent an insurer from adequately meeting its customers' needs.

   d. In extreme cases, inefficiency can lead to insolvency and a consequent failure to meet legal and regulatory goals.

2. Expertise

   a. The insurance business is complex, and considerable expertise is required to successfully operate an insurer.

   b. Lack of expertise could prevent an insurer from making a profit or meeting customers' needs, or it could eventually cause the insurer to fail to attain any of its goals.

   c. The insurer should make sure that the current staff has the skills needed to perform their jobs adequately.

3. Size

An insurer's size affects its ability to meet its goals.

   a. A small insurer has more challenges than a large insurer in terms of available resources.

   b. Large insurers can take advantage of economies of scale and may have more financial resources to update technology or reach additional markets.

   c. One advantage for a small insurer is that it can be more nimble, allowing it to respond quickly to an emerging trend or a change in the external insurance environment.

4. Financial resources

   a. When financial resources become strained, insurers are unable to effectively train staff, make new capital investments, or reach new markets.

   b. The economic strain of the past decade, and especially the recession that began in late 2007, have caused some insurers to suffer reduced financial resources through underwriting losses, investment losses, or both.

5. Other internal constraints

Other internal constraints can interfere with achieving goals.

   a. A newly established insurer might lack the name recognition necessary to achieve its profit goals even if it has the expertise and financial resources to do so.

   b. Another internal constraint is a reputation damaged by past problems. Overcoming a poor reputation requires work on the part of all employees within the organization.

B. External Constraints

In addition to internal constraints, insurers contend with several external constraints that may prevent them from meeting their goals:

1. Regulation

   a. Insurance operations are closely regulated, extending from incorporation to liquidation and encompassing most activities in between.

   b. Insurance regulators monitor insurers' solvency to protect the insurer's policyholders and members of the public who benefit from the existence of insurance.

   c. Regulation can also extend to the insurance rates and forms insurers use.

   d. Regulation varies by state, and federal regulation adds another layer of complexity.

   e. Regulation imposes a major constraint on insurers, requiring significant personnel and financial resources that can inhibit the insurer's ability to achieve its profit goals.

2. Rating agencies

   a. Financial rating agencies, such as A.M. Best Company, Standard & Poor's, and Moody's, rate insurers based on financial strength as an indication of an insurer's ability to meet policyholder obligations.

   b. Rating agencies are also placing new demands when assessing insurers' financial health. Rating agencies now require insurers to boost their capital to handle higher catastrophe risk.

   c. An insurer's financial rating can also be a potential constraint for insurers whose rating has declined. A decrease in customers often causes financial ratings to decline further.

3. Public opinion

   a. Public opinion about the insurance industry as a whole can act as a constraint for individual insurers in meeting goals.

   b. Matters of ethics are major components in managing an insurer's reputation.

   c. When the insurance industry is viewed negatively by the public, it contradicts the idea of serving in the public's best interests.

4. Competition

   Insurance industry underwriting cycles (or market cycles) are referred to as either hard cycles or soft cycles.

   a. Hard cycles are characterized by periods of decreased competition and rising rates leading to increased profitability and high rates of return.

   b. Soft cycles are when prices moderate or decline as competition increases and, eventually, profitability diminishes.

   c. Excessive competition can entice some insurers to bend the rules, making insurers unable to attain their legal and regulatory goals.

5. Economic conditions

   a. Insurers' investment operations can be affected severely by economic downturns.

   b. Insurers can be adversely affected during inflationary cycles as well. Inflation affects the cost of insurance losses through increased medical costs, construction costs, and other loss-related costs.

6. Insurance marketing and distribution

   a. Insurers distribute their products through many types of distribution systems using different types of sales and service personnel and distribution channels to promote products and services as well as communicate with existing and prospective insureds.

   b. Each distribution system or channel meets the needs of some customers, and each fails to meet the needs of others.

7. Other external constraints

   a. Other external constraints can hinder an insurer's ability to reach its goals.

   b. Some of these constraints are natural or man-made catastrophe losses, which increased dramatically in the mid-2000s; disregard for law and order, particularly in some larger cities; and legal changes that affect liability claims.

Educational Objective 4

Describe the measurements used to evaluate how successful an insurer is at meeting its established goals.

Key Points:

Insurers use measurements that are specific to their industry to determine their success at meeting established goals.

A. Meeting Profitability Goals

An understanding of how insurers make a profit is crucial to understanding how they meet their profitability goals. A review of these topics assists in understanding insurer profitability:

1. Premiums and investment

    a. Premiums are the amounts that insurers charge insureds for insurance coverages.

        • Insurers use rates based on the insured's loss exposures to determine the premium to charge for insurance policies.

        • Insurers must charge premiums to have the funds necessary to make loss payments.

    b. Insurance operations generate substantial amounts of investable funds, primarily from loss reserves, loss adjustment expense reserves, and unearned premium reserves.

    c. Measures of insurer profitability based on premiums consider premium growth issues and the rate of growth that is sustained over time.

        • Premium growth, or the lack thereof, must be evaluated in light of current market conditions. An insurer should consider whether growth resulted from a competitive advantage, relaxed underwriting, inadequate insurance rates, or a combination of these factors.

        • Evaluating the rate of premium growth sustained over time helps determine insurer profitability. Growth that is slower than the industry average or substantially higher than the industry average may indicate problems.

2. Underwriting performance

An insurer's underwriting performance can be measured in terms of net underwriting gain or loss.

    a. Because net underwriting gain or loss ignores investment income (or investment losses) and investment expenses, it represents the extent of the insurer's profit or loss derived strictly from the sale of insurance products.

      b. The formula for calculating net underwriting gain or loss can be expressed as: net underwriting gain or loss = earned premiums – (incurred losses + underwriting expenses).

      c. Three specific ratios are used to measure an insurer's underwriting performance: the loss ratio, the expense ratio, and the combined ratio (trade basis).

  3. Overall operating performance

      a. The formula for overall gain or loss from operations is expressed as: overall gain or loss from operations = net underwriting gain or loss + investment gain or loss.

      b. After an insurer pays losses, expenses, and taxes, and reserves money to pay additional incurred losses, the remainder is net operating income, which belongs to the company's owners.

        • The owners (stockholders or policyholders) may receive a portion of this remainder as dividends.

        • The amount that is left after dividends are paid is added to the policyholders' surplus.

      c. Insurers may lose money on their underwriting activities and yet still generate a profit on investments.

      d. The investment income ratio, overall operating ratio, and return on equity are more specific measures of an insurer's operational performance.

  4. Estimation of loss reserves

      a. Loss reserves are generally the largest liability in the insurer's balance sheet and can have a significant effect on the insurer's overall profitability.

      b. Errors in estimating outstanding loss amounts, by either underestimating or overestimating the final cost of claims, can distort the insurer's reported profits.

        • If an insurer does not have adequate reserves, it may not have the funds necessary to pay claims.

        • If the loss reserves are overestimated, the statutory limits on premiums that could be written may be less, and the premiums may be inflated for new and existing risks.

B. Meeting Customer Needs

  1. Complaints and praise

      a. All insurers receive complaints, and each complaint should be evaluated.

      b. Insurance producers can also be a source of information for evaluating an insurer's success in this area, as they are in frequent contact with customers and hear their complaints about and praise of insurers.

2. Customer satisfaction data

   a. Many insurers emphasize a customer focus to maintain and raise levels of customer satisfaction with the insurer's products and services.

   b. Insurers can use response cards and phone surveys and conduct customer focus groups or interviews.

3. Insurer's retention ratio and lapse ratio

   These are two particularly telling measurements of customer satisfaction:

   a. The retention ratio is the percentage of expiring insurance policies that an insurer renews, and it can be measured by policy count, premium volume, or both.

   b. The lapse ratio is calculated by dividing the number of policies that lapse during a period by the total number of policies written at the beginning of that period.

4. Insurer-producer relationships

   a. Insurers that market products through independent agents and brokers usually view this network of producers as their customers, in addition to the ultimate insurance customer.

   b. These insurers recognize that many other insurers are available to producers and that a competitive marketplace exists within their industry.

5. State insurance department statistics

   Several state insurance departments tabulate complaints they receive and publish lists showing the number of complaints received for each insurer.

6. *Consumer Reports*

   a. Consumers Union periodically surveys its membership to determine its level of satisfaction with the performance of auto and homeowners insurers.

   b. The results are published in that organization's magazine, *Consumer Reports*, including a list of the most satisfactory and least satisfactory insurers as indicated by the survey responses.

C. Meeting Legal Requirements

   1. An insurer's success or failure in meeting legal requirements is indicated by the number of criminal, civil, and regulatory actions taken against the insurer.

   2. State insurance departments monitor the treatment of insureds, applicants for insurance, and claimants, and they oversee four insurer operational areas: sales and advertising, underwriting, ratemaking, and claim settlement.

3. Financial rating agencies provide summary information about insurer financial strength in the form of a financial rating.

4. The prospective outcome of such actions affects the ratings that these organizations assign to insurers and are another indicator of how well an insurer meets its legal requirements.

D. Meeting Social Responsibilities

   1. No standards exist for judging an insurer's performance in this area, and little information on an individual insurer's performance is publicly available.

   2. Many insurers use their Web sites to indicate their participation in home and workplace safety programs, support of community projects, and involvement in other social programs.

   3. Another possible indicator of social responsibility is the benefits that an insurer provides for its employees.

   4. Comparative information for employee benefits is available from the United States Chamber of Commerce and from various insurer trade associations.

   5. Expenditures on loss control activities may also indicate an insurer's level of humanitarian concern; some insurers go beyond typical efforts in loss control to improve safety conditions for their insureds.

   6. Additionally, "green" initiatives are emerging for many insurers as they recognize their responsibility to preserve our environment.

Educational Objective 5
Describe the core and supporting functions performed by insurers.

Key Points:

The functional view of insurance examines the many and varied functions an insurer performs as it conducts its business operations.

A. Core Functions

Although insurers may use varying organizational structures, three core functions exist within the structure of a typical insurer.

1. Marketing and Distribution

    a. Marketing and distribution involves determining what products or services customers want and need, advertising the products (communicating their value to customers), and delivering them to customers.

    b. The insurer cannot make a profit if it does not provide the products and services customers need.

    c. The goals of the marketing and distribution function must be balanced with other insurer goals.

2. Underwriting

    a. It is the job of the underwriting function to determine whether and under what conditions the insurer is willing to provide insurance products and services to potential customers.

    b. The goal of underwriting is to write a profitable book of business for the insurer, which supports the insurer's profit goal.

    c. Underwriting serves both insurers and insurance buyers by helping the insurer avoid adverse selection.

3. Claims

    a. The purpose of the claims function is to fulfill the insurer's promise to make a payment to, or on behalf of, the insured if a covered event occurs.

    b. The claims function is staffed by employees who are trained in the skills necessary to evaluate and settle claims and to negotiate or litigate the settlement of claims by or against insureds through the claim handling process.

    c. The claim handling process is designed to achieve a fair settlement in accordance with the applicable insurance policy provisions.

d. Insurers have developed expertise in claim handling in all categories of loss exposures.

B. Supporting Functions

1. To support the core functions of marketing and distribution, underwriting, and claims, insurers provide a variety of supporting functions, including risk control, premium auditing, actuarial functions, reinsurance, and information technology.

2. These functions are not only necessary to the efficient operation of insurers, but are also used by a variety of other risk financing organizations, such as captives, pools, risk retention groups, and self-insurers:

   a. Risk control—An insurer's risk control function provides information to the underwriting function to assist in selecting and rating risks. The risk control function also works with commercial insureds to help prevent losses and to reduce the effects of losses that cannot be prevented.

   b. Premium auditing—Although the premium for many types of insurance is known and guaranteed in advance, the premium is variable for some lines of insurance and cannot be precisely calculated until after the end of the policy period.

   c. Actuarial—Actuarial functions include calculating insurance rates, developing rating plans, estimating loss reserves, and providing predictive modeling services. The actuarial function also conducts sensitivity analysis to determine the financial security of the insurer.

   d. Reinsurance—When an insurer accepts a risk that is larger than it is willing or able to support, it can transfer all or part of that risk to other insurers through reinsurance transactions.

   e. Information technology—The information technology function provides the infrastructure that supports all of an insurer's internal and external communications.

C. Other Common Functional Areas

1. In addition to the core and supporting functions, insurers perform a host of other functions or outsource them to an external organization.

2. Some common functions include these:

   a. Investments—An insurer's investment operations enable it to earn investment income on the funds generated by its underwriting activities. This investment income enables the insurer to reduce the premium that it must charge in exchange for the risks it assumes.

b. Accounting and finance—The primary responsibilities of the accounting and finance function are to ensure that the organization has funds to meet its obligations and to fairly and fully disclose the financial position of the insurer in conformance with generally accepted accounting principles (GAAP).

c. Customer service—Some insurers have customer service personnel assigned to specific work areas such as customer billing, claims services, underwriting support, agency relations or billing, agency technology support, customer Internet support, and information technology support services for internal users. The customer service function could apply to specific functions or to the entire organization.

d. Legal and compliance—The legal and compliance function provides legal counsel, support, and service to other functions within the insurer and ensures that statutory and administrative requirements are met.

e. Human resources—The human resources function involves the selection, training, and dismissal of employees.

f. Special investigation units (SIUs)—These units are established to combat insurance fraud, which includes any deliberate deception committed against an insurer or an insurance producer for the purpose of unwarranted financial gain.

Key Words and Phrases:

 Key Words

Proprietary insurer
Insurer formed for the purpose of earning a profit for its owners.

Mutual insurer
An insurer that is owned by its policyholders and formed as a corporation for the purpose of providing insurance to them.

Reciprocal insurance exchange (interinsurance exchange)
An insurer owned by its policyholders, formed as an unincorporated association for the purpose of providing insurance coverage to its members (called subscribers), and managed by an attorney-in-fact. Members agree to mutually insure each other, and they share profits and losses in the same proportion as the amount of insurance purchased from the exchange by that member.

Fair Access to Insurance Requirements (FAIR) plans
An insurance pool through which private insurers collectively address an unmet need for property insurance on urban properties, especially those susceptible to loss by riot or civil commotion.

Residual market
The term referring collectively to insurers and other organizations that make insurance available through a shared risk mechanism to those who cannot obtain coverage in the admitted market.

Surplus lines broker
A person or firm that places business with insurers not licensed (nonadmitted) in the state in which the transaction occurs but that is permitted to write insurance because coverage is not available through standard market insurers.

Independent agency and brokerage marketing system
An insurance marketing system under which producers (agents or brokers), who are independent contractors, sell insurance, usually as representatives of several unrelated insurers.

Direct writer marketing system
An insurance marketing system that uses sales agents (or sales representatives) who are direct employees of the insurer.

Exclusive agency marketing system
An insurance marketing system under which agents contract to sell insurance exclusively for one insurer (or for an associated group of insurers).

Distribution channel
The channel used by the producer of a product or service to transfer that product or service to the ultimate customer.

Probable maximum loss (PML)
The largest loss that an insured is likely to sustain.

Underwriting
The process of selecting insureds, pricing coverage, determining insurance policy terms and conditions, and then monitoring the underwriting decisions made.

Book of business
A group of policies with a common characteristic, such as territory or type of coverage, or all policies written by a particular insurer or agency.

Underwriting guidelines (underwriting guide)
A written manual that communicates an insurer's underwriting policy and that specifies the attributes of an account that an insurer is willing to insure.

Adverse selection
In general, the tendency for people with the greatest probability of loss to be the ones most likely to purchase insurance.

Insurance Regulation

2

Educational Objective 1

Describe the effect each of the following had on insurance regulation:

- **Paul v. Virginia**

- **Sherman Antitrust Act**

- **South-Eastern Underwriters Association Decision**

- **McCarran-Ferguson Act**

- **Insurance Services Office (ISO) and the Attorneys General Lawsuit**

- **Gramm-Leach-Bliley Act**

Key Points:

Insurance regulation in the United States began when the Constitution gave Congress the right to regulate commerce among the states. Six subsequent legal events significantly influenced the three major issues of insurance regulation—locus of regulatory control, extent of regulation, and collaboration among insurers.

A. *Paul v. Virginia*

  1. This 1869 legal decision determined that insurance was not interstate commerce.

  2. In a long line of subsequent cases, usually involving an insurer seeking to defeat state regulation, *Paul v. Virginia* was cited as the precedent for upholding state regulation of insurance.

  3. By implication, despite few explicit judicial statements, this decision came to be relied on as support for the premise that the federal government has no authority over insurance.

  4. In 1871, New York's insurance commissioner met with regulatory representatives from nineteen other states to address their common problems. By 1872, thirty states had become members of this initial regulators' association, known as the National Insurance Convention (NIC).

Study Tips

When reviewing, focus on concepts you haven't mastered yet, rather than those you already know well.

B. Sherman Antitrust Act

1. This 1890 Congressional act prohibited collusion to gain a monopoly. The act prevented insurers from banding together to control insurance rates and coverages.

2. The Sherman Act applies to practices beyond collusive pricing activities, and it remains in effect today.

3. Insurance consumers hoped that these state and federal antitrust laws would limit the ability of insurers to raise rates, but applying antitrust laws to insurance was complicated because of the nature of insurance operations.

4. In periods of intense competition, insurers cut prices to levels that had the potential to lead to insurer insolvencies. Insurers tried to organize the market to control rates and break the destructive patterns of the property-casualty underwriting cycle.

5. One way to organize the market was to devise a rate "tariff" listing the prescribed rates for different types of loss exposures.

6. By 1912, twenty-three states had passed legislation to prohibit insurer compacts or associations from controlling rates.

7. In 1923, the National Convention of Insurance Commissioners (NCIC, the renamed NIC) passed a resolution to repeal state anticompact laws. Insurance regulators had concluded that rating bureaus and insurer compacts or associations were necessary if insurers were to develop and maintain adequate and appropriate rates.

C. South-Eastern Underwriters Association Decision

1. The South-Eastern Underwriters Association (SEUA) consisted of nearly 200 private stock insurers that controlled 90 percent of the fire and allied lines insurance market in six southeastern states.

   a. The state of Missouri wanted the federal government to challenge rating bureaus, and the SEUA seemed like an ideal target.

   b. A federal investigation ensued, and criminal indictments were brought against the SEUA, twenty-seven of its officers, and all of its members.

   c. The case was dismissed, but, on appeal, the U.S. Supreme Court agreed to hear the SEUA case in 1944.

2. This 1944 legal decision turned the U.S. insurance world upside down by making insurance subject to federal regulation.

3. This decision, contrary to legal precedent, eliminated the role of state insurance regulators and made insurance subject to federal regulation that prohibited many collaborative activities that the states had previously approved and encouraged.

4. The immediate effect of the Court's decision was that these federal acts now applied to insurance:
    a. The Sherman Act (1890)—This act prohibits collusion to gain a monopoly. Any activity that restrains trade or commerce and any attempt to monopolize are illegal.
    b. The Clayton Act (1914)—This act, together with its amendment, the Robinson Patman Antidiscrimination Act (1936), prohibits activities that lessen competition or create monopoly power, including price discrimination, tying (requiring the purchase of one product when purchasing another product) and exclusive dealing, and mergers between competitors.
    c. The Federal Trade Commission (FTC) Act (1914)—This act prohibits unfair methods of competition and unfair or deceptive trade practices, and therefore it promotes competition and protects consumers.

D. McCarran-Ferguson Act
    1. This 1945 Congressional act restored most insurance regulatory responsibilities to the states. This act allows the states to regulate and tax the business of insurance.
    2. One condition of the McCarran Act is that the Sherman Act, the Clayton Act, the FTC Act, and the Robinson-Patman Act do not apply to the "business of insurance" unless the states are not regulating the activities described in the acts.
    3. Federal regulation that applies to boycott, coercion, and intimidation and federal regulation that deals only with insurance (and not business in general) supersedes state regulation.
    4. Based on the court decisions that have been rendered, the "business of insurance" is defined as any activity that has one or more of these three characteristics:
        a. The risk of the policyholder or insured is shared and underwritten by the insurer.
        b. The insurer and the insured have a direct contractual connection.
        c. The activity is unique to entities within the insurance business.
    5. Under the McCarran Act, the states had until 1948 to pass legislation to regulate insurance, thereby limiting federal regulation.
    6. In 1947, the NAIC adopted the Act Relating to Unfair Methods of Competition and Unfair Deceptive Acts and Practices in the Business of Insurance. The NAIC and the states believed that they had succeeded in preempting federal legislation.

E. ISO and the Attorneys General Lawsuit

   1. In 1971, six separate national service bureaus (then known as rating bureaus) consolidated to form Insurance Services Office (ISO). By the end of 1971, nine local or regional property bureaus also joined ISO.

   2. In 1987, ISO was a national, not-for-profit corporation that provided statistical information to insurers and insurance regulators; developed and implemented policy coverage provisions; distributed industry-wide advisory rate information and, where appropriate, filed that information with state insurance regulators.

   3. This 1988 lawsuit alleged that insurers and industry associations conspired to draft restrictive policy language that created a liability crisis in the late 1980s.

   4. One result of the out-of-court settlement of this lawsuit was to restrict insurer collaboration in the development of insurance rates.

   5. ISO's board was reconstituted to comprise three insurance company executives, seven executives from noninsurance companies, and ISO's president serving as chairman.

      a. Insurer committees were dissolved and replaced with insurer advisory panels, whose members make recommendations in their areas of expertise.

      b. Rate and form decisions are made not by insurer committees but by ISO staff.

   6. Currently, ISO is a for-profit corporation, and the rating information it provides involves loss costs rather than advisory rates.

   7. ISO continues to develop insurance policy forms and coverage programs that are adopted by many property-casualty insurers and continues its role as a statistical agent for regulators in almost every state.

F. Gramm-Leach-Bliley Act

   1. This 1999 Congressional act, also known as the Financial Services Modernization Act, repealed the Glass-Steagall Act; facilitated affiliations among banks, insurers, and other financial service providers; and introduced the concept of functional regulation.

   2. The act reaffirmed the McCarran-Ferguson Act, reiterating that states would continue to have primary regulatory authority for all insurance activities.

3. The Gramm-Leach-Bliley (GLB) Act essentially repealed the Depression-era Glass-Steagall Act by permitting different types of financial services organizations, such as commercial banks, investment banks, and insurers, to merge or diversify across functional boundaries.

4. The GLB Act also treats insurance underwriting differently from insurance sales and marketing.

    a. National banks are prohibited from underwriting insurance through an operating subsidiary.

    b. National banks can arrange for a financial holding company to create an insurance affiliate. This arrangement makes it more difficult for a failing bank to use insurer assets.

5. The GLB Act also compels states to facilitate insurance producers' ability to operate in more than one state. The GLB Act contains a provision that gives states three years to adopt full reciprocal licensing agreements.

Educational Objective 2

Explain how insurance regulation protects consumers, contributes to maintaining insurer solvency, and assists in preventing destructive competition.

Key Points:

The insurance industry is regulated primarily for three reasons.

A. Protect Consumers

1. The primary reason for insurance regulation is consumer protection.

2. Regulators help to protect consumers by reviewing insurance policy forms to determine whether they benefit consumers and comply with state consumer protection laws.

3. State legislatures can set coverage standards and specify policy language for certain insurance coverages.

4. State insurance regulators can review policy language and disapprove policy forms and endorsements that are inconsistent with state consumer protection laws.

5. Departments of insurance receive complaints about these behaviors:

   a. Producers have intentionally sold unnecessary insurance.

   b. Producers have misrepresented the nature of coverage to make a sale.

   c. Producers have stolen or misused insured or insurer funds.

   d. Claim representatives have engaged in unfair claim practices, refusing to pay legitimate claims or unfairly reducing claim payments.

   e. Insurance managers have contributed to the insolvency of insurers through their dishonesty.

6. Insurance regulators also provide information about insurance matters so that consumers can make more informed decisions.

B. Maintain Insurer Solvency

1. Solvency regulation protects insureds against the risk that insurers will be unable to meet their financial obligations.

  2. Insurance regulators try to maintain a sound financial condition of private insurers for several reasons:

   a. Insurance provides future protection—Premiums are paid in advance, but the period of protection extends into the future. If insurers become insolvent, future claims may not be paid, and the insurance protection already paid for may become worthless.

   b. Regulation is needed to protect the public interest—Large numbers of individuals and the community at large are adversely affected when insurers become insolvent.

   c. Insurers have a responsibility to insureds—Insurers hold substantial funds for the ultimate benefit of insureds. Government regulation is necessary to safeguard such funds.

  3. The goal of regulation is not to eliminate all insolvencies but rather to minimize the number of insolvencies.

C. Prevent Destructive Competition

  1. Regulators are responsible for determining whether insurance rates are high enough to prevent destructive competition.

  2. At times, some insurers underprice their products to increase market share by attracting customers away from higher-priced competitors.

   a. This practice drives down price levels in the whole market.

   b. When insurance rate levels are inadequate, some insurers can become insolvent, and others might withdraw from the market or stop writing new business.

   c. An insurance shortage can then develop, and individuals and firms might be unable to obtain the coverage they need.

  3. Certain types of insurance can become unavailable at any price.

Educational Objective 3

Identify the regulatory activities of state insurance departments and the duties typically performed by state insurance commissioners.

Key Points:

Insurance is regulated primarily by state insurance departments. State regulators, in turn, are members of the National Association of Insurance Commissioners (NAIC), a nonprofit corporation that has no regulatory authority of its own but that plays an important coordinating role.

A. State Insurance Departments

1. Every state has three separate and equal branches of government:

a. The legislative branch makes the laws.

b. The judicial branch (the court system) interprets the laws.

c. The executive branch implements the laws.

2. State insurance departments fall within the executive branch of each state government.

a. State insurance departments enforce insurance laws enacted by the legislature.

b. Under the insurance commissioner's direction, a state insurance department engages in a wide variety of regulatory activities that typically include these:

- Licensing insurers
- Licensing producers, claim representatives, and other insurance personnel
- Approving policy forms
- Holding rate hearings and reviewing rate filings
- Evaluating solvency information
- Performing market conduct examinations
- Investigating policyholder complaints
- Rehabilitating or liquidating insolvent insurers
- Issuing cease-and-desist orders
- Fining insurers that violate state law
- Publishing shoppers' guides and other consumer information (in some states)
- Preventing fraud

3. Every state insurance department is headed by an insurance commissioner, superintendent, or director appointed by the governor or elected by the voting public.

   a. The duties a typical state insurance commissioner delegates to those in the state insurance department include these:

   - Overseeing the state insurance department's operation
   - Promulgating orders, rules, and regulations necessary to administer insurance laws
   - Determining whether to issue business licenses to new insurers, producers, and other insurance entities
   - Reviewing insurance pricing and coverage
   - Conducting financial and market examinations of insurers
   - Holding hearings on insurance issues
   - Taking action when insurance laws are violated
   - Issuing an annual report on the status of the state's insurance market and insurance department
   - Maintaining records of insurance department activities

   b. Disagreement exists regarding which selection method (appointing or voting) of the insurance commissioner better serves the public interest.

4. State insurance departments are partly funded by state premium taxes, audit fees, filing fees, and licensing fees, but premium taxes are the major source of funding.

B. The National Association of Insurance Commissioners (NAIC)

   1. The NAIC meets three times per year to discuss important problems and issues in insurance regulation.

   2. The NAIC developed uniform financial statement forms that all states require insurers to file.

   3. It collects and compiles financial information from insurers and warehouses the financial data for use by insurance regulators.

   4. It assists state insurance departments by sharing financial information about insurers that are potentially insolvent and by developing model laws and regulations.

   5. State insurance departments must meet three criteria to satisfy the NAIC's Financial Regulation Standards and to be accredited:

      a. The state's insurance laws and regulations must meet basic standards of NAIC models.

      b. The state's regulatory methods must be acceptable to the NAIC.

      c. The state's insurance department practices must be adequate as defined by the NAIC.

C. Federal Regulation

   1. The McCarran Act reverses the usual state-federal allocation of regulatory powers only for the business of insurance, and this does not include everything that insurers do. For example:

      a. As employers, insurers are subject to federal employment laws just like any other business.

      b. As businesses that sell their stock to the public to raise capital, stock insurers are subject to regulations like any other such business.

   2. The Insurance Fraud Protection Act protects consumers and insurers against insolvencies resulting from insurance fraud.

      a. The act prohibits anyone with a felony conviction involving trustworthiness from working in the business of insurance unless he or she secures the written consent of an insurance regulator.

      b. The act identifies these crimes involving the business of insurance:

         • Making false statements or reports to insurance regulators—including overvaluing assets—to influence regulatory decisions

         • Making false entries in books, reports, or statements to deceive anyone about an insurer's financial condition or solvency

         • Embezzling from anyone who is engaged in the business of insurance

         • Using threats or force or "any threatening letter or communication to corruptly influence, obstruct, or impede" insurance regulatory proceedings

Educational Objective 4

Describe the arguments for and against federal regulation of insurance.

Key Points:

The question of which level of government—state or federal—should regulate insurance is far from settled. With strong arguments on both sides, the debate is likely to continue.

A. Proponents of federal regulation present these arguments:

1. Federal regulation would provide regulatory uniformity across the states.
2. Federal regulation would be more efficient.
3. Federal regulation would attract personnel with a high level of expertise.

B. Opponents of federal regulation present these arguments:

1. State regulation is more responsive to local needs.
2. Uniformity of state laws can be attained through the National Association of Insurance Commissioners (NAIC).
3. Greater opportunities for innovation are possible with state regulation.
4. State regulation is already in place, and its strengths and weaknesses are known.
5. State regulation results in a desirable decentralization of political power.
6. State regulation results in multiple eyes looking at an issue.
7. State regulators have been responsive in reducing the complexity of regulation.

C. A new Federal Insurance Office (FIO) will be created to facilitate some of the regulatory coordination and provide a source of information to Congress about the insurance industry. The FIO will have a role in negotiating agreements with other nations related to insurance.

Educational Objective 5

Describe the licensing requirements for insurers and insurance personnel.

Key Points:

At the beginning of any business development plan, insurers and insurance personnel should consider insurance regulation.

A. Licensing Insurers

1. By issuing a license to an insurer, a state indicates that the insurer meets minimum standards of financial strength, competence, and integrity.

   a. A license indicates that the insurer has complied with the state's insurance laws and is authorized to write certain types of insurance in the state.

   b. Once licensed, the insurer is subject to all applicable state laws, rules, and regulations.

   c. In response to complaints about the length of time regulators took to license a new insurer, regulators developed the Uniform Certificate of Authority Application (UCAA) to streamline the process.

2. Domestic insurers

   a. An insurer licensed in its home state is called a domestic insurer. If a domestic insurer obtains licenses in states other than its state of domicile, it is a foreign insurer in those other states.

   b. A domestic insurer's license generally has no expiration date. Licenses of foreign insurers and alien insurers generally must be renewed annually.

   c. An applicant for an insurer license must apply for a charter.

   - The applicant must provide the names and addresses of the incorporators, the name of the proposed corporation, the territories and types of insurance it plans to market, the total authorized capital stock (if any), and its surplus.

   - The state insurance commissioner reviews the application to see whether the applicant also meets the state's licensing requirements.

   d. State laws require that domestic stock insurers satisfy certain minimum capital and surplus requirements before a license is granted. Minimum initial capital and paid-in surplus requirements vary widely.

    e. For mutual or reciprocal insurers, the minimum financial requirement applies only to surplus because a mutual insurer does not have capital derived from the sale of stock.

- Most states require mutuals to have an initial surplus equal to the minimum capital and paid-in surplus requirement for stock insurers writing the same type of insurance.
- Some states have set a minimum surplus requirement for mutuals that is lower than the minimum capital and paid-in surplus requirement for stock insurers.

    f. Many states require the organizers of a mutual insurer to have a minimum number of applications with deposit premiums for a minimum number of separate loss exposures and aggregate premium exceeding a specific amount.

    g. In addition to financial requirements, states impose other requirements on new insurers. Some examples include:

- The proposed name for a new mutual insurer must include the word "mutual."
- The proposed name of a new insurer must not be so similar to that of any existing insurer that it would be misleading.

    h. Some states even permit the commissioner to deny a license to an otherwise worthy applicant if the commissioner believes that no additional insurers are needed in the state.

3. Foreign insurers

    a. To be licensed in an additional state, an insurer first must show that it has satisfied the requirements imposed by its home state.

    b. A foreign insurer must generally satisfy the minimum capital, surplus, and other requirements imposed on the state's domestic insurers.

4. Alien insurers

    a. Alien insurers (insurers domiciled outside the United States) must satisfy the requirements imposed on domestic insurers by the state in which they want to be licensed.

    b. They must usually establish a branch office in any state and have funds on deposit in the U.S. equal to the minimum capital and surplus required.

5. Nonadmitted insurers

An admitted insurer is licensed by a state insurance department to do business in the insured's home state. A nonadmitted insurer is not licensed (not authorized) in the insured's home state; it may be an admitted insurer in other states, and it may even be an alien insurer.

a. A nonadmitted insurer is typically a surplus lines insurer.

- The surplus lines insurance mechanism allows U.S. consumers to buy property-casualty insurance from nonadmitted insurers when consumers are unable to purchase the insurance they need from admitted insurers.
- The business that surplus lines insurers generally accept includes distressed risks, unique risks, and high-capacity risks.
- Surplus lines coverages commonly include products liability, professional liability, employment practices liability, special events, and excess and umbrella policies.

b. Under surplus lines laws, a nonadmitted insurer might be permitted to transact business through a specially licensed surplus lines producer if these are true:

- The insurance is not readily available from admitted insurers.
- The nonadmitted insurer is "acceptable."
- The producer has a special license authorizing him or her to place such insurance.

c. An "acceptable" nonadmitted insurer generally must complete a number of tasks:

- File a financial statement that the insurance commissioner finds satisfactory
- Supply documentation of transactions to state regulators
- Obtain a certificate of compliance from its home state or country
- Maintain a trust fund in the U.S., if an alien insurer

d. The National Association of Insurance Commissioners (NAIC) maintains an International Insurers Department that helps insurance regulators evaluate the financial status of alien insurers.

e. The International Insurers Department prepares and disseminates a quarterly listing (Non-Admitted Insurers Quarterly Listing) of alien nonadmitted insurers to assist state insurance regulators, surplus lines brokers, and the public in evaluating whether to do business with one of the insurers on the listing.

f. A nonadmitted insurer writing business in the surplus lines market does not face regulatory constraints on insurance rates and forms.

- From the insured's perspective, a distinct disadvantage of surplus lines insurance is that it is not usually protected by the state's guaranty fund.

- The requirements for capital and trust accounts provide assurance for insureds that nonadmitted insurers will be able to pay their claims.

6. Risk retention groups

   a. A risk retention group is a special type of assessable mutual insurer enabled by the 1986 Liability Risk Retention Act.

      - Risk retention groups are often formed under state captive laws, which generally maintain lower capital and surplus requirements for captives than for traditional property-casualty insurers.

      - Once licensed as a commercial liability insurer under the laws of at least one state, a risk retention group can write insurance in other states without a license by filing the appropriate notice and registration forms with the nonchartering state.

      - A risk retention group can write only commercial liability insurance for its members and may not write other lines of business.

      - In a nonchartering state, a risk retention group might be subject to some state laws, such as unfair claim settlement practice laws, and to premium taxes.

      - The risk retention group might also be required to become a member of a joint underwriting association (JUA).

   b. Some state regulators have expressed concerns about the financial security of risk retention groups, particularly when the group providing the insurance is licensed in another state. Congress assisted with addressing these concerns by allowing the licensing state to request and mandate an examination of a group's financial condition.

B. Licensing Insurance Personnel

   States license many of the people who sell insurance, give insurance advice, or represent insurers, including producers, claim representatives, and insurance consultants.

   1. Producers

      a. Producers must be licensed in each state where they do business.

      b. To obtain a license to sell a particular type of insurance, a producer must pass a written examination.

      c. Provisions in the Gramm-Leach-Bliley (GLB) Act have led to greater licensing reciprocity among states.

    d. The development of the National Insurance Producer Registry (NIPR) has eliminated many of the inconveniences that arise from a multi-state regulatory system. The NIPR supports the work of the states and the NAIC in making the producer licensing process more cost-effective, streamlined, and uniform for the benefit of regulators, insurance producers, insurers, and consumers.

    e. The NIPR developed and implemented the Producer Database (PDB) and the NIPR Gateway.

- The PDB is an electronic database consisting of information relating to insurance producers that links participating state regulatory licensing systems into one common repository of producer information.
- The NIPR Gateway is a communication network that links state insurance regulators with the entities they regulate to facilitate the electronic exchange of producer information.

2. Claim representatives

    a. Some states require claim representatives to be licensed so that those who make claim decisions for insurers are aware of prohibited claim practices, have a minimum level of technical knowledge and skill, and understand how to handle insureds' claims fairly.

    b. Licensing of claim representatives in most states includes an examination, which is important because of the complex and technical nature of insurance policies and the claim process.

    c. Public adjusters, who represent insureds for a fee, are generally required to be licensed to ensure technical competence and to protect the public.

3. Insurance consultants

    a. Insurance consultants give advice, counsel, or opinions about insurance policies.

    b. Some states require insurance consultants to be licensed, and requirements for a consultant's license vary by state.

Educational Objective 6

Describe the methods that regulators use to maintain the solvency of insurers and to manage insolvencies, and the reasons why insurers become insolvent.

Key Points:

Individual consumers and most businesses do not have the skills or resources to analyze claim-paying ability when selecting an insurer. However, because insurers hold large sums of money paid by consumers for long periods of time, their financial strength must be carefully monitored to ensure their continued ability to pay covered claims, both in the present and in the future. The United States regulatory framework helps to maintain insurers' solvency and thus protect consumers.

A. Methods to Maintain Solvency

1. The U.S. regulatory framework is a national system of state-based regulation where the regulatory responsibility for insurer solvency monitoring rests with the state insurance regulator.

2. The state insurance regulators are assisted by the National Association of Insurance Commissioners (NAIC), an organization of the chief insurance regulatory official in each state, the District of Columbia, and five U.S. territories.

3. The mission or purpose of U.S. insurance regulation is to protect the interests of the insured and those who rely on the insurance coverage provided to the insured, while also facilitating an effective and efficient marketplace for insurance products.

4. The U.S. regulatory framework relies on an extensive system of peer review, featuring frequent communication and collaboration to provide the necessary checks and balances needed to make the system work.

5. Uniformity of approach to financial regulation has been facilitated by the NAIC accreditation program.

    a. To become accredited, the state must submit to a full on-site accreditation review.

    b. To remain accredited, an accreditation review must be performed at least once every five years with interim annual reviews. The evaluation looks at these factors:

    • The adequacy of the state's solvency laws and regulations to protect consumers

- The ability of the regulator to meet standards regarding effective and efficient financial analysis and examination processes based on the priority status of insurers
- The ability and willingness of the state regulator to cooperate and share pertinent information with other state, federal, or foreign regulatory officials
- The ability of a state to take timely and effective action when an insurer is identified as financially troubled or potentially troubled
- The quality of the state regulator's organizational and personnel practices
- The effectiveness of the state's processes for company licensing and review of proposed changes in control

    c. At the present time, all fifty states and the District of Columbia are accredited.

6. The NAIC's U.S. Insurance Financial Solvency Framework *Financial Solvency Core Principles* are these:

    a. Regulatory reporting, disclosure, and transparency

    b. Off-site monitoring and analysis

    c. On-site, risk-focused examinations

    d. Reserves, capital adequacy, and solvency

    e. Regulatory control of significant, broad-based, risk-related transactions/activities

    f. Preventive and corrective measures, including enforcement

    g. Exiting the market and receivership

7. The U.S. regulatory framework has evolved over time into the risk-focused approach used by regulators today, and is built on a set of solvency requirements for insurers. These are some examples of solvency requirements:

    a. Insurers must submit annual and quarterly financial statements to the domestic regulator and the NAIC using a prescribed format called the "annual statement" or the "blank."

    b. Insurers are required to use the NAIC's Accounting Practices and Procedures Manual and the Annual Statement Blank and Instructions for consistency of accounting treatment and financial reporting.

    c. The accounting practices have been codified, and an insurer using a state-approved permitted practice must disclose the differences so that anyone using the financial statement can make the appropriate adjustments to remove the effect of the permitted practice.

d. Most insurers (excepting the very small) must submit their financial statement to a Certified Public Accountant (CPA) for audit.

e. Most insurers must have their reserves evaluated by an actuary and have the actuary attest to the accuracy of the reserve estimates.

B. Liquidation of Insolvent Insurers

    1. If an insurer falls into insolvency, the insurance commissioner places it in receivership.

    2. With proper management, successful rehabilitation might be possible. If the insurer cannot be rehabilitated, it is liquidated according to the state's insurance code.

    3. Many states now liquidate insolvent insurers according to the Uniform Insurers Liquidation Act drafted by the NAIC.

        a. Under this act, creditors in each state in which the insolvent insurer has conducted business are treated equally; creditors in the state where the insurer is domiciled do not receive preferential treatment.

        b. Some states prioritize claimants who are entitled to the failed insurer's assets.

C. State Guaranty Funds

    1. Guaranty funds do not prevent insurer insolvency, but they mitigate its effects.

    2. All states have property-casualty insurance guaranty funds that pay some of the unpaid claims of insolvent insurers licensed in the particular state.

    3. Insurers can recoup all or part of the assessments by insurance rate increases, special premium tax credits, and refunds from the state guaranty fund.

D. Characteristics of State Guaranty Funds

    1. State guaranty funds vary by state. However, these characteristics are common:

        a. Assessments are made only when an insurer fails (except in New York)—The definition of "failure" varies by state.

        b. Policies usually terminate within thirty days after the failure date—Unpaid claims before termination, however, are still valid and paid from the guaranty fund of the insured's state of residence if the insolvent insurer is licensed in the state.

        c. Claim coverage varies by state—No state guaranty fund covers reinsurance or surplus lines insurance (except New Jersey).

      d. Claims are subject to maximum limits—The maximum limit is usually the lesser of $300,000 or the policy limit.

      e. Most states provide for a refund of unearned premiums—A few states have no unearned premiums claim provision.

      f. Most states apply a $100 deductible to unpaid claims—Many states exempt workers compensation claims from a deductible.

      g. Most states divide their guaranty funds into separate accounts, usually auto, workers compensation, and other types of insurance—Auto or workers compensation assessments can be limited to insurers that write only that line of insurance.

      h. Assessment recovery varies by state—Thirty-two states permit insurers to recover assessments by an insurance rate increase.

  2. Self-insured groups are not protected by guaranty funds.

  3. Risk retention groups are prohibited by federal law from participating in the state guaranty fund system.

E. Reasons for Insolvency

  1. Increased competition among insurers, leading to lower premium prices during soft phases of the underwriting cycle, often contributes to an increase in insurer insolvencies.

  2. Some insolvencies occur when an insurer is overexposed to losses resulting from a major insured catastrophe, especially during periods when intense competition causes lower insurance prices.

  3. Experts have identified these factors that frequently contribute to an insurer's insolvency:

      a. Rapid premium growth

      b. Inadequate insurance rates

      c. Inadequate reserves

      d. Excessive expenses

      e. Lax controls over managing general agents

      f. Uncollectible reinsurance

      g. Fraud

  4. If inadequate insurance rates and lax underwriting standards are not detected and corrected promptly, the decay in the quality of a business accelerates.

  5. Rapid premium growth precedes nearly all major insolvencies. It reduces the margin for error in insurers' operations.

  6. If insurance rates are inadequate and losses understated, net losses and capital deterioration rise more quickly than management can effectively respond to.

Educational Objective 7

Describe the goals of insurance rate regulation, the major types of state rating laws, and the reasons supporting and opposing rate regulation.

Key Points:

Insurers must comply with rate regulatory laws in each state in which they write insurance. Additionally, insurers are often required to satisfy social concerns that are not included in state statutes. The primary goal of rate regulation is insurer financial stability and, as a result, consumer protection.

A. Insurance Rate Regulation Goals

The three major goals of rate regulation are to ensure that rates are adequate, not excessive, and not unfairly discriminatory.

1. Adequate

a. Rates for a specific type of insurance should be high enough to pay all claims and expenses for that type of insurance.

b. If an insurer fails because its rates are inadequate, it cannot pay for losses of its insureds and third-party claimants.

c. These are examples of factors that complicate the regulatory goal of rate adequacy:

- An insurer usually does not know what its actual expenses will be when a policy is sold. Premiums are paid in advance, but they might be insufficient to pay all related claims and expenses that occur later. An unexpected increase in claim frequency or severity can make the rate inadequate.

- Insurers might charge inadequate rates in response to strong price competition in order not to lose business.

- State rate approval systems may not approve insurers' requests for adequate rates for public policy reasons or because of disagreement over the level of requested rates.

- Unanticipated events could lead to higher losses than those projected when rates were set.

- Regulatory actuaries and insurer actuaries may disagree about the assumptions used to determine trends or account for socioeconomic components of a proposed rate change.

2. Not excessive

a. Insurers should not earn excessive or unreasonable profits.

    b. Regulators have considerable latitude and discretion in determining whether rates are excessive for a given type of insurance. These are examples of factors they may consider:

- Number of insurers selling a specific coverage in the rating territory
- Relative market share of competing insurers
- Degree of rate variation among the competing insurers
- Past and prospective loss experience for a given type of insurance
- Possibility of catastrophe losses
- Margin for underwriting profit and contingencies
- Marketing expenses for a given type of insurance
- Special judgment factors that might apply to a given type of insurance

    c. Regulators sometimes use the fair rate of return approach in determining whether an insurer's rates are adequate or excessive.

3. Not unfairly discriminatory

Rates that are adequate and are not excessive must also not be unfairly discriminatory.

    a. Insurers' discrimination must be fair and consistent. This means that insureds with loss exposures that are roughly similar, regarding expected losses and expenses, should be charged substantially similar rates.

    b. The use of sophisticated computer simulation modeling for catastrophes and the use of innovative risk classification systems, such as credit-based insurance scores, have greatly complicated regulatory evaluation of whether rates are unfairly discriminatory.

    c. If loss exposures are substantially different in terms of expected losses and expenses, then different rates can be charged.

B. Types of Rating Laws

1. A state's rating laws influence how it achieves its three major rate regulation goals and the rates property-casualty insurers can charge. Rating laws apply not only to rates for a new type of insurance, but also to rate changes. The major types of state rating laws consist of:

    a. Prior-approval laws require rates and supporting rules to be approved by the state insurance department before they can be used.

    b. File-and-use laws allow the insurer to use the new rates immediately after filing with the state insurance department.

    c. Use-and-file laws are a variation of file-and-use laws that allow insurers to use the new rates and later submit filing information that is subject to regulatory review.

    d. No filing laws (information filing or open competition) do not require insurers to file rates with the state insurance department.

    e. Flex rating laws require prior approval only if the new rates exceed a certain percentage above (and sometimes below) the rates filed previously.

2. Most consumer advocacy groups and regulatory agencies support prior-approval systems allowing regulators to determine the adequacy and fairness of rates for reasons including these:

    a. Prior-approval systems require insurers to justify requests for rate increases with supporting actuarial data.

    b. Prior-approval systems help maintain insurer solvency through regulatory review of data to analyze the adequacy of rates for reported losses.

3. Most insurers and economists favor competitive rating systems where the market determines rates for reasons including these:

    a. Prior-approval systems may cause rates to be inadequate for writing profitable business because of the time required for the regulatory review and approval process.

    b. Competitive rating systems are less expensive to administer and allow regulators to focus their resources on other areas.

Educational Objective 8

Explain how the contract language contained in insurance policies is regulated.

Key Points:

Insurance policies are complex documents. Regulation of insurance policies helps to protect insurance consumers, who often may not understand their policies. Also, insurance policies are usually drafted by insurers, who sell them to the public on a take-it-or-leave-it basis. Regulation can protect insureds from policies that are narrow, restrictive, or deceptive, or that fail to comply with state laws and regulations.

A. Legislation

   1. Insurance policy regulation starts with a state legislature passing laws that control the structure and content of insurance policies sold in the state.

   2. Legislative policy regulation affects these five areas:

      a. Standard forms

      A standard policy is one policy all insurers must use if a coverage is sold in the state.

      b. Mandatory provisions

      Legislation might also require that certain standard mandatory policy provisions appear in certain types of insurance policies. The required and optional provisions might be based on a model bill developed by the National Association of Insurance Commissioners (NAIC).

      c. Prohibited provisions

      State laws and regulations might list certain provisions that are prohibited in insurance contracts.

      d. Forms approval

      Legislation might mandate that policies be filed and/or approved by the state to protect policyholders against ambiguous, misleading, or deceptive policies.

        • If a specified period elapses and the policy has not been disapproved, the policy is considered approved. The purpose is to encourage a prompt review. (Some states permit the state insurance department to extend the review period.)

- The NAIC has implemented a series of operational efficiencies along with the System for Electronic Rate and Form Filings (SERFF). SERFF has dramatically improved the timeliness of product filings.

    e. Readability standards

    Legislation may specify policy style and form as well as the size of print. Readability tests do not necessarily measure how well the policies can be understood.

B. Policy Rules, Regulation, and Guidelines

1. State insurance departments implement specific directives from the legislature or exercise the general authority they have to regulate insurance policies.

2. Administrative rules, regulations, and guidelines can be stated in:

    a. Regulations communicated by the state insurance department to insurers

    b. Informal circulars or bulletins from the same source

    c. Precedents set during the approval process

C. Courts

1. Although the courts do not directly regulate insurers, they do influence the insurer by determining whether insurance laws are constitutional and whether administrative rulings and regulations are consistent with state law.

2. The courts also interpret ambiguous and confusing policy provisions, determine whether certain losses are covered by the policy, and resolve other disputes between insurers and insureds over policy coverages and provisions.

3. Court decisions often lead insurers to redraft their policy language and to modify provisions.

Educational Objective 9

Explain how the market conduct areas in insurance are regulated and how regulatory activities protect consumers.

Key Points:

Regulation of the insurance industry's market conduct is concerned with consumer protection. By overseeing producers, sales and advertising, underwriting, ratemaking, and claim settlement procedures and activities, state departments of insurance help protect insurance consumers from such practices as unfair discrimination, insurer fraud, and excessive rates. Additionally, market conduct regulation promotes competition within the insurance marketplace.

A. Monitoring Market Conduct

   1. Laws regarding unfair trade practices prohibit abusive practices.

   2. If an insurer is found to be in violation of the unfair trade practices act, the insurer is subject to one or both of two penalties:

   a. Fine per violation—The fine is often increased significantly if the activity is considered flagrant, with conscious disregard for the law.

   b. Suspension or revocation of license—This may occur if the practice occurred frequently and if the insurer's management knew or should have known of the unfair trade practice.

   3. The National Association of Insurance Commissioners (NAIC) Model Unfair Trade Practices Act prohibits insurers from any activity that would restrain trade or competition in the business of insurance. The act also prohibits an insurer from misrepresenting its own or another insurer's financial status.

   4. Producer practices

   A producer might be penalized for engaging in practices that violate the state's unfair trade practices act, such as these:

   a. Dishonesty or Fraud—A producer might embezzle premiums paid by insureds or misappropriate some claim funds.

   b. Misrepresentation—A producer might misrepresent the losses that are covered by an insurance policy, which might induce a client to purchase that policy under false pretenses.

    c. Twisting—A producer might induce an insured to replace one policy with another, to the insured's detriment. This is a special form of misrepresentation called "twisting."

    d. Unfair Discrimination—A producer might engage in any number of acts that favor one insured unfairly over another.

    e. Rebating—A producer might engage in rebating, the practice of giving a portion of the producer's commission or some other financial advantage to an individual as an inducement to purchase a policy.

5. Underwriting practices

To protect consumers, insurance regulators take actions such as these:

    a. Constrain insurers' ability to accept, modify, or decline applications for insurance—To increase insurance availability, states often require insurers to provide coverage for some loss exposures they might prefer not to cover.

    b. Establish allowable classifications—Regulators limit the ways in which insurers can divide consumers into rating classifications.

    c. Restrict the timing of cancellations and nonrenewals—All states require insurers to provide insureds with adequate advance notice of policy cancellation or nonrenewal so that insureds can obtain replacement coverage.

6. Claim practices

    a. Regulatory controls on claim practices are intended to protect insureds and maintain public confidence in the promise of insurance to pay valid claims promptly and fairly.

    b. Apart from regulatory penalties, failure to practice good faith claim handling can lead to claims for damages that allege bad faith on the insurer's part.

    c. Unfair claim practices laws prohibit unethical and illegal claim practices. The laws generally are patterned after the NAIC Model Unfair Claims Settlement Practices Act.

    d. In some cases, courts have ruled that an insurer's improper claim handling constitutes the tort of bad faith. An insurer that violates good-faith standards can be required to honor the policy's intent and pay extracontractual damages, such as emotional distress and attorney fees.

B. Market Analysis

1. Market analysis allows regulators to identify general market disruptions, promotes uniform analysis by applying consistent measurements between insurers, and facilitates communication and collaboration among regulators from different states.

2. A fundamental component of market analysis is the collection of regulatory information from insurers using the Market Conduct Annual Statement (MCAS). As a work-in-progress at the time of this writing, regulators are engaged in these activities:

   a. Defining the scope of the market analysis program

   b. Determining minimum required skills and essential education necessary for market analysis professionals

   c. Developing, prioritizing, and coordinating data collection and analysis techniques

   d. Making recommendations regarding the expansion of the data elements for MCAS

   e. Developing analysis techniques to ensure states expand their focus from company-specific issues to general market problems

C. Ensuring Consumer Protection

   1. In a sense, all insurance regulatory activities protect insurance consumers. However, certain activities are designed specifically to support consumers.

   2. State insurance departments often assist with complaints about rates or policy cancellations or with consumers' difficulty in finding insurance.

   3. To help make consumers more knowledgeable about the cost of insurance, some states publish shoppers' guides and other forms of consumer information, and much of this information can be found on the Internet.

Educational Objective 10
Explain how organizations that act as unofficial regulators affect insurance activities.

Key Points:
Insurance regulation involves numerous entities that interact to influence insurer activities.

A. Financial Rating Organizations

1. Several financial rating agencies provide insurer financial ratings, including these:
   a. A.M. Best Company
   b. Duff and Phelps
   c. Moody's
   d. Standard & Poor's
   e. Weiss Ratings, Inc.

2. Generally, these organizations provide summary information about insurer financial strength in the form of a financial rating, typically a letter grade.

3. Corporate risk managers, independent insurance producers, consumers, and others consult these ratings when choosing an insurer.

4. Banks and other lending institutions typically require mortgagors to provide evidence of insurance from an insurer with a specified minimum financial rating.

5. Insurers pay close attention to the factors financial rating agencies consider and endeavor to avoid an adverse rating.

6. An insurer whose financial rating is threatened can implement remedial measures, such as purchasing more reinsurance; limiting new business; selling a portion of its book of business; selling stock to raise additional capital; or merging with another, more financially secure, insurer.

7. A "poor" rating does not mean an insurer will become insolvent, and a "good" rating does not guarantee that the insurer will never become insolvent.

B. Insurance Advisory Organizations
Insurance advisory organizations are companies that work with, and on behalf of, insurers.

1. Advisory organizations develop standard insurance policy forms and provide data regarding rates or prospective loss costs.

2. They may also file loss costs and policy forms with the state on behalf of their member and subscribing insurers.

3. They may provide other valuable services, such as these:
    a. Developing rating systems
    b. Collecting and tabulating statistics
    c. Researching important insurance topics
    d. Providing a forum for discussing important issues
    e. Educating members, the industry, insurance regulators, and the public about relevant issues
    f. Monitoring regulatory issues of concern to members

4. Well-known insurance advisory organizations include Insurance Services Office (ISO), the American Association of Insurance Services (AAIS), and the National Council on Compensation Insurance (NCCI).

5. By developing rate information and standard insurance forms, advisory organizations provide a degree of uniformity that can benefit consumers and regulators as well as serve insurers.

C. Insurance Industry Professional and Trade Associations

1. Professional organizations' members are individuals who share a common profession, whereas the trade associations' members are companies that share a common industry.

2. Trade and professional associations have similar activities, and their main purpose is to advance the success of members as well as uphold ethical standards.

3. Professional associations in the property-casualty insurance industry provide educational, leadership, and ethical development for individual members and their employers.

4. For a fee, members have timely access to legislative developments on the national level and can use association personnel to help them lobby on behalf of the industry group.

5. Trade association members can also participate on trade association committees to help draft new legislation or to influence pending legislation.

6. Trade associations operate not only on the national level but also at state and local levels.

7. Trade associations at the national, state, and local levels influence the NAIC, state and federal legislators, and state insurance regulators.
    a. Trade associations can provide accurate information to legislators and regulators about critical issues in time to influence the development of legislation, regulations, and rules.

b. Trade associations can sometimes persuade legislators and regulators that the insurance industry can solve a problem without legislation.

D. Consumer Groups

Consumers, through consumer groups, have had a major influence on state insurance departments, state and federal legislators, the NAIC, and insurance consumers themselves.

1. Some consumer groups focus solely on insurance issues, while others tackle a variety of public interest issues.

2. Consumer complaints made to state insurance departments can trigger market conduct examinations that may lead to actions ranging from insurer warnings to revocation of an insurer's license.

3. Consumers and consumer groups often influence state insurance commissioners to hold hearings on specific issues, which can lead insurers to take corrective action or lead regulators to develop legislative proposals.

Key Words and Phrases:

 Key Words

National Association of Insurance Commissioners (NAIC)
An association of insurance commissioners from the fifty U.S. states, the District of Columbia, and the five U.S. territories and possessions, whose purpose is to coordinate insurance regulation activities among the various state insurance departments.

Model law
A document drafted by the NAIC, in a style similar to a state statute, that reflects the NAIC's proposed solution to a given problem or issue and provides a common basis to the states for drafting laws that affect the insurance industry. Any state may choose to adopt the model bill or adopt it with modifications.

Model regulation
A draft regulation that may be implemented by a state insurance department if the model law is passed.

Systemic risk
The potential for a major disruption in the function of an entire market or financial system.

Domestic insurer
An insurer doing business in the jurisdiction in which it is incorporated.

Foreign insurer
An insurer licensed to operate in a state but incorporated in another state.

Alien insurer
An insurer domiciled in a country other than the United States.

Capital stock
A balance sheet value that represents the amount of funds that a corporation's stockholders have contributed through the purchase of stock.

Paid-in surplus
The amount stockholders paid in excess of the par value of the stock.

Reciprocal insurer
An insurer owned by its policyholders, formed as an unincorporated association for the purpose of providing insurance coverage to its members (called subscribers), and managed by an attorney-in-fact. Members agree to mutually insure each other, and they share profits and losses in the same proportion as the amount of insurance purchased from the exchange by that member.

Insolvency
A situation in which an entity's current liabilities (as opposed to its total liabilities) exceed its current assets.

Guaranty fund
A state-established fund that provides a system for the payment of some of the unpaid claims of insolvent insurers licensed in that state, generally funded by assessments collected from all insurers licensed in the state.

Good faith claim handling
The manner of handling claims that requires an insurer to give consideration to the insured's interests that is at least equal to the consideration it gives its own interests.

Bad faith (outrage)
A breach of the duty of good faith and fair dealing.

Mortgagor
The person or organization that borrows money from a mortgagee to finance the purchase of real property.

Advisory organization
An independent organization that works with and on behalf of insurers that purchase or subscribe to its services.

Prospective loss costs
Loss data that are modified by loss development, trending, and credibility processes, but without considerations for profit and expenses.

Insurance Marketing and Distribution

3

Key Points:

The property-casualty insurance marketplace is the highly competitive meeting point between customers' needs and insurers' abilities to meet those needs.

A. Characteristics of Property-Casualty Insurance Customers

Customers' characteristics are significant to insurers because they directly affect the products and services they supply to each type of customer group.

1. Individuals

From an insurance perspective, individuals generally share the same needs for property coverage to protect real and personal property and liability coverage for losses arising out of their personal actions and their ownership and use of property.

a. Insurers are able to pool individual insureds' loss exposures based on relevant underwriting factors to determine the appropriate premiums for their policies.

b. Individuals often need to rely on the expertise of a producer to help them decide which types of coverages, policy limits, and deductible levels are most appropriate for their individual circumstances.

c. Individuals have few risk financing alternatives available besides retention and insurance. Mortgagors and lenders often require insurance, and states require auto liability coverage.

d. Individuals have little negotiating power in insurance transactions. If the individual customer is not satisfied with the policy's terms or price, typically his or her only option is to look to other insurers for coverage.

Study Tips

Are you interested in joining a formal class on this material? Go to our Web site, www.TheInstitutes.org, for a complete listing of public classes.

2. Small business

In general, "small business" describes organizations with few employees and limited revenue. Small businesses do not usually have any employees with full-time risk management responsibilities.

   a. The insurance needs of small businesses can usually be covered by a limited number of commercial insurance policies, such as a businessowners policy, a workers compensation policy, and commercial auto policies.

   b. Small businesses have little negotiation power with insurers and a limited number of choices when it comes to risk financing alternatives. Some small businesses have been able to join with similar organizations to form small risk retention groups or purchasing groups as alternatives to the standard commercial insurance market.

3. Middle markets

Organizations that can be classified as middle markets are larger organizations with insurance needs that vary considerably according to the products or services they provide.

   a. Middle-market organizations are often large enough that their loss histories provide credible statistics for use in projecting future losses. They may have a risk manager.

   b. These organizations typically have some negotiating power with insurers because they have a more credible loss history, generate more premium income for the insurer, and have broker representation that can assist in their presentations to insurers.

   c. Middle-market organizations have increasing access to risk financing alternatives such as captives, protected-cell companies, risk retention groups, and contingent capital programs.

4. National accounts

The national accounts segment contains the largest organizations seeking insurance coverage. These organizations have the most complex insurance needs, the most comprehensive knowledge of the insurance market (with a large risk management department and regional or national broker representation), and the widest variety of risk financing alternatives.

   a. National accounts often generate millions of dollars in premiums annually, giving national account brokers the most negotiating power with insurers.

b. National account organizations are likely to have complex insurance programs that combine commercial insurance coverages with sophisticated retention plans and captive insurers.

- Captives provide additional flexibility to bypass the standard commercial insurance market and access reinsurance markets directly.
- Unique loss exposures are often insured by a consortium of insurers that work together to provide the necessary insurance program.

B. Property-Casualty Insurer Marketing Differentiations

An insurer's marketing differentiations uniquely match the characteristics of the customer groups or segments of those groups that they target for sales.

1. Customer focus

a. An insurer must understand the characteristics of specific customer groups and provide products and services that respond to those characteristics.

b. Customer focus is improved through market intelligence, which provides information that is relevant to understanding customers' current and future needs, preferences, attitudes, and behaviors.

2. Products and services

a. Personal or commercial lines insurers may focus on property or liability insurance, package policies, or specialty lines, but often sell a range of insurance products that meet the needs of their customers.

b. Services are also tailored to respond to customers' needs identified through market intelligence.

3. Size

a. An important driver of competition is the size of the organizations in an industry. For a given number of organizations, the level of competition is usually greater if all organizations are approximately the same size than if there are two or three large organizations and many small ones.

b. An insurer's size influences its decision in the market it enters and the customer groups to which it chooses to market.

- If a market is dominated by a large organization, a smaller insurer might select a subsection of the market or niche market to target and tailor its product to better meet the closely defined needs of that group.

- A small insurer might avoid the national accounts market, where large written premiums must be reinsured or offset by significant reserve levels, reducing an insurer's ability to write a substantial number of other accounts.

4. Geographic area

   a. Although thousands of insurers may compete in the United States, not all of them compete nationally. Many insurers are small organizations that compete in only one or a limited number of states.

   b. An insurer's decision regarding geographic area is based on its size, its level of expertise in writing coverage in broader geographic areas, the level of competition in those areas, and its customer focus.

5. Distribution system

   a. An insurer's choice of marketing system(s) is influenced by its customers' knowledge of insurance products and the risk financing alternatives available.

      - Insurers focused on mature customers with homes, autos, and valuable personal property may choose a distribution system based on exclusive agents or independent agents.

      - Alternatively, an insurer targeting sales of personal auto insurance to young drivers who have a high probability of selecting the lowest-priced coverage might choose an Internet-based distribution system.

   b. Similar decisions regarding the selection of marketing systems are made for small-business, middle-market, and national accounts.

C. Unique Factors in the Insurance Marketplace

All marketplaces are influenced by changes in the economy. The property-casualty insurance marketplace is also shaped by unique economic forces, regulatory controls, and technology demands that set the parameters within which insurers must operate.

1. Economic forces

   a. Property-casualty insurers manage a narrow margin of underwriting profitability to remain competitive.

   b. Inflation is a factor in increasing the costs of losses and the costs of an insurer's operations. Similarly, the availability of reinsurance influences the price and the cost of insurer operations.

   c. When investment earnings are diminished or the prospect of catastrophe losses increase, insurers must raise premiums to sustain risk-appropriate rates of return.

2. Regulatory controls

State-based insurance regulations stipulate the financial requirements that insurers must sustain to operate within a state and the marketing conduct to which insurers must adhere.

3. Demands for technology

  a. The demand for technology is a powerful factor in the insurance marketplace because of the computer networks that interconnect insurers and producers as well as the technological connections between insurers and customers through the Internet.

  b. The primary demand for technology in these marketing applications is ease of use.

4. Underwriting cycles

  a. Underwriting cycles create additional competitive shifts to which insurers continuously adapt.

  b. Because underwriting cycles have numerous causes, they have varying duration and depth. As a result, insurers must also adapt as the cycle patterns reveal themselves to remain competitive.

5. Unanticipated catastrophic losses

  a. Insurers maintain reserves and reinsurance to pay catastrophe losses. However, catastrophes of unanticipated severity can cause losses that exceed maximum anticipated losses.

  b. Unplanned losses can result in insurer insolvencies, withdrawal of insurers from geographic markets, and reinsurance shortages. The market must respond with improved catastrophe ratemaking and forecasting that anticipates even greater unforeseen events.

Educational Objective 2

Explain how typical insurer marketing activities are performed and why they are performed.

Key Points:

Activities performed by marketing can be divided into these categories:

A. Marketing Research

Marketing research is the systematic gathering and analyzing of data to assist in making decisions. Marketing research is typically done on a project basis with a stated objective, research design, data collection, analysis, and formal report. Effective marketing research results include conclusions and implications or recommendations.

1. Market research methods

The best marketing research is conducted as scientifically as possible. A researcher should strive for objectivity.

a. The research may consist of qualitative studies, such as focus groups and observer impressions, and quantitative studies that use survey research techniques and statistical analysis of the data included in corporate databases.

b. The two broad categories of market data are secondary data and primary data.

- Research typically begins with secondary data, which is data collected by other parties, because it is immediately available at little or no cost.

- Primary data collection is more expensive, but it addresses issues specific to the marketing research project.

c. Increasingly, insurers are applying predictive analytics to improve the outcome of market research.

- Most predictive models generate a score, with the higher score indicating a higher likelihood that the given behavior or event will occur.

- A predictive model weighs the importance of each relevant variable to provide an estimate of the likely profitability of each characteristic.

- Insurers can take advantage of additional applications for predictive analytics in marketing, such as cross-selling, target marketing, individualized customer support, new agent contracting, and designing and evaluating marketing campaigns.

2. Market segmentation

Insurers use market segmentation to differentiate themselves from other insurance providers to meet the needs of customer groups.

- **a.** Target marketing is a practice of more closely defining a group of customers within a market segment.
- **b.** Niche marketing is a well-defined, often small, marketing segment of the population that has specific needs.
- **c.** The more closely a group of customers is defined, the more closely an insurer can develop expertise regarding the customers' needs and tailor products and services to meet those needs.
- **d.** As groups are more closely defined, insurers are less likely to encounter competition for that group than in the open market.
- **e.** Marketers commonly use four bases of segmentation, among others:
  - Behavioristic segmentation—the division of a total consumer market by purchase behavior
  - Geographic segmentation—the division of markets by geographic units
  - Demographic segmentation—the division of markets based on demographic variables, such as age, gender, education, occupation, ethnicity, income, family size, and family life cycle
  - Psychographic segmentation—the division of markets by individuals' values, personalities, attitudes, and lifestyles
- **f.** Each marketing segment should be accessible, substantial, and responsive.

B. Market Development

Market development activities provide leadership when an insurer enters a new market, which may be a new territory, customer type, or product.

1. Market development involves actions required to ensure the success of the venture, including training programs, problem resolution, process documentation, funding assistance, technical assistance, and public relations campaigns.

2. The market development staff includes project managers who generate and screen ideas. Project managers are also skilled in developing project scope documents, decision grids, task outlines, progress reports, and project reports.

C. Marketing Information

Marketing information activities develop and maintain information needed in market planning to support management at all levels in answering specific questions concerning markets, customers, producers, and competitors. It is divided into two major types of systems:

1. The internal accounting system provides report and analysis capability based on transactions associated with sales activity. Much of the essential information on production, retention, and policies in force is available as a byproduct of the systems that keep track of commissions and billings.

2. The marketing monitoring system provides intelligence about the external environment to inform senior management about important developments and changing conditions. The market monitor should provide current, unfiltered, and unbiased information about customers, producers, and competitors.

D. Marketing Planning

Marketing planning provides the tools and facilitation skills to assist management in developing fact-based marketing plans. This activity also assists in developing and updating the company's strategic plans.

1. Before introducing a new insurance product or service, the insurer completes a comprehensive marketing plan, which identifies the product or service to be promoted, the customers to be targeted, and the resources and strategies that will be used to create, price, promote, and sell the product or service.

2. A marketing plan for a typical insurance product or service might include, but is not limited to, these items:
   a. Product proposal and sales goals
   b. Situational analysis
   c. Marketing goals
   d. Marketing strategies
   e. Projected outcome

E. Product Development

Insurers usually follow a series of steps in product development:

1. Opportunity assessment
   a. Monitor market
   b. Identify opportunity

     c. Relate opportunities to business strategy

     d. Develop specifications

     e. Secure senior management approval to proceed

  2. Development of contract, underwriting, and pricing

     a. Develop coverage and policy forms

     b. Develop guidelines for underwriting and claims

     c. Develop classifications

     d. Develop pricing structure

     e. Secure approval from functional managers to proceed

  3. Business forecast

     a. Review the product plan with profit center management

     b. Identify requirements for statistics

     c. Develop business forecast

     d. Secure senior management approval to proceed

  4. Regulatory requirements

     a. File with regulators

     b. Develop statistical information systems

     c. Communicate regulatory approval

  5. Distribution requirements

     a. Develop advertising and sales promotional information

     b. Develop sales training

     c. Plan roll-out strategy

  6. Introduction

     a. Implement sales training and promotion

     b. Measure and compare results to plan

F. Advertising and Promotion

  1. The advertising function is responsible for managing the company's communications through mass media with its chosen target markets.

  2. Sales promotion, including brochures and giveaway items, reinforces the image and positioning created by the insurer's advertising efforts when carried down to the agency level.

G. Customer and Public Relations

  1. The customer relations function manages communications with individual customers from the home office.

     a. This functional area ensures that all written communications seen by customers are understandable and consistent in quality and tone.

     b. The customer relations function also provides a forum for communications to the insurer initiated by customers, including complaints, suggestions, and questions.

2. Public relations activities include communications with the public on behalf of the insurer to ensure a strong public image.

    a. The public relations staff provides periodic information to the insurer's community about the organization's activities.

    b. In times of crisis, the public relations staff coordinates a consolidated message to the media to provide consistent communication as well as to respond to negative publicity, if necessary.

H. Sales Fulfillment

    1. Sales fulfillment is the satisfactory delivery of the products and services that result from the product development activity.

    2. Fulfillment of a product plan affects many of an insurer's functional areas. Each functional area must determine the impact of the plan on operations, budget, and performance standards.

    3. Milestones should be established for the functional areas with metrics to periodically check the results of the marketing plan and take action in any area where goals are not met.

Educational Objective 3

Describe the main types of insurance distribution systems and channels, including the principal characteristics that distinguish one distribution system from another.

Key Points:

Insurers use many types of distribution systems based on their organizational structure, business and marketing plans, growth goals, technological capabilities, staffing, and other resources necessary to support the selected system(s).

A. Independent Agency and Brokerage Marketing Systems

The independent agency and brokerage marketing system uses agents and brokers. These independent agents and brokers are usually free to represent as many or as few insurers as they want.

1. Independent agents and brokers

a. An independent agency is a business, operated for the benefit of its owner (or owners), that sells insurance, usually as a representative of several unrelated insurers.

b. An insurance broker is an independent business owner or firm that sells insurance by representing customers rather than insurers. Brokers shop among insurers to find the best coverage and value for their clients.

c. One of the main distinguishing features between independent agents and brokers and other distribution systems is the ownership of the agency expiration list.

- If the insurer ceases to do business with an agency, the agency has the right to continue doing business with its existing customers by selling them insurance with another insurer.

- The ownership of expiration lists is an agency's most valuable asset. An independent agency has the right to sell its expiration lists to another independent agent.

d. Compensation for independent agents and brokers is typically in two forms:

- A flat percent commission on all new and renewal business submitted

- A contingent or profit-sharing commission based on volume or loss ratio goals

2. National and regional brokers

   a. National and regional brokers generally represent commercial insurance accounts that often require sophisticated knowledge and service.

   b. In addition to insurance sales, large brokerage firms may provide extensive risk control, appraisal, actuarial, risk management, claim administration, and other insurance-related services that large businesses need.

   c. They can tailor insurance programs for customers or groups of customers who require a particular type of coverage for multiple locations.

   d. The brokers receive negotiated fees for the services they provide, or they receive fees in addition to commissions, subject to state regulation.

3. Independent agent networks

   a. Independent agent networks, also known as agent groups, agent clusters, or agent alliances, consist of independent agencies and brokerages that join together to gain advantages normally available only to large national and regional brokers.

   b. By combining individual agency forces into a single selling, negotiating, and servicing unit, an agent network can offer many benefits to its agent members, including obtaining access to an increased number of insurers, meeting counter-signature law requirements for businesses in multiple states, and combining premium volume to meet insurer requirements for profit-sharing.

4. Managing general agents (MGAs)

   a. MGAs serve as intermediaries between insurers and the agents and brokers who sell insurance directly to the customer, similar to wholesalers in the marketing system for tangible goods.

   b. The exact duties and responsibilities of an MGA depend on its contracts with the insurers it represents.

   c. An insurer operating through an MGA reaps the advantages of a low fixed cost, specialty expertise, and the assumption of insurer activities.

5. Surplus lines brokers

   a. A surplus lines broker places business with insurers not licensed in the state in which the transaction occurs but that are permitted to write insurance because coverage is not available through standard market insurers.

    b. The circumstances under which business can be placed with an unlicensed (or nonadmitted) insurer through a surplus lines broker vary by state. Normally, a reasonable effort to place the coverage with a licensed insurer is required.

    c. The agents and brokers, who must be licensed to place surplus lines business in that state, may be required to certify that a specified number (often two or three) of licensed insurers have refused to provide the coverage.

    d. Surplus lines insurance is appropriate for customers who require high limits of insurance or unusually broad or specialized insurance, have an unusual or unique loss exposure, or have an unfavorable loss exposure.

B. Exclusive Agency Marketing System

    1. The exclusive agency marketing system uses independent contractors called exclusive agents (or captive agents), who are not employees of insurers.

    2. Exclusive agents are usually restricted by contract to representing a single insurer.

    3. Insurer management can exercise greater control over exclusive agents than over independent agents. However, some exclusive agency companies allow their agents to place business with other insurers if the exclusive agency insurer does not offer the product or service needed.

    4. Exclusive agents typically do not own expirations as independent producers do. However, some insurers that market through the exclusive agency system do grant agents limited ownership of expirations.

        a. Usually, when the agency contract is terminated, the ownership of expirations reverts to the insurer.

        b. The agent does not have the option of selling the expirations to anyone other than the insurer.

    5. The exclusive agency insurer handles many administrative functions for the exclusive agent, including policy issuance, premium collection, and claim processing.

C. Direct Writer Marketing System

    1. This system uses sales agents (also known as sales representatives) who are employees of the insurers they represent.

    2. Sales agents usually do not have any ownership of expirations and are usually restricted to representing a single insurer or a group or insurers.

3. When a customer needs a type of policy not available from the direct writer insurer, the sales agent may act as a broker by contacting an agent who represents another insurer and apply for insurance through that agent.

D. Distribution Channels

Insurers' increasing use of multiple distribution channels has been driven by technology and customer preference.

1. Internet

    The Internet can be used to varying degrees by all parties to the insurance transaction. Interactions range from exchanges of e-mail to multiple-policy quoting, billing, and policy issuance.

2. Call centers

    Call centers sell insurance products and services through telemarketing. The best-equipped call centers can replicate many of the activities of producers. In addition to making product sales, call center staff can respond to general inquiries, handle claim reporting, answer billing inquiries, and process policy endorsements.

3. Direct response

    The direct response distribution channel markets directly to customers. No agent is involved; rather, the direct response relies primarily on mail, phone, and/or Internet sales. With direct response, commission costs, if any, are greatly reduced. However, a disadvantage is that advertising costs are typically higher.

4. Group marketing

    Group marketing sells insurance products and services through call centers, the Internet, direct mail response, or a producer to individuals or businesses that are all members of the same organization.

5. Financial institutions

    Insurers and producers can elect to market their products and services through a bank or another financial services institution, either exclusively or through using additional distribution channels. Insurers view financial institutions as beneficial strategic partners because of their strong customer base and predisposition to product cross-selling, among other reasons.

E. Mixed Marketing System

1. The term mixed marketing system refers to an insurer's use of more than one distribution system or channel to attract a wider range of customers.

2. Combining insurance distribution systems and channels requires consideration of several issues:
   a. Maintaining consistent customer communications
   b. Providing a consistent customer experience
   c. Matching the type of insurance with an appropriate distribution system and channel

Educational Objective 4
Describe the functions performed by insurance producers.

Key Points:

The functions insurance producers perform vary widely from one marketing system to another and from one producer to another within a given marketing system. Generally, producers are the initial contact with insurance customers and provide expertise and ongoing services.

A. Prospecting

Prospecting involves locating persons, businesses, and other entities that might be interested in purchasing the insurance products and services offered by the producer's principals.

B. Risk Management Review

Risk management review is the principal method of determining a prospect's insurance needs.

1. Individual or family

For an individual or a family, the risk management review process might be relatively simple, requiring an interview or completion of a questionnaire that assists in identifying the prospect's loss exposures, which are often associated with property ownership and activities.

2. Businesses

a. The risk management review process for businesses is likely to be more complex because they have property ownership, products, services, employees, and liabilities that are unique to the size and type of organization.

b. A loss run report can guide the producer in helping the business owner develop risk management plans, track the results of current risk management efforts, identify problem areas, and project costs.

C. Sales

1. Selling insurance products and services is one of the most important activities of an insurance producer.

2. Steps in the sales process include contacting the prospective client, determining the prospect's needs, preparing and presenting a proposal, and closing the sale.

D. Policy Issuance

  1. At the producer's request, insurers issue policies and their associated forms, either mailing them directly to policyholders or sending them to the producer for delivery.

  2. Some producers use their own agency management systems to generate computer-issued policies on site.

E. Premium Collection

  Producers who issue policies might also prepare policy invoices and collect premiums.

  1. After deducting their commissions, they send the net premiums to the insurers, a procedure known as the agency bill process. For business that is agency billed, there are three widely used methods of transmitting premiums to the insurer:

  a. Item basis

  The premium (less commission) is forwarded to the insurer when the producer collects it or when it becomes due.

  b. Statement basis

  The insurer sends a statement to the producer showing the premiums that are due. The producer is obligated to pay the premiums indicated as due or to show that the statement is in error.

  c. Account current basis

  The producer periodically prepares a statement showing the premiums due to the insurer, after deducting appropriate commissions, and transmits that amount to the insurer. The producer must pay the insurer when the premium is due, even if the policyholders have not paid the producer.

  2. For small commercial accounts and the vast majority of personal insurance, the customer is usually directed to send premium payments to the insurer, bypassing the producer in a procedure known as the direct bill process.

F. Customer Service

  Customer service activities that producers perform can include responding to billing inquiries, performing customer account review, engaging in field underwriting, answering questions regarding existing coverage and additional coverage requirements, and corresponding with premium auditors and risk control representatives.

G. Claim Handling

  All producers are likely to be involved to some extent in handling claims filed by their policyholders.

1. The producer might simply give the policyholder the telephone number of the claim department.

2. The producer might obtain some basic information about the claim from the policyholder, relay it to the insurer, and arrange for a claim representative to contact the insured.

3. Some producers are authorized by their insurers to adjust some types of claims.

H. Consulting

Many producers offer consulting services, for which they are paid on a fee basis.

Educational Objective 5

Describe the key factors an insurer should evaluate during the distribution-system and distribution-channel selection process.

Key Points:

The key factors in selecting distribution systems and channels are based on customers' needs and characteristics as well as the insurer's profile.

A. Customers' Needs and Characteristics

The needs and characteristics of customers, both existing and those in target markets, are key factors in an insurer's selection of distribution systems and channels because their satisfaction drives their purchase decisions. These are examples of customer needs and characteristics:

1. Products and services
   a. Customers with low service expectations may be satisfied with the ease of comparison shopping over the Internet for direct writers' policies.
   b. A large commercial account's risk manager will seek the expertise of an agent or broker.

2. Price
   a. Some consumers' paramount concern is the price of insurance. Others are concerned with price to a degree, but are unlikely to make changes if they are satisfied with a product.
   b. Others seek risk management alternatives, including insurance that will minimize the adverse effects of losses for the organization over the long term.

3. Response time
   a. For those customers whose inquiries and transactions can be addressed by telephone or via the Internet, a variety of distribution systems and channels can meet those needs.
   b. Speed can be an issue in attracting commercial accounts that demand extensive services if producers are not in the territory of the businesses' facilities.

B. Insurer's Profile

The insurer must evaluate these key factors in selecting distribution systems and channels:

1. Insurer strategies and goals
    a. An insurer's strategies, defined by high-level organizational goals, provide purposeful direction for the organization.
    b. These strategies and goals often address issues regarding market share size, sales, service, and the markets in which the insurer competes. They may also relate to acquisitions, strategic alliances, or mergers.
    c. Changes in market strategies or aggressive goals can be a catalyst for an insurer to reexamine its distribution systems and channels, if current approaches are inadequate to achieve required results.

2. Insurer strengths
    Organizations evaluate their internal and external environments to assess their strengths and weaknesses compared to external opportunities and threats. After determining where its strengths lie, an insurer selects those distribution systems and channels that maximize its opportunities to capture market share and minimize its weaknesses. In doing so, the insurer may analyze these factors:
    a. Financial resources
        • The initial fixed cost of entering the market through the exclusive agency system or direct writer system is greater than doing so through the independent agency system.
        • The insurer must hire, train, and financially support the direct writer and exclusive agency producers at substantial cost before they become productive. Similarly, Internet-based distribution channels have high start-up costs for supporting information systems.
        • Insurers with the financial resources to initiate distribution systems and channels with high start-up costs have the option of competing in markets that are best served by those marketing methods.
    b. Core capabilities
        • Core capabilities include the abilities of an organization's staff, processes, and technology.
        • Complex commercial accounts require personalized service and are well served by agents and brokers, who can provide advice and ongoing service to expand the types of businesses to which the insurer markets or its geographic market.
    c. Expertise and reputation of producers
        The level of expertise required of a producer depends on the lines of insurance written.

- Specialty target markets, such as international manufacturing, high-net-worth individuals, and large public entities require knowledgeable and prominent producers to advise them. Having producers with those attributes in a direct writer distribution system allows the insurer to expand into similar or secondary markets.
- An insurer attempting to enter specialty markets without the skill base or staff must compete for agents and brokers who can provide the needed expertise and reputation.

3. Existing and target markets
   a. The characteristics of an insurer's existing book of business should be considered in any change in distribution system or channel. If agents or brokers own the expirations for current accounts, the insurer must either give up that business and start over or purchase the expirations from producers.
   b. Disruptions in communication channels can also cause changes in communication patterns that can result in policyholder dissatisfaction and lost accounts.
      - Insurers change market systems and channels for existing customers with great caution.
      - Some catalysts are sufficiently threatening to cause an insurer to change marketing approaches. For example, an insurer that is losing market share to an aggressive new competitor has ample incentive to change its approach to better address customers' needs and characteristics.
   c. The insurer carefully balances the cost of changing its distribution systems and channels with expected benefits resulting from the new accounts it will write.

4. Geographic location
   The geographic location of existing policyholders or target markets is a key concern in selecting a distribution system and channels because the insurer's fixed costs of establishing an exclusive agent or direct-writer agent in a territory are substantial.
   a. Exclusive agent or direct writer marketing systems can be successful only when a sufficient number of prospects exist within a relatively small geographic area.
   b. The cost of appointing an independent agent or using the direct response system is generally lower than the cost of appointing an exclusive or direct-writer agent.
   c. Some insurers that traditionally used either the exclusive agency system or the direct writer system have elected to use the independent agency system in rural areas and small towns because of the lower startup costs.

5. Degree of control required

The extent of control the insurer wants to exercise over its marketing operations may influence its choice of a distribution system:

  a. An insurer can exercise the greatest control over producers in the direct writer system. Under that system, the producer is an employee of the company, and the company can exercise control over both the results achieved and the methods used to achieve them.

  b. Under both the agency and brokerage system and the exclusive agency system, the producers are independent contractors. The insurer can control only the results they produce, not the methods by which they produce them.

  c. Producers are not involved in the direct response system. Consequently, the insurer has complete control of its distribution system.

Key Words and Phrases:

Key Words

Producer
Any of several kinds of insurance personnel who place insurance business with insurers and who represent either insurers or insureds, or both.

Market intelligence
Information gathered and analyzed regarding a company's markets to improve competitive decision-making.

Underwriting cycle
A cyclical pattern of insurance pricing in which a soft market (low rates, relaxed underwriting, and underwriting losses) is eventually followed by a hard market (high rates, restrictive underwriting, and underwriting gains) before the pattern again repeats itself.

Focus group
A small group of customers or potential customers brought together to provide opinions about a specific product, service, need, or other issue.

Predictive analytics
Statistical and analytical techniques used to develop models that predict future events or behaviors.

Market segmentation
The process of identifying and dividing the groups within a market that share needs and characteristics and that will respond similarly to a marketing action.

Target marketing
Focusing marketing efforts on a specific group of consumers.

Niche marketing
A type of marketing that focuses on specific types of buyers who are a subset of a larger market.

Distribution system
The necessary people and physical facilities to support the sale of insurance products and services.

Agency expiration list
The record of an insurance agency's present policyholders and the dates their policies expire.

Countersignature laws
Laws that require all policies covering subjects of insurance within a state to be signed by a resident producer licensed in that state.

Managing general agent (MGA)
An authorized agent of the primary insurer that manages all or part of the primary insurer's insurance activities, usually in a specific geographic area.

Direct response distribution channel
An insurance distribution channel that markets directly to the customer through such distribution channels as mail, telephone, or the Internet.

Affinity marketing
A type of group marketing that targets various groups based on profession, association, interests, hobbies, and attitudes.

Cold canvass
Contacting a prospect without an appointment.

Loss run
A report detailing an insured's history of claims that have occurred over a specific period, valued as of a specific date.

Agency bill
A payment procedure in which a producer sends premium bills to the insured, collects the premium, and sends the premium to the insurer, less any applicable commission.

Direct bill
A payment procedure in which the insurer assumes all responsibility for sending premium bills to the insured, collecting the premium, and sending any commission payable on the premium collected to the producer.

The Underwriting Function

4

Educational Objective 1
Describe the purpose of underwriting.

Key Points:

The overarching purpose of underwriting is to develop and maintain a profitable book of business for the insurer. To achieve profitability, the underwriting function serves additional purposes:

A. Guarding Against Adverse Selection

   1. Underwriters are an insurer's guard against adverse selection (the tendency for people with the greatest probability of loss to be the ones most likely to purchase insurance).

   2. Underwriters minimize the effects of adverse selection by these methods:

     a. Carefully selecting the applicants whose loss exposures they are willing to insure

     b. Charging appropriate premiums for the applicants that they do accept

     c. Monitoring applications and books of business for unusual patterns of policy growth or loss

B. Ensuring Adequate Policyholders' Surplus

   1. An insurance company must have adequate policyholders' surplus if it wishes to increase its written premium volume.

   2. An insurer's capacity is limited by regulatory guidelines and often by its own voluntary constraints.

   3. If an insurer's underwriting practices generate policy premiums that exceed losses and expenses, the policyholders' surplus will increase, thereby increasing capacity.

C. Enforcing Underwriting Guidelines

   1. Underwriting guidelines reflect the levels of underwriting authority that are granted to varying levels of underwriters, producers, and managing general agents (MGAs).

Study Tips

The review questions help reinforce this material. Take some time now to complete them.

2. If loss exposures, risks, or policy limits on an application exceed an underwriter's authority, he or she will seek approval through supervisory and management ranks within the underwriting department.

Educational Objective 2

Describe the underwriting activities typically performed by line and staff underwriters.

Key Points:

In insurance organizations, underwriting responsibilities are delegated by members of senior management to line and staff underwriters who coordinate the day-to-day risk selection decisions and the management-level underwriting activities. This coordinated effort is crucial to the achievement of the insurer's profitability goals.

A. Line Underwriting Activities

Most line underwriters are responsible for these major activities:

1. Select insureds

   a. Line underwriters select new and renewal accounts that meet the criteria established in underwriting guidelines.

   b. Effective account selection is essential to attaining these goals:

   - Avoiding adverse selection
   - Charging adequate premiums for accounts with a higher-than-average chance of loss
   - Selecting better-than-average accounts for which the premium charged will be more than adequate
   - Rationing an insurer's available capacity to obtain an optimum spread of loss exposures by location, class, size of risk, and line of business

2. Classify and price accounts

   a. Account classification is the process of grouping accounts with similar attributes so that they can be priced appropriately.

   b. Line underwriters are responsible for ensuring that all the information needed for classification is obtained and that accounts are priced properly.

   - Accounts that are misclassified and priced too low are a bargain for the policyholder, but the insurer receives premiums that are inadequate for the loss exposures they assume.
   - Policyholders may move accounts that are overcharged, because of a misclassification, to another insurer once the policyholder discovers a better price.

- Insurers submit classification plans to state insurance regulators; those who do not implement their classification plan as filed are subject to possible fines.

3. Recommend or provide coverage

   a. Determining an applicant's coverage needs is generally the responsibility of the insurance agent or broker or the insured's risk manager.

   b. Line underwriters support the producers and policyholders by inquiring about an insured's risk management program to ensure that they are using other risk management techniques to address gaps in insurance coverage.

   c. Sometimes an underwriter must narrow an insured's coverage.

      - Rather than decline the application, the underwriter may offer a more limited form of coverage involving higher deductibles or covering fewer causes of loss.

      - The producer has an opportunity to provide reduced coverage that may be acceptable to the applicant rather than reject the applicant altogether.

   d. Line underwriters also have a role in ensuring that applicants obtain the coverage they request. Line underwriters must explain the types of losses the coverage forms are designed to cover and the endorsements that must be added to provide the coverage desired.

   e. For some complex or unique accounts, the line underwriter will draft a manuscript policy or endorsement that is worded to address the specific coverage needs of the insured.

4. Manage a book of business

   a. Underwriting management usually reinforces departmental goals through individual line underwriters.

   b. Some insurers also make line underwriters responsible for the profitability of a book of business accepted from a producer, or written in a territory or line of business.

5. Support producers and customers

   a. Some insurers rely on customer service departments to respond to routine inquiries and requests.

   b. Insurers operating through independent agents often rely on their sales force to perform many policy service functions.

   c. Line underwriters are usually directly involved with producers in preparing policy quotations.

6. Coordinate with marketing efforts

   Insurer marketing efforts should conform to the insurer's underwriting policy.

    a. Producers are discouraged from submitting accounts that are clearly outside the insurer's underwriting guidelines.

    b. Some insurers rely on special agents or field representatives to market the insurer and its products to agents and brokers.

    c. Some insurers have blended the responsibilities of special agents and line underwriters into the position of production underwriter.

B. Staff Underwriting Activities

Staff underwriters work closely with underwriting management to perform activities essential for profitable risk selection.

  1. Research the market

    a. Insurers must continually research fundamental issues such as which markets the insurer should target.

    b. Research includes an ongoing evaluation of these items:
- Effect of adding or deleting entire types of business
- Effect of expanding into additional states or retiring from states presently serviced
- Optimal product mix in the book of business
- Premium volume goals

  2. Formulate underwriting policy

    a. An insurer's underwriting policy, also referred to as underwriting philosophy, guides individual and aggregate decision making.

    b. Underwriting policy is communicated through underwriting guidelines.

    c. Staff underwriters work with employees from other departments to formulate underwriting policy.

    d. No single underwriting policy is appropriate for all insurers. Insurers often develop their underwriting policy within the context of these markets they serve:
- Standard market—better-than-average accounts for which the average premium is more than adequate
- Nonstandard market—higher-risk applicants who are charged a higher-than-average premium
- Specialty market—accounts that have unique needs, such as professional liability, that are not adequately addressed in the standard market

  3. Revise underwriting guidelines

Staff underwriters are usually responsible for revising underwriting guidelines so that they accurately reflect changes in underwriting policy.

    a. The underwriting guides identify the major elements that line underwriters should evaluate for each type of insurance.

    b. Some underwriting guides include systematic instructions for handling particular classes of commercial accounts.

    c. Guides may identify specific hazards to evaluate, alternatives to consider, criteria to use when making the final decision, ways to implement the decision, and methods to monitor the decision.

4. Evaluate loss experience

Staff underwriters evaluate an insurer's loss experience to determine whether changes should be made in underwriting guidelines.

    a. Staff underwriters research loss data to determine the specific source of the excess losses.

    b. Part of this research includes an analysis of insurance industry loss experience that may reveal trends affecting the insurer's products.

5. Research and develop coverage forms

    a. Insurance advisory organizations have a significant role in the development of commonly used coverage forms.

    b. Staff underwriters work cooperatively with the actuarial and legal departments to develop new coverages and modify existing coverage forms developed by advisory organizations.

6. Review and revise pricing plans

Staff underwriters review and update rates and rating plans continually, subject to regulatory constraints, to respond to changes in loss experience, competition, and inflation.

    a. Historical loss data are gathered by the insurer or by advisory organizations to develop prospective loss costs.

    b. Staff underwriters combine prospective loss costs with an insurer-developed profit and expense loading to create a final rate used in policy pricing.

    c. Production efficiencies or a superior account-selection process is reflected in lower expense loadings, which can lead to a pricing plan that provides the insurer with a competitive advantage.

    d. For those coverages for which advisory organizations do not develop loss costs, the insurer must develop its own rates.

7. Arrange treaty reinsurance

Staff underwriters are responsible for securing and maintaining treaty reinsurance.

    a. Staff underwriters' responsibility includes determining the insurer's needs for reinsurance, selecting reinsurers, negotiating the terms and conditions of reinsurance treaties, and maintaining the insurer's relations with its treaty reinsurers.

    b. For commercial property accounts, many staff underwriters maintain a line authorization guide, which serves as a control on the property limits accepted based on the treaty reinsurance agreement.

8. Assist others with complex accounts

    a. Staff underwriters often serve as consultants to other underwriters.

    b. Staff underwriters also function as "referral underwriters"—that is, when an application exceeds a line underwriter's authority, a referral underwriter can review and approve the risk.

9. Conduct underwriting audits

Staff underwriters are often responsible for monitoring line underwriter activities and adherence to underwriting authority by conducting underwriting audits.

    a. The audits focus on proper documentation; adherence to procedure, classification, and rating practices; and conformity of selection decisions to the underwriting guide and bulletins.

    b. Staff underwriters also monitor underwriting activity by analyzing statistical results by type of insurance, class of business, size of loss exposure, and territory.

10. Participate in industry associations

    a. Many insurers are members of national and state associations that address insurance industry concerns. Staff underwriters typically represent the insurer as a member of these organizations.

    b. Staff underwriters may also serve on an advisory organization's committees that study standard policy forms and recommend changes.

11. Conduct education and training

Staff underwriters are usually responsible for determining the education and training needs of line underwriters.

    a. Training needs can be addressed in several ways:

- Through a formal training program that all newly hired underwriters must complete
- Through classes that address a specific underwriting issue or procedure, if the training need is transitory
- Through programs provided by the insurer's human resources department

    b. Staff underwriters often develop courses and serve as instructors in technical insurance subjects.

Educational Objective 3
Describe the importance of compliance with underwriting authority in individual account selection.

Key Points:
The levels of underwriting authority granted to underwriters reflect their experience and knowledge in risk selection decisions. Authority may also be granted to producers and managing general agencies. Compliance with levels of authority is crucial to maintaining the appropriate controls over risk selection.

A. Levels of Authority
1. As their levels of underwriting authority increase, underwriters' responsibility for accurately applying experience and judgment also increases.
2. Before accepting an applicant, a line underwriter must determine whether he or she has the necessary underwriting authority to make the decision.

B. Authority Requirements
Underwriting authority requirements are usually communicated to an underwriter through the insurer's underwriting guidelines.
1. A notation next to a specific classification in the underwriting guide, for example, might indicate that a senior underwriter must review and approve an application from that classification before it is processed further.
2. Another approach to controlling underwriting authority is to specify in the underwriting guidelines the policy limits at which the accounts must be submitted to a higher authority.
3. In addition, certain rating plans, endorsements, or coverage forms might require higher underwriting.

C. Granting Authority
1. To place controls on levels of underwriting authority, insurers generally grant authority in these ways:
   a. Underwriters gain underwriting authority with experience and positive results.
   b. Producers may gain underwriting authority based on experience, profitability, and contractual arrangements.
   c. Managing general agents (MGA), when appointed, assume decentralized underwriting authority, which capitalizes on an MGA's familiarity with local conditions.

2. Insurers with conservative internal underwriting philosophies and specialty insurers may not grant underwriting authority to any entities beyond their own internal underwriters.

Educational Objective 4

Describe the constraining factors considered in the establishment of underwriting policy.

Key Points:

An insurer's underwriting policy promotes the type of insurance anticipated to produce a growing and profitable book of business. However, various factors constrain what an underwriting policy can accomplish.

A. Financial Capacity

An insurer's financial capacity refers to the relationship between premiums written and the size of the policyholders' surplus, which is an insurer's net worth.

1. The National Association of Insurance Commissioners (NAIC) has developed a series of financial ratios that it uses in conjunction with analytical evaluations to identify insurers that should receive additional solvency surveillance from regulators.

   a. The premiums-to-surplus ratio is considered too high when it exceeds 300 percent, or 3-to-1.

   b. Because of conservative statutory accounting principles used in insurance, rapid growth results in a reduction in policyholders' surplus to pay for expenses generated by that growth.

2. Insurers recognize the limitations of their capacity and seek to write those lines of business or accounts that maximize return on equity. These activities help realize maximization:

   a. Setting return thresholds

   b. Redirecting focus on target business classes

   c. Adjusting underwriting policy based on jurisdiction

3. Return on equity is a fundamental measure of insurer profitability. This financial ratio relates net operating gain (after taxes) as a percentage of prior-year capital and surplus.

   a. The statutory accounting principles (SAP) and generally accepted accounting principles (GAAP) approaches to calculating return on equity differ.

   b. Stock insurers calculate both ratios and mutual insurers calculate only the SAP.

B. Regulation

1. States promulgate insurance regulations that take the form of statutes enacted by state legislatures and regulations adopted by the state insurance department. Regulation is not applied uniformly across states.

2. Regulation affects underwriting policy in several ways:

   a. Insurers must be licensed to write insurance in each state in which they write insurance.

   b. Rates, rules, and forms must be filed with state regulators.

   c. Some states specifically require underwriting guidelines to be filed.

   d. If consumer groups believe that the insurance industry has not adequately served certain geographic areas, regulatory focus on insurance availability can lead to requirements to extend coverage to loss exposures that an insurer might not write otherwise.

3. State regulators perform market conduct examinations to ensure that insurers adhere to the classification and rating plans they have filed.

C. Personnel

1. Insurers require the talent of specialists. An insurer must have a sufficient number of properly trained underwriters to implement its underwriting policy.

2. The insurer must have the personnel where they are needed.

   a. As a general practice, an insurer should obtain premiums from a broad range of insureds to create the widest possible distribution of loss exposures.

   b. Regulatory expenses and policyholder service requirements make it difficult for small insurers to efficiently handle a small volume of business in many widespread territories.

D. Reinsurance

1. The availability and cost of adequate reinsurance can influence underwriting policy.

2. Reinsurance treaties may exclude certain types of insurance or classes of business, or the cost of reinsurance may be prohibitive.

3. Reinsurers are also concerned about the underlying policy forms offered by the insurer and may exclude reinsurance coverage for loss exposures covered by manuscript forms developed for a particular insured or covered by forms developed independently of an advisory organization.

Educational Objective 5

Describe the purposes that underwriting guidelines and underwriting audits serve.

Key Points:

Staff underwriters develop underwriting guidelines, which distill underwriting policies into directions for line underwriters' policy selection. Underwriting audits ensure that established underwriting standards are reasonably consistent.

A. Purposes of Underwriting Guidelines

An insurer's underwriting policy is communicated to underwriters through underwriting guidelines, which are continually updated to reflect changes in policy.

1. Underwriting guidelines identify the major elements that underwriters should evaluate for each type of insurance, as well as boundaries, such as maximum coverage limits, for application selection.

2. Underwriting guidelines serve these eight purposes:

   a. Provide for structured decisions

   - Underwriting guidelines provide a structure for underwriting decisions by identifying the major considerations underwriters should evaluate for each type of insurance the insurer writes.

   - By identifying the principal hazards associated with a particular class of business, underwriting guidelines ensure that underwriters consider the primary hazard traits of the exposures they evaluate.

   b. Ensure uniformity and consistency

   Underwriting guidelines help ensure that selection decisions are made uniformly and consistently by all of the insurer's underwriters.

   c. Synthesize insights and experience

   For many insurers, underwriting guidelines serve as a repository for an insurer's cumulative expertise.

   d. Distinguish between routine and nonroutine decisions

   - Routine decisions are those for which the line underwriter clearly has decision-making authority according to the underwriting guidelines.

   - Nonroutine decisions involve submissions that fall outside the underwriter's authority.

e. Avoid duplication of efforts

- If the problems inherent in a particular situation have been identified and solved, the solution should apply to all similar situations that might arise in the future.
- Underwriting guidelines contain the information necessary to avoid costly duplication of effort.

f. Ensure adherence to reinsurance treaties and planned rate levels

- Compliance with underwriting guidelines ensures that coverage limits and accepted loss exposures will not exceed the insurer's treaty reinsurance, because staff underwriters reflect those treaty limitations in the guidelines.
- Compliance with underwriting guidelines also ensures selection of loss exposures in an overall book of business commensurate with the planned rate levels for those policies.

g. Support policy preparation and compliance

- Underwriting guides provide information to assist underwriters and support staff in policy preparation.
- Underwriting guidelines also support compliance with state regulatory requirements, as staff underwriters incorporate applicable regulations in the guidelines.

h. Provide a basis for predictive models

Underwriters use predictive modeling to identify applications that present lower underwriting risk. Predictive models function in this way:

- Multiple data variables of individual risks are developed to rank the relative likelihood of insurance loss.
- Data variables are based on underwriting guidelines along with the insurer's loss experience, loss data collected from external sources, and underwriting expertise.
- The ranking or score developed from the data variables is a predictive measure of future profit potential based upon the account's characteristics.

B. Purpose of Underwriting Audits

1. Audits are a management tool used to achieve uniformity and consistency in the application of underwriting standards.

2. A typical underwriting audit may involve selecting accounts at random or reviewing files that had experienced notable claims. Feedback from the audit of individual files provides individual line underwriters with strategies to improve future underwriting decisions.

3. Underwriting audits can also be used to monitor statistics for books of business. This can provide indications of applications written in excess of underwriting guidelines.

4. An underwriting audit provides staff underwriters with information on the effectiveness of the underwriting guidelines. Underwriting guidelines that are not being following may be either outdated or considered unrealistic.

Educational Objective 6
Describe the steps in the underwriting process.

Key Points:

The underwriting process incorporates these underlying concepts into a series of steps and tasks:

- The purpose of underwriting is to develop and maintain a profitable book of business.
- Underwriting activities include line underwriting activities, which are focused on evaluating new applications and renewal policies, and staff underwriting activities, which are focused on managing the risk selection process.
- Levels of underwriting authority are based on experience and knowledge.
- Underwriting policy should support an insurer's mission.

Whether relying on independent judgment or the guidance of expert systems, underwriters engage in a series of steps and tasks designed to ensure that, ultimately, insurers are able to each their business goals.

A. Evaluate the Submission

The first step in the underwriting process is evaluating a submission's loss exposures and associated hazards. Underwriters must understand the activities, operations, and character of every applicant. To evaluate a submission, underwriters perform two tasks:

1. Weigh the need for information

   a. Underwriters apply information efficiency to weigh the need for information against the cost to obtain it.

   b. Underwriters may also use these categories intuitively or consciously when determining whether the additional information should be obtained:

- Essential information—information that is absolutely necessary to arrive at the decision and is often specified in the underwriting guidelines
- Desirable information—information that is not absolutely necessary but would be helpful in evaluating the account if the information can be obtained at an acceptable cost and without any undue delay
- Available information—information that may or may not be helpful and is not worth making any special effort to obtain

2. Gather the necessary information

Underwriters compile information from a number of sources to develop a profile of a submission.

   a. Underwriters pay close attention to a submission's hazards to determine whether those hazards are typical of similarly classified accounts.

- A physical hazard is a tangible characteristic of property, persons, or operations to be insured that increases the frequency or severity of loss.
- A moral hazard is a condition that increases the likelihood that a person will intentionally cause or exaggerate a loss.
- A morale hazard is a condition of carelessness or indifference that increases the frequency or severity of loss.
- A legal hazard is a condition of the legal environment that increases loss frequency or severity.

   b. These are the principal sources of underwriting information:

- Producers—Underwriters rely more on the producer than on any other source for information about the account.
- Applications—Insurance applications provide general information required to process, rate, and underwrite loss exposures of the applicant.
- Inspection reports—Independent inspections or risk control reports provide underwriting information about the property's physical condition, the business operations' safety record, and the policyholder's management.
- Government records—Government records that provide underwriting information include motor vehicle reports; criminal court records; and civil court records, including records of suits filed, mortgages and liens, business licenses, property tax records, United States Securities and Exchange Commission (SEC) filings, and bankruptcy filings.
- Financial rating services—An applicant's financial status provides important underwriting information. Dun & Bradstreet (D&B), Standard & Poor's, and Experian are some of the major financial rating services that underwriters use.

- Loss data—Loss data are a significant underwriting tool for predicting future losses. The policyholder's loss runs provide information on loss frequency and severity, types of losses, possible seasonality, trends in loss experience, and indications of management's attention to prompt loss reporting. Loss data also provide important information for policy pricing.

c. Field marketing personnel—Insurers often employ field marketing personnel (such as marketing representatives or special agents) who can provide both specific and general underwriting information.

d. Premium auditor—A premium auditor examines the policyholders' operations, records, and books of account to determine the actual loss exposure for the coverage already provided.

e. Claim files—When renewing existing policies, an underwriter can obtain insights into the policyholder's character by reviewing the policyholder's claim files.

f. Production records—Records on individual producers, indicating loss ratio, premium volume, mix of business, amount of supporting business, length of service, and industry experience, help underwriters make decisions about the quality of the applicants that the producer is submitting.

g. Consultants' reports—Large and specialized commercial accounts may require special expertise to fully underwrite loss exposures and hazards from emerging issues.

3. Many tools are available to help underwriters evaluate, select, and price submissions, such as telematics, predictive analytics, predictive modeling, and catastrophe modeling.

B. Develop Underwriting Alternatives

The underwriter must consider each alternative carefully and choose the optimal one for the circumstances. The underwriter may accept a submission as is, reject the submission, or accept the submission subject to certain modifications. There are four major types of modifications.

1. Require risk control measures

The first type of modification for an unacceptable submission is a counteroffer with a requirement for the applicant to implement additional risk control measures.

a. Some risk control measures are relatively inexpensive and simple to implement, while others, such as sprinklers, require considerable capital investment.

b. Some applicants welcome an insurer's recommendations and understand that implementation reduces ultimate business costs. Other applicants view risk control requirements unfavorably and consider them unnecessary expenses.

2. Change insurance rates, rating plans, or policy limits

The second type of modification for a submission is a counteroffer to change insurance rates, rating plans, or policy limits.

    a. A submission that is not desirable at standard rates may be desirable if the underwriter can charge a different rate, use a different rating plan, or provide a different limit of coverage.

    b. A rate modification could either increase or decrease the premium.

    c. Underwriters have greater price discretion in commercial insurance than in personal insurance.

    d. Several rating plans are available for commercial applicants:

      • Experience rating uses the policyholder's past loss experience to develop a premium modification factor to adjust the manual rate upward or downward.

      • Schedule rating awards debits and credits to a submission based on categories of business characteristics, such as the care and condition of the premises and the selection and training of employees.

      • Retrospective rating is an individual rating plan that uses the current year as the experience period to develop the experience modification factor.

    e. If high policy limits are requested, the underwriter may suggest lower limits or may use facultative reinsurance.

    f. When dealing with property insurance, the underwriter must be alert for overinsurance that could indicate a moral hazard and might lead to a fraudulent loss.

3. Amend policy terms and conditions

    a. The third type of modification for an unacceptable submission is a counteroffer to amend policy terms and conditions.

    b. An unacceptable submission may become acceptable by modifying the policy to exclude certain causes of loss, add or increase a deductible, or make another coverage change.

    c. The underwriter's flexibility varies by type of insurance.

4. Use facultative reinsurance

    a. The fourth type of modification for an unacceptable submission is an insurer's internal decision to use facultative reinsurance if treaty reinsurance is not available.

b. The underwriter may be able to transfer a portion of the liability for the applicant's loss exposure to a facultative reinsurer.

C. Select an Underwriting Alternative

  1. An underwriter must decide whether to accept a submission as offered, reject it, or accept it subject to modifications.

  2. These additional factors need to be considered before selecting an underwriting alternative:

    a. Underwriting authority—Before accepting a submission, an underwriter must determine whether he or she has the necessary underwriting authority.

    b. Supporting business—A submission that is marginal by itself might be acceptable if the other insurance components of the applicant's account (the supporting business) are desirable.

    c. Mix of business— The mix of business is the distribution of individual policies that constitute the book of business of a producer, territory, state, or region among the various types of insurance and classifications of insureds.

    d. Producer relationships—Some producers pressure underwriters to accept a marginal submission as an accommodation. The relationship between the underwriter and the producer should be based on mutually shared goals.

    e. Regulatory restrictions—State regulations restrict underwriters' ability to accept or renew business.

D. Determine an Appropriate Premium

  1. Insurance loss costs are typically based on an elaborate classification system in which similar loss exposures are combined into the same rating classification.

  2. Combining loss exposures into rating classifications enables the insurer to appropriately match potential loss costs with an applicant's particular loss exposures.

  3. Accurate classification ensures a pooling of loss exposures whose expected loss frequency and loss severity are similar.

  4. For most types of personal insurance, workers compensation, and some other commercial insurance, proper classification automatically determines the premium.

  5. Many insurers operate subsidiary insurers with different rating plans that reflect the loss exposures of different groups of insureds.

6. The underwriter must be certain in each case that the characteristics of the applicant's loss exposures justify the placement and must document that any adjustment is consistent with the insurer's rating plan.

E. Implement the Underwriting Decision

Implementing underwriting decisions generally involves three tasks:

1. Communicate the decision—The underwriting decision is communicated to the producer. If the decision is to accept the submission with modifications, the reasons must be clearly communicated to the producer and applicant, and the applicant must agree to accept or implement any modifications made as a counteroffer. If the underwriter decides to reject the application, he or she must communicate the rejection to the producer in a positive way to preserve their long-term relationship.

2. Issue documents—In accepting a submission, the underwriter might need to issue a binder. For some types of business, the underwriter might also need to prepare certificates of insurance.

3. Record information—Information about the policy and the applicant are recorded for policy issuance, accounting, statistical, and monitoring purposes.

F. Monitor the Underwriting Decisions

After an underwriting decision has been made on a new-business submission or a renewal, the underwriter has two tasks to ensure that satisfactory results are achieved: monitor activity for individual policies, and monitor books of business.

1. Monitor individual policies

Monitoring existing policies usually occurs in response to these triggering events:

a. Substantive policy changes—Adding a new location to a property policy or a new driver to an auto policy can cause the underwriter to investigate whether the additions significantly change the loss exposures.

b. Significant and unique losses—A notice of loss provides the underwriter with another opportunity to review the account and to determine whether that loss is the type the underwriter expected.

c. Preparation for renewal—As a policy's expiration date approaches, the underwriter may need to repeat the underwriting process before agreeing to renew the policy for another term.

    d. Risk control and safety inspections—A risk control and safety inspection might have contained recommendations that were requirements for policy issuance. A follow-up investigation could reveal that only some of the requirements were met.

    e. Premium audits—Premium audits usually lag behind a renewal policy by several months. The audit report could disclose larger loss exposures than originally contemplated, unacceptable operations, new products, new operations, or financial problems.

2. Monitor books of business

    a. Monitoring a book of business means evaluating the quality and profitability of all the business written for any group of policies.

    b. The evaluation should identify specific problems for each type of insurance, which can be subdivided into class of business, territory, producer, and other policy subgroups.

    c. Underwriters use premium and loss statistics to identify aggregate problems in a deteriorating book of business.

    d. Special attention is given to some books of business when they are defined by these characteristics:

- Class of business—A poor loss ratio in a particular class of business can indicate inadequate pricing or a disproportionate number of high-hazard policyholders relative to the average loss exposure in the classification.

- Territories or geographic areas—A territory can be defined in various ways to reflect an insurer's operations.

- Producers—Ideally, each producer's book of business should be evaluated annually. The producer's premium volume, policy retention, and loss ratio are evaluated both on an overall basis and by type and class of business.

Educational Objective 7

Explain how an insurer's underwriting results are measured and how financial measures can be distorted.

Key Points:

An insurer's underwriting results are a key indicator of its profitability. Without a clear understanding of their underwriting performance, insurers may not be able to respond to conditions that adversely affect them or recognize opportunities to improve their performance.

A. Financial Measures

   1. Many insurers use the combined ratio (or combined loss and expense ratio) to measure the success of underwriting activities.

      a. From an insurer's perspective, the lower the combined ratio, the better.

- When the combined ratio is exactly 100 percent, every premium dollar is being used to pay claims and cover operating costs, with nothing remaining for insurer profit.
- When the combined ratio is greater than 100 percent, an underwriting loss occurs because more dollars are being paid out than are being taken in as premiums.
- When the combined ratio is less than 100 percent, an underwriting profit occurs because not all premium dollars taken in are being used for claims and expenses.

      b. Although the combined ratio is the most often cited measure of underwriting success, the results that it produces are generally subject to an additional analysis of its components.

      c. Changes in premium volume, major catastrophic losses, and delays in loss reporting can distort the combined ratio, making it difficult to evaluate the effectiveness of underwriting.

   2. Distortions created by changes in premium volume

      a. An insurer's combined ratio must be evaluated, taking into consideration fluctuations in premium volume and the distortions that they can create.

      b. Restrictive underwriting policy usually reduces premium volume.

      c. Changes in underwriting policy often do not have the immediate effect desired.

3. Distortions created by major catastrophic losses
   a. Underwriting results are usually evaluated annually. However, major hurricanes, major earthquakes, and other natural catastrophes occur too irregularly to be predicted annually.
   b. Ideally, insurance rates allow for unpredicted losses. Still, a major catastrophe is likely to cause an underwriting loss for that year for most, if not all, affected insurers.
   c. Failure to predict the unpredictable does not necessarily indicate inadequate underwriting.
4. Distortions created by delays in loss reporting and loss development
   a. Delays in loss reporting reduce the value of the information provided by the combined ratio.
   b. Insurers establish a loss reserve amount when a claim is reported.
      • Reserved losses are included in incurred losses and reflected in the combined ratio.
      • The type of loss usually determines how quickly the insurer is notified of a claim and how quickly the reserve is replaced with the amount of final payment.
   c. Delays in loss reporting and loss settlement can result in an understatement of losses in one year and an overstatement in another year that appear in the combined ratio.
5. Distortions created by underwriting cycle
   a. Insurance industry underwriting cycles have consisted of a period of underwriting profits followed by a period of underwriting losses, as measured by the combined ratio.
   b. At times of underwriting losses, insurers may need to increase premium rates and restrict the availability of coverage to increase underwriting profits. These tactics may be necessary for the insurer to maintain the policyholders' surplus it needs to support its level of business.
   c. Insurance regulators are concerned about the effects of the underwriting cycle on insurance availability and affordability.
   d. Individual insurers cannot change the underwriting cycle.
   e. Effective underwriting and financial management can enable an insurer to periodically reposition itself through changes in its underwriting guidelines and allocation of capital to underwriting.

B. Nonfinancial Measures

The success of an insurer depends on the ability of every under-writer to attain and maintain profitable results over the long term. This goal is accomplished in part by using nonfinancial measures to assess performance. Some of these nonfinancial measures apply only to commercial lines underwriting departments. Others apply to both personal and commercial lines. Portions of both types may be automated using expert systems. Some measures can be evaluated during an underwriting audit.

1. Selection

   a. Insurers often establish selection goals for underwriters to ensure that the quality of the underwriter's book of business does not deteriorate.

   b. Selection standards for individual underwriters usually support overall underwriting goals and are evaluated during an underwriting audit.

2. Product or line of business mix

   a. Measuring product or line of business mix is one way to evaluate an underwriter's contribution to a profitable book of business.

   b. Building a proper mix in a book of business requires that underwriters have a thorough knowledge of the insurer's business goals, including the types of products it prefers to write and the "appetite" the insurer has for certain types of risks.

3. Pricing

   a. Pricing standards enable insurers to determine levels of premium adequacy by comparing premiums charged to the established pricing standards.

   b. Insurers also track through information systems the extent to which their underwriters deviate from the insurer's established pricing for specific classifications.

4. Accommodated accounts

   a. Making an underwriting accommodation usually means accepting substandard exposures in return for other, more profitable accounts.

   b. Evaluating the accommodation notes in the files or the log as part of underwriting audits and reviews can reveal whether the underwriter is making excessive accommodations and can ensure that the producer has increased volume or has fulfilled some other promise in exchange for the accommodations.

5. Retention ratio
   a. The retention ratio is the percentage of expiring policies that an insurer renews.
   b. Retention can be measured by policy count, premium volume, or both.
   c. A low retention rate might indicate serious deficiencies in the way insurers do business, including poor service to producers, noncompetitive pricing, or unfavorable claim service.

6. Hit ratio
   a. The hit ratio, sometimes called the "success ratio," is a non-financial measure used to determine how well underwriters (or the insurer as a whole) are meeting their sales goals.
   b. Ratios that are either inordinately high or low might require further investigation.
   c. A high hit ratio might indicate any of these conditions:
      • Competition is easing.
      • Rates are inadequate or lower than other insurers' rates.
      • Coverage is broader than that of other insurers.
      • The underwriter has the skill set for production underwriting.
      • Underwriting selection criteria are deteriorating.
      • An extremely good relationship exists between the insurer and the producer.
   d. A low hit ratio might indicate one of more of these conditions:
      • Competition is increasing.
      • Rates are higher than other insurer's rates.
      • Coverages or forms are too restrictive.
      • The underwriter does not have the skill set for production underwriting.
      • Selection criteria are too stringent.
      • Service is poor.
      • A poor relationship exists between the insurer and the producer.

7. Service to producers
   a. This standard requires establishing a set of minimum acceptable standards for certain types of service to producers.
   b. The actual performance of each underwriter, branch, or region being evaluated is then compared with the targeted level of performance.

8. Premium to underwriter

    a. The volume of premium an underwriter is able to handle is an often-used measure of performance.

    b. Underwriting management uses this measure to determine whether individual underwriters are assuming their share of work compared with other underwriters in the same company handling similar accounts.

Key Words and Phrases:

Policyholders' surplus
Under statutory accounting principles (SAP), an insurer's total admitted assets minus its total liabilities.

Capacity
The amount of business an insurer is able to write, usually based on a comparison of the insurer's written premiums to its policyholders' surplus.

Underwriting authority
The scope of decisions that an underwriter can make without receiving approval from someone at a higher level.

Line underwriter
Underwriter who is primarily responsible for implementing the steps in the underwriting process.

Staff underwriter
Underwriter who is usually located in the home office and who assists underwriting management with making and implementing underwriting policy.

Manuscript policy
An insurance policy that is specifically drafted according to terms negotiated between a specific insured (or group of insureds) and an insurer.

Underwriting policy (underwriting philosophy)
A guide to individual and aggregate policy selection that supports an insurer's mission statement.

Loss development
The increase or decrease of incurred losses over time.

Trending
A statistical technique for analyzing environmental changes and projecting such changes into the future.

Treaty reinsurance
A reinsurance agreement that covers an entire class or portfolio of loss exposures and provides that the primary insurer's individual loss exposures that fall within the treaty are automatically reinsured.

Underwriting audit
A review of underwriting files to ensure that individual underwriters are adhering to underwriting guidelines.

Premium-to-surplus ratio or capacity ratio
A capacity ratio that indicates an insurer's financial strength by relating net written premiums to policyholders' surplus.

Statutory accounting principles (SAP)
The accounting principles and practices that are prescribed or permitted by an insurer's domiciliary state and that insurers must follow.

Return on equity (ROE)
A profitability ratio expressed as a percentage by dividing a company's net income by its net worth (book value). Depending on the context, net worth is sometimes called shareholders' equity, owners' equity, or policyholders' surplus.

Market conduct examination
An analysis of an insurer's practices in four operational areas: sales and advertising, underwriting, ratemaking, and claim handling.

Predictive modeling
A process in which historical data based on behaviors and events are blended with multiple variables and used to construct models of anticipated future outcomes.

Underwriter
An insurer employee who evaluates applicants for insurance, selects those that are acceptable to the insurer, prices coverage, and determines policy terms and conditions.

Underwriting submission
Underwriting information for an initial application, or a substantive policy midterm or renewal change.

Expert systems, or knowledge-based systems
Computer software programs that supplement the underwriting decision-making process. These systems ask for the information necessary to make an underwriting decision, ensuring that no information is overlooked.

Loss exposure
Any condition or situation that presents a possibility of loss, whether or not an actual loss occurs.

Hazard
A condition that increases the frequency or severity of a loss.

Information efficiency
The balance that underwriters must maintain between the hazards presented by the account and the information needed to underwrite it.

Application
A legal document that provides information obtained directly from an applicant requesting insurance and that an insurer can use for underwriting and claim handling purposes.

Counteroffer
A proposal an offeree makes to an offeror that varies in some material way from the original offer, resulting in rejection of the original offer and constituting a new offer.

(a) rated classification
The rate classifications provided by the ISO Commercial Lines Manual that describe operations with unique characteristics or for which inadequate statistical experience exists.

Estimated loss potentials (ELP)
Rate development factors used for operations with unique characteristics or for which inadequate statistical experience exists. ELPs are multiplied by loss cost multipliers to develop rates.

Experience rating
A ratemaking technique that adjusts the insured's premium for the upcoming policy period based on the insured's experience for the current period.

Schedule rating
A rating plan that awards debits and credits based on specific categories, such as the care and condition of the premises or the training and selection of employees, to modify the final premium to reflect factors that the class rate does not include.

Retrospective rating
A ratemaking technique that adjusts the insured's premium for the current policy period based on the insured's loss experience during the current period; paid losses or incurred losses may be used to determine loss experience.

Facultative reinsurance
Reinsurance of individual loss exposures in which the primary insurer chooses which loss exposures to submit to the reinsurer, and the reinsurer can accept or reject any loss exposures submitted.

Account underwriting
A method of underwriting in which all of the business from a particular applicant is evaluated as a whole.

Unfair trade practices
Methods of competition or advertising or procedures that tend to deprive the public of information necessary to make informed insurance decisions.

Binder
A temporary written or oral agreement to provide insurance coverage until a formal written policy is issued.

Certificate of insurance
A brief description of insurance coverage prepared by an insurer or its agent commonly used by policyholders to provide evidence of insurance.

Combined ratio
A profitability ratio that indicates whether an insurer has made an underwriting loss or gain.

Production underwriting
Performing underwriting functions in an insurer's office as well as traveling to visit and maintain rapport with agents and sometimes clients.

Hit ratio
The ratio of insurance policies written to those that have been quoted to applicants for insurance.

Underwriting Property and Liability Insurance

5

Educational Objective 1

Describe in detail each of the COPE factors used to evaluate property loss exposures.

Key Points:

The COPE model is a common tool underwriters use to evaluate exposures related to fire and other causes of loss. COPE is an acronym that stands for the four property risk characteristics an underwriter reviews when evaluating a submission for property insurance.

Study Tips

Set aside a specific time each day to study.

A. Construction

The building's construction characteristics relate directly to its ability to withstand damage by fire and other causes of loss and to protect its contents.

1. Construction classes

Construction classes reflect the construction materials' ability to resist fire damage. These are the six Insurance Services Office (ISO) construction classes:

a. ISO Class 1 is frame construction. In addition to the direct damage caused by a fire, frame construction can suffer structural damage because the weight-bearing supports are combustible.

b. ISO Class 2 is joisted masonry construction.

- Exterior walls can be fire-resistive construction with a fire-resistance rating of at least one hour, or they can be masonry construction.

- Mill construction, also known as heavy timber construction, is a type of joisted masonry construction in which no concealed areas exist under the roof and floors that might permit a fire to go undetected.

c. ISO Class 3 is noncombustible construction. Although these buildings are noncombustible, they are not fire resistive. The buildings' unprotected steel structural supports twist and bend when subjected to the heat of a typical fire.

d. ISO Class 4 is masonry noncombustible construction. In masonry noncombustible construction, the building's exterior walls are made of self-supporting masonry materials, and the floors and roof are made of metal or some other noncombustible or slow-burning material.

e. ISO Class 5 is modified fire-resistive construction. It is similar to fire-resistive construction, except that the material's fire-resistance rating is one to two hours.

f. ISO Class 6 is fire-resistive construction. In a building of fire-resistive construction, the structure's load-bearing members can withstand fire damage for at least two hours. The construction materials are either of these:

- Noncombustible with a fire-resistance rating of at least two hours
- Protected by a noncombustible covering such as concrete, masonry, plaster, or gypsum that provides at least a two-hour fire-resistance rating

2. Construction materials

   a. The interior finishing materials used on walls, floors, and ceilings; the insulation; and the roofing also affect a structure's combustibility and underwriting desirability.

- Relatively noncombustible interior finishes include plaster, gypsum, and wallboard.
- Combustible interior finishes include wood or plywood, fiber ceiling tiles, and plastic wall coverings.

   b. Insulation is another construction material that can be problematic. Insulation can contain the heat of a fire within a building, concentrating it on structural members.

   c. In addition to considering the construction materials used for interior finishes and insulation, underwriters should consider the construction materials used in roofing.

   d. A roof's exterior surface not only keeps out the weather but also provides a barrier against fires in adjacent or nearby buildings, as sparks and embers falling from fires outside the building can make contact with roofs. Roof coverings vary in the fire resistance they provide.

3. Building age

   a. The age of a building is the first additional construction characteristic that underwriters should consider. These age factors should be noted:

- A different building code might have been in effect when the building was constructed. Consequently, the building might lack protective features and systems generally considered essential today.

- Complying with current building codes might increase the cost of making repairs after a loss.
- Heating, cooling, electrical, and fire protection systems might be obsolete.
- The building might have been intended for a different occupancy and might not be suitable for its current use.
- Conversion and remodeling might have created concealed spaces in which fire could burn undetected and spread rapidly.
- Alterations and repairs made over the years might have left unprotected openings in vertical and horizontal firestops.
- The building's condition might have deteriorated for numerous reasons, including normal wear and tear, hard use, or lack of maintenance.
- The value of an older building might be difficult to determine, especially if the builder used construction techniques and materials that are no longer available.

   b. Construction methods and materials have changed over time.

   c. Although proper maintenance mitigates the effects of age and deterioration, all buildings eventually wear out.

4. Building height

   a. Building height is the second additional construction characteristic that underwriters should consider.

   b. Buildings present unique problems when their height restricts the capability of the local fire service to fight fires from outside.

   c. In a high-rise building, the fire department has to fight the fire from inside—if possible.

   d. Controlling combustible contents in high-rise buildings is crucial.

   e. Property underwriters must realize that the fire department's first priority is the safety of a building's occupants.

5. Fire divisions

A building's fire divisions are the third additional construction characteristic that underwriters should consider.

   a. Fire divisions are the analogous solution for fires in buildings with large horizontal areas.

   b. A fire wall restricts the spread of fire by serving as a fire-resistive barrier.

- A fire wall must be free standing, which means that it must support its own weight without assistance from other building components.

- Building codes typically specify that fire walls have a parapet eighteen to thirty-six inches above a combustible roof.
- Extensions of the fire wall through the outer walls are known as fender walls.

   c. A firestop is an element of fire-resistant construction, inserted in concealed spaces or between structural elements of a building, either a floor, or wall, or roof area, that prevents the passage of flame from one point to another.

6. Building openings

Building openings are the fourth additional construction characteristic that underwriters should consider.

   a. Openings that pierce fire walls or firestops increase fire loss potential.

   b. In addition to containing ducts and passageways, buildings contain many openings that, without additional protection, can compromise the integrity of a fire division. In most circumstances, fire doors can protect these openings.

- Fire doors are approved when they meet the National Fire Protection Association (NFPA) design specifications. The NFPA's classification scheme ranges from doors that withstand fire for three hours to those that withstand fire for one-third of an hour.
- Each door must be automatically self-closing and unobstructed.

   c. A vertical opening such as an elevator or a stairwell is protected only when it is completely segregated into a separate fire division.

7. Building codes

Building codes are the fifth additional construction characteristic that underwriters should consider.

   a. Building codes can provide the underwriter with information regarding the construction of buildings erected under the provisions of those codes.

   b. A tool that underwriters can use to evaluate the effectiveness of building codes in general and in a particular community is ISO's Building Code Effectiveness Grading Schedule (BCEGS).

   c. The BCEGS program includes grades from 1 to 10, indicating the effectiveness of a community's building code.

B. Occupancy

The underwriter needs to know information about the activities and operations taking place in the building.

1. Occupancy categories

   Underwriters have traditionally grouped occupancies into six categories to help analyze their hazards:

   a. Habitational occupancies include apartments, hotels, motels, and nursing homes.

   b. Office occupancy is a relatively low-hazard category. Materials found in offices are usually of limited combustibility and are relatively less susceptible to damage than those found in other occupancies.

   c. Institutional occupancies include schools, churches, hospitals, and property owned by governmental entities.

   d. Mercantile occupancies include businesses that buy and sell goods and merchandise, whether wholesale or retail.

   e. Service occupancies include businesses that perform an activity or a service for the customer rather than create or sell a product. This category includes a long list of service businesses such as dry cleaners, auto service stations, barbers, and car washes, and it contains a diverse assortment of occupancies.

   f. Manufacturers' operations involve converting raw stock into finished products. The hazards of occupancies in this category vary widely according to the product being manufactured.

2. Characteristics of contents

   a. Different types of occupancies present different types of underwriting concerns based on the characteristics of the contents at the insured location.

   b. The loss potential of a particular occupancy can be evaluated by examining the contents' ignition sources, combustibility, and susceptibility.

   c. Ignition sources provide the means for a fire to start. Potential ignition sources include these:

      • Friendly fires that escape containment—Hostile fires can result from "friendly" open flames (such as in a fireplace) and heaters, smoking, lamps, furnaces, and ovens and space heaters, as well as from welding and cutting torches.

      • Friction that generates enough heat to ignite nearby combustible material—Sources of friction include hot bearings, rubbing belts, grinding, shredding, picking, polishing, cutting, and drilling.

- Electricity that produces sparks or heat that can ignite exposed combustibles—Static electricity frequently causes sparks. Lighting fixtures, overloaded circuits, and worn wiring can release potentially damaging amounts of heat.
- Certain chemical reactions, called exothermic reactions, that produce heat sufficient to cause ignition—Sources of exothermic reactions include substances such as magnesium or phosphorus, resulting in fires that are difficult to contain and extinguish.

   d. Combustibility determines how quickly the material ignites, the rate at which a fire spreads, and the intensity or amount of heat a fire generates. Materials that are highly combustible include these:
- Light combustible materials such as thin plywood, shingles, shavings, paper, cotton, and other fibers
- Combustible dusts such as those produced when refinishing bowling alley lanes or refining flour
- Flammable liquids
- Combustible gases such as hydrogen
- Materials subject to spontaneous combustion
- Explosive materials, acids, and oxidizing agents

   e. Susceptibility measures the extent to which fire and its effects, either direct or resultant, will damage personal property—either merchandise or materials—typical of the occupancy.

   f. The susceptibility of contents is also a major underwriting consideration when determining the probable maximum loss.

3. Occupancy hazards

   a. The physical hazards that any occupancy presents can be classified into three categories: common hazards, special hazards of the class, and special hazards of the risk.

   b. Hazards that increase the probable frequency or severity of loss but that are typical for the type of occupancy are called special hazards of the class.

   c. Some businesses engage in activities that are not typical of other businesses in their class. Those activities create special hazards of the risk.

C. Protection

The quantity and quality of fire protection available to individual properties vary widely. Fire protection is of two types:

1. Public fire protection
   a. The organization of public fire protection varies by community.
   b. Municipalities and sometimes counties often provide protection to all properties within their political boundaries.
   c. The American Association of Insurance Services (AAIS) personal and commercial insurance fire rates recognize these fire protection classifications:
      - Protected—This classification is divided into five tiers (Protected 1, Protected 2, Protected 3, Protected 4, and Protected 5) based on how far the building is from a responding fire department.
      - Partially protected—Building is located more than 1,000 feet from a fire hydrant and is within five road miles of a responding fire department.
      - Unprotected—Building is located in an area that is classified as neither protected nor partially protected.
   d. ISO independently collects and evaluates information on a community's public fire protection using its Fire Suppression Rating Schedule (FSRS).
   e. The schedule measures the major elements of a community's fire suppression system and develops a numerical grading called a public protection classification (PPC) for each community.
   f. The PPC classification system rates the quality of a public fire service on a scale of 1 to 10.
   g. Geographic features sometimes prevent prompt fire service response to property in some areas, and water mains and hydrants in some areas might not extend to all properties that a given fire service protects.
   h. A given property might also have a public protection class inferior to the community as a whole, for two principal reasons:
      - The property might present a loss exposure to fires that are more challenging than the fire service is equipped to handle.
      - The fire service might lack adequate year-round access to the property, especially when the property owner maintains private access roads.
2. Private fire protection: prevention
   a. Fires can be prevented by controlling heat sources and by separating fuel and heat. Fires can also be prevented by controlling arson.
   b. Heat sources can sometimes be reduced or eliminated.

c. Fuel and heat can often be separated by ensuring that flammable or combustible materials are kept away from fixed-location heat sources.

3. Private fire protection: detection

a. Early fire detection is important because the size of a fire increases exponentially with time, and large fires are more difficult to suppress than small fires.

b. The major detection systems are described here:

- Guard service with a clock system—The effectiveness of a guard service depends on its guards' alertness.

- Private patrol service—Small merchants or businesses often employ private patrol services to check for break-ins.

- Smoke detectors—The use of smoke detectors in private residences and businesses has increased significantly with the development of inexpensive, battery-powered smoke detectors.

- Heat detectors—Heat detectors can be operated independently of suppression devices but are most frequently combined with devices like automatic sprinkler systems.

c. To perform their intended function, smoke and heat detectors must be connected to an alarm, which can be a:

- Local fire alarm system—A local fire alarm system is a type of automatic fire detection system that relies on occupants or passersby to report the alarm to fire or police officials.

- Central station system—A central station system is a private service with personnel who monitor the systems of commercial establishments and, sometimes, residences.

- Remote station system and proprietary alarm system— These are similar to central station systems, except that they do not signal a commercially operated central station.

4. Private fire protection: suppression

a. Private fire suppression systems consist of equipment and personnel that the insured uses to suppress a fire before the municipal fire service arrives.

b. Private fire suppression methods fall into four categories:

- Portable fire extinguishers.

- Standpipe and hose systems—These consist of water supply pipes located inside buildings and equipped with standard fire department connections at regular intervals.

- Automatic sprinkler systems—These consist of a series of interconnected valves and pipes with sprinkler heads.
- Private fire brigades.

   c. There are various approaches to delivering fire extinguishment materials through sprinkler systems.

- Most automatic fire sprinkler systems are wet pipe sprinkler systems.
- Pre-action sprinkler systems are used where property is highly susceptible to water damage from damaged sprinklers or piping.
- Deluge sprinkler systems are similar to pre-action systems, except that sprinkler heads are always open.

   d. Depending on the occupancy, and where water damage to sensitive property is a concern, it may be appropriate to have specialized sprinkler systems that use gas extinguishing agents—typically halon, carbon dioxide, or environmentally friendly agents such as Inergen.

   e. Private fire brigades are found only in the largest industrial complexes, such as petrochemical plants, and rural areas where municipal fire protection is unavailable or considered inadequate.

D. External Exposure

External exposure refers only to fires that originate outside the insured premises.

  1. Single-occupancy loss exposures

   a. A single-occupancy loss exposure exists when the property being underwritten consists of a single building, fire division, or group of buildings, all owned or controlled by the insured.

   b. An exposing building is one that significantly increases the possibility of a fire in the insured building. A fire that erupts in an exposing building is an exposure fire.

  2. Multiple-occupancy loss exposures

   a. In a multiple-occupancy building, persons other than the insured own or control portions of the fire division that contains the insured property.

   b. When evaluating a multiple-occupancy building, underwriters consider the occupancy class of the other occupants.

Educational Objective 2

Explain how insurable interest, policy provisions for valuing losses, and insurance to value affect a loss payment amount under property insurance.

Key Points:

Determining the quality of a property claim submission begins with assessing the amount that the policy will obligate the insurer to pay in the event of the loss.

A. Insurable Interest

  1. Subject to the limits of coverage, coinsurance provisions, and the deductible, standard commercial property forms limit the insured's recovery to the amount of its insurable interest at the time of the loss.

  2. The most common interest in property comes from outright ownership.

  3. Other forms of ownership exist in which the insured may have something less than an insurable interest in the entire property or may have an insurable interest for only a period of time.

B. Policy Provision for Valuing Losses

  1. The method prescribed by the policy provisions is important when determining the acceptability of a new submission or a renewal and for properly underwriting property coverage.

  2. The most common property valuation methods are replacement cost and actual cash value.

   a. While actual cash value is the standard valuation approach in many commercial property forms, most underwriters regard replacement cost as the valuation most appropriate.

   b. The replacement cost option in commercial property forms typically reimburses the insured fully for any losses sustained, eliminates uncertainty in loss adjustment, and creates a contract that fulfills a reasonable customer's expectations.

C. Insurance to Value

  1. Underwriters use the value of the covered property to determine whether the insured carries an adequate amount of insurance.

  2. To encourage purchasing insurance to value, insurance policies include coinsurance clauses and other insurance-to-value provisions.

3. Insurance to value provides better policyholder protection against a total loss, and policyholders who are insured to value will not face a coinsurance penalty at the time of loss.

4. The insurer benefits when underwriters encourage insurance to value because these results are then promoted:

   a. Higher limits of property insurance—Insurance to value promotes higher limits of property insurance, which in turn generate higher property insurance premiums that properly reflect the insurer's loss exposures.

   b. An adequately insured book of business—An underinsured book of business generates inadequate premiums that, in turn, can contribute to an underwriting loss.

   c. Competitive status for the insurer—An underwriting loss caused by underinsurance can indicate the need for higher property insurance rates, which, in turn, make the insurer less competitive.

5. When working to prevent underwriting losses, it is preferable to insure to value with rates that reflect the loss exposure than to underinsure property at inflated rates.

6. At policy renewal, the underwriter should reassess the values exposed to loss and adjust limits accordingly.

Educational Objective 3

Explain how underwriters use policy amount, amount subject, normal loss expectancy (NLE), probable maximum loss (PML), and maximum foreseeable loss (MFL) to measure potential loss severity.

Key Points:

Underwriters use several measures to determine the potential severity of a loss. Different underwriters arrive at different estimates. Estimates by any two underwriters with a common employer, however, should be consistent if not identical because insurers ordinarily establish rules for determining both values.

A. Policy Amount

1. The amount of insurance the policy provides (or its limit of liability) is the easiest to calculate and is the only measure of potential severity on which underwriters tend to agree.

2. The amount of insurance is also the least useful figure for determining potential loss severity, because the amount of insurance purchased could have little bearing on the amount of the loss.

B. Amount Subject

Amount subject measures the exposure to a single loss.

1. For fire insurance, the amount subject is almost always the value of all insured property exposed within a single fire division. Underwriters often use the expression "within four walls" to explain the concept of amount subject.

    a. It requires subjective judgment to measure the boundaries of a fire division.

    b. Not all underwriters agree about what constitutes an acceptable firewall.

2. Underwriters must also consider how ventilating systems and electrical conduits affect the ability of a fire to spread from one part of a building to another.

C. Normal Loss Expectancy

Normal loss expectancy (NLE) is defined as the loss expected under normal operating conditions with all fire protection services working. In determining the NLE for a risk, several elements are used for consideration:

1. Construction

2. Protection (positive pressure ventilation/sprinklers)

3. Business interruption contingency plans

4. Fire divisions

5. Susceptibility of contents to damage and combustibility

6. Operational hazards

D. Probable Maximum Loss

Probable maximum loss (PML) is the underwriter's estimate of the largest loss likely to occur. PML calculations are subjective estimates.

1. To many underwriters, PML is meaningful only for fire-resistive buildings and their contents. For other types of construction, underwriters consider PML equal to the amount subject and make only one calculation.

2. Amount subject considers the benefit of horizontal fire divisions, but PML includes the effects of building features that impede the vertical spread of fire from one floor to the next.

3. For fire-resistive construction, insurer underwriting guidelines might establish PML as the value of a certain number of floors, expressed as maximum and minimum values.

4. To establish an accurate PML for a fire-resistive building, the underwriter must also consider how a fire can spread vertically from floor to floor and how fire can damage property on the floors that it never reaches. The underwriter must also allow for smoke and water damage on floors the fire never reaches.

5. Accurately calculating the amount subject and PML is also important for complying with state insurance codes and satisfying reinsurance arrangements. Statutes generally prohibit an insurance company from exposing more than 10 percent of its policyholders' surplus to a single loss net of authorized reinsurance.

6. PML also influences the availability of both treaty and facultative reinsurance. Reinsurers have designed many property treaties to facilitate writing large amounts of insurance on a single risk while limiting the reinsurer's exposure within the PML.

E. Maximum Foreseeable Loss

Generally applied to fire losses, maximum foreseeable loss (MFL) is an estimate of the financial cost of the loss that would occur if all protection measures (automatic and manual) were to fail and no effective fire department response occurred.

1. It assumes that only passive protection measures, such as separation and barrier walls, limit the loss.

2. Some insurers underwrite to the MFL only and do not consider the PML. Others underwrite to the PML only and limit losses through policy limits.

Educational Objective 4
Describe the underwriting considerations for business income and extra expense coverage.

Key Points:

Coverage for income lost and associated expenses the business incurs as it recovers is a significant consideration for underwriting business income and extra expense coverage.

A. Probable Maximum Loss

Underwriters can estimate the probable maximum loss (PML) for business income coverage in three steps:

1. Determine the most serious direct loss

    a. The direct PML is the logical starting point for estimating the business income PML.

    b. When the direct PML is used to estimate future business income losses, the dollar amount of the direct loss is not important.

    c. The extent of the damage and its location will determine how much time is necessary for repairs and how long the time element loss will continue.

2. Calculate the longest period of restoration that this loss can reasonably be expected to cause.

3. Compute the largest loss of business income that the insured is likely to sustain during a period of this length.

B. Factors Affecting the Period of Interruption

Underwriters must consider the time frame when underwriting time element coverages. Any factor that would lengthen the likely period of interruption increases the insured's potential loss amount.

1. Rebuilding time

    a. The time required to repair, replace, or rebuild the insured's building or the building containing the insured's premises is a major factor in determining loss exposure.

    b. Specialized structures requiring long construction periods, lengthy delays in obtaining permits, severe climatic conditions inhibiting construction during certain times of the year, and congested urban locations are all factors that increase loss exposure.

2. Seasonality
   a. A seasonal business such as a toy store or ski resort with, for example, 80 percent of its business concentrated in a three-month peak season, could suffer a severe business income loss from a relatively short shutdown at an inopportune time of year.
   b. The time of year when a loss occurs has little effect on a nonseasonal business whose income stream is spread evenly across the year.

3. Bottlenecks
   A bottleneck can apply to a machine, process, or building that is essential to the continued operation of an entire facility or manufacturing plant.
   a. A relatively minor direct damage loss involving a bottleneck can lead to a severe business income loss.
   b. If a vital process is duplicated on machines in separate fire divisions, the loss exposure is greatly reduced.
   c. Although bottlenecks usually result from manufacturing processes, a congested area or an unusual building configuration can also create them.

4. Computer systems
   a. Computer systems play a central role in many business operations.
   b. Relatively minor damage to a computer system can halt an entire operation.

5. Long production processes
   If the insured's normal manufacturing or processing operation takes an unusually long time to complete, the underwriter must consider the time required to get stock in process back to the point at which it had been before the loss. For example, if a product must be aged or seasoned, destruction of the facility could lead to a lengthy interruption.

6. Availability of substitutes
   a. When replacing damaged or destroyed property takes a long time, the insured might not have to wait to resume full operations.
   b. In many cases, other property can be substituted.
   c. The substitute can be permanent or temporary.

7. Business continuity and disaster recovery planning
   A business continuity plan (BCP) allows an organization to anticipate its response to potential disruption and determine the critical functions that must continue so that it survives, recovers, and resumes growth.

a. A crucial element of a BCP is a disaster recovery plan, which includes detailed written plans to restore the production process if part or all of the facility and equipment were destroyed.

b. The disaster recovery plan should indicate what would be necessary if each part of the process were destroyed.

c. The plan could also indicate whether continuation of the operation is feasible following certain types of damage. If it is, extra expense insurance might be indicated.

Educational Objective 5

Describe the underwriting considerations and risk control techniques associated with employee dishonesty and crimes committed by others.

Key Points:

Crime is a significant cause of loss for commercial insureds. It is important for underwriters to assess crime loss potential by examining both the characteristics of the property subject to loss and the characteristics of the account itself.

A. Employee Dishonesty

1. Employee dishonesty loss exposures have unique characteristics:

   a. Employees have ready access to money and other valuable property. They learn the company's routines and schedules and the habits of fellow employees. They can discover the controls employers have to prevent crime and how well those controls work.

   b. Losses can be hidden from discovery.

   c. Once losses occur, they are often large. A thief's access to property continues until the crime is discovered. The length of time of access, in turn, contributes to the size of the loss.

   d. Employers are often reluctant to believe that employees may steal from them. That reluctance leads to practices that create opportunities for theft, greatly increases exposures to loss, and creates a problem of adverse selection for the insurer.

   e. Employers might be reluctant to prosecute employees who steal.

2. Many commercial insureds overlook the employee dishonesty loss exposure, and only a small percentage of mercantile establishments purchase employee dishonesty coverage.

3. Underwriting employee dishonesty loss exposures

   a. Employee dishonesty insurance is often included in businessowners policies and commercial package policies.

   b. Before issuing a policy, underwriters should be satisfied that certain conditions exist:

      • There is no evidence of a moral hazard.

      • Burglary and robbery risk control systems should be in place and maintained. Defenses against external crime also deter employee crime.

- As with other coverages, amounts of insurance should fall within the limits prescribed by the insurer's underwriting guidelines.
- The organization should be managed soundly. Management controls provide evidence of management's care and concern.

4. Controlling employee dishonesty losses

a. Minimizing employee dishonesty losses requires strict adherence to management controls.

b. These controls, applicable to almost all organizations, improve underwriting acceptability:

- New hires are screened for prior criminal activity, and their references are checked.
- Seasoned employees are evaluated before they are promoted, especially for moves into sensitive positions.
- A substance-abuse screening program is in place.
- The rate and level of employee turnover is appropriate given the insured's business.
- Termination procedures are well defined.
- Management is sensitive to dramatic changes in employee behavior, such as sudden or drastic lifestyle changes, which might indicate employee dishonesty.
- Periodic audits are conducted to evaluate accounts receivable, cash accounts, inventories, and disbursements.
- Bank reconciliations are done to ensure that company records and bank records agree.
- Employees monitor one another through a division of authority among employees.
- Annual vacations of a minimum length of time are required.
- Duties are rotated, a practice that helps to uncover irregularities or embezzlement.
- Two-person or dual control systems are in place on some items, such as the vault, cash, and other items susceptible to theft.

B. Crimes Committed by Others

Crime committed by others includes acts such as robbery, burglary, and theft.

1. Underwriting crimes committed by others loss exposure

Underwriters analyzing crimes committed by others loss exposures consider six factors:

    a. Susceptibility and marketability
- The size, weight, portability, visibility, and accessibility of property determine how susceptible it is to being stolen.
- Property that is widely used has more potential customers, and property that is difficult to trace is more marketable.

    b. Property location
- Topography, neighborhood, climate, and the local crime rate can tell underwriters what kind of losses to expect.

    c. Nature of the occupancy
- Some occupancies generally have a great deal of cash or other valuable property on hand.
- Some businesses are conducted in obscure locations where criminal activity might not be readily detected, or they operate during hours when few people are around to deter criminals.

    d. Moral and morale hazards
- A dishonest insured can readily dispose of inventory and arrange a fraudulent claim.
- A lax attitude toward loss might mean that precautions and protective measures are not consistently adhered to, thereby creating an environment in which a loss is more likely to occur.

    e. Public protection

    The quality of police protection varies by community.

    f. Coverage and price modifications

    Possible modifications include changing coverage, limits, pricing, deductibles, and adding endorsements requiring protective safeguards.

2. Controlling crime committed by others loss exposures

    a. Crime loss exposures respond well to risk control efforts. Private protection systems to prevent or reduce loss include these:
- Safes and vaults
- Cages, special rooms, and limited-access areas
- Indoor and outdoor lighting
- Fences and walls
- Protection of openings on the premises (gates, doors, windows, and skylights)
- Guard services
- Alarm systems
- Electronic surveillance systems

- Inventory control and other management activities

b. Private protection systems generally serve two important functions: to prevent crime losses and to reduce losses that do occur.

c. The two main categories of private protection devices are detection devices and barriers to criminal access.

Educational Objective 6

Describe the loss exposures and the underwriting considerations for commercial general liability insurance.

Key Points:

When evaluating a commercial general liability submission, an underwriter must consider a variety of loss exposures and hazards.

A. Premises and Operations Liability Underwriting Considerations

1. The primary loss exposures facing most businesses are those for either their premises or their operations.

2. Premises liability loss exposures arise from the insured's ownership or possession of real property.

3. Operations liability loss exposures arise from an insured's business operations conducted away from its own premises and from uncompleted work.

4. Liability underwriters tend to evaluate a business's loss exposures in terms of its "premises risks" or "operations risks."

5. Extent of public exposure

   a. Underlying an underwriter's evaluation of an account for general liability insurance is the extent of its liability exposure to the public.

      • The public includes customers, representatives of suppliers, anyone else associated with the business, and the general public.

      • Underwriters should determine whether the account's exposure is common for the classification and how much variation in the exposure is likely.

   b. In many cases, the hazards inherent in the insured's operations bear little or no relation to the extent to which the public is exposed to them.

   c. The differences in exposure between two premises may be a result of location, type of business, or time in business, or a combination of the three.

   d. A higher level of customer traffic suggests higher premises loss exposures.

   e. A store's location may create an increase in traffic and thus increase the extent of public exposure.

    f. Underwriters must also consider the legal status of persons likely to be on the premises. The underwriter can compare the insured's required degree of care with that of an average risk in the same classification.

6. Physical Hazards

    a. The physical hazards relating to premises and operations liability loss exposures fall into three categories:

- Common hazards—physical hazards common to many premises, such as those that induce slips and falls
- Special hazards of the class—physical hazards, such as chemicals, dust, and explosives, that occur only in certain types of businesses
- Special hazards of the risk—physical hazards found in businesses that conduct operations that are not typical of the class to which they belong

    b. To properly evaluate the physical hazards of premises loss exposures, underwriters consider the entire premises. When the primary loss exposures arise from the premises' interior, underwriters cannot overlook the exterior loss exposures.

    c. In addition to evaluating bodily injury loss exposures, an underwriter considers the physical hazards that can cause property damage losses.

    d. Operations-oriented accounts generally have a greater potential for causing property damage losses than do premises-oriented risks.

- Use of heavy equipment may cause serious property damage, but the major sources of property damage losses are fire, collapse, water damage, and, in some cases, pollution.
- Generally, businesses with substantial premises loss exposures, such as apartment houses and office buildings, have minimal operations loss exposures.

    e. The hazards related to operations loss exposures vary more than those related to premises loss exposures.

7. Contractors and subcontractors

    a. A contractor is covered by its CGL policy for its vicarious liability for the acts of its subcontractors.

    b. A subcontractor must purchase its own CGL policy to cover itself against liability claims arising out of its work for the general contractor.

    c. Contractors use subcontractors so frequently that they are evaluated based on the quality of work, timeliness, and availability—not by the adequacy of their insurance.

d. Premium payment disputes may be isolated incidents, but they could also be symptomatic of the contractor's poor management of the operation.

e. Underwriting subcontractors is nearly impossible.
  - The insured might not know at the outset of the policy term exactly which subcontractors will be used.
  - Depending upon the number of subcontractors used, it is often not feasible for a contractor to notify its insurer every time a new subcontractor is hired.
  - The underwriter must rely on the insured's reputation in hiring competent subcontractors.
  - At the least, the underwriter can convey its requirements for adequate insurance to the insured and insist that certificates of insurance be obtained from each subcontractor.

B. Products and Completed Operations Liability Underwriting Considerations

Products liability and completed operations liability are considered together because both address exposures to accidents or damage caused by a defect in finished work that is away from the insured's premises and over which the insured has relinquished control.

1. Sources of products liability

Liability for sale, manufacture, or distribution of products can arise from three areas:

a. Breach of warranty

A warranty can be an explicit guarantee of safety. An express warranty is a statement or representation about a product's quality or suitability for its intended use. An implied warranty is an obligation that the courts impose on a seller to warrant certain facts about a product. In all states, common law and the Uniform Commercial Code recognize two implied warranties in any contract of sale:
  - The implied warranty of merchantability represents that the product is reasonably fit for the ordinary purpose for which it was intended.
  - The implied warranty of fitness for a particular purpose applies when the buyer relies on the seller's knowledge in selecting a particular product for a particular purpose.

b. Negligence

Negligence can occur at many different steps in the product process, from the design, manufacture, or inspection of the product to the instructions or warnings that accompany it. Regardless of the source of negligence, the result is a defect in the product.

    c. Strict liability in tort

        Strict liability in tort is the most common basis for products liability suits; it imposes liability on any person who produces an unreasonably dangerous product.

2. Underwriting products liability loss exposures

    a. The underwriter is concerned about the product's potential to harm the public—that is, the product's loss frequency and severity.

        • Determining the inherent hazards of a product is the first and most important step in underwriting a product.

        • A product that is not inherently hazardous has a relatively minor loss exposure. The reverse is also true.

    b. The applicant's business, the limits of liability, and the business's size and scope are important in underwriting products.

    c. Plaintiffs increase their chances of winning a products liability lawsuit when they assert more than one ground for recovery, thereby increasing underwriting losses.

3. Underwriting completed operations loss exposures

    a. Completed operations loss exposures include construction, service, repair, and maintenance activities.

    b. Businesses with operations loss exposures are likely to have completed operations loss exposures.

    c. How work is performed is important to the underwriter in evaluating loss exposures of both operations in progress and completed operations.

    d. Careless or faulty work is likely to increase loss frequency to the same degree for both operations in progress and completed operations.

    e. When evaluating an applicant for completed operations coverage, the underwriter must determine the likelihood and severity of potential losses by evaluating the applicant's business.

    f. The completed operations loss exposures the underwriter should consider vary by class of business, and completed operations loss exposures for a given business can be considerably different from the completed operations loss exposures for other businesses in the same class.

C. Personal and Advertising Injury Liability Underwriting Considerations

    1. Personal and advertising injury is automatically included as Coverage B in the ISO CGL coverage form, unless it is specifically excluded by attaching an endorsement to the policy.

2. Personal injury loss exposures include the insured's legal liability arising out of libel; slander; false arrest; wrongful eviction; invasion of the right of private occupancy; and infringement of copyright, trade dress, or slogan.

3. The coverage provided under the CGL form for advertising liability excludes personal injury and advertising injury committed by an insured whose business is advertising, broadcasting, publishing, or telecasting.

4. This coverage is intended for businesses that purchase advertising to sell their own products or services, not for a company that is in the advertising business.

D. Premises Medical Payments Liability Underwriting Considerations

1. Medical payments coverage is also automatically included as Coverage C in the CGL coverage form.

2. Underwriters do not individually underwrite this loss exposure but do consider the medical payments loss exposure as part of the premises or operations loss exposures.

3. Medical payments coverage applies to medical expenses of persons other than the insured who are injured on the insured's premises or because of the insured's operations.

4. Medical payments coverage does not require the insured to be legally liable to pay for them. Because of this, the limits for medical payments coverage are usually much lower than those for bodily injury or property damage.

5. Medical payments coverage can be excluded by attaching an endorsement to the policy, but this is rarely done.

Educational Objective 7
Describe the underwriting considerations for personal and commercial auto insurance.

Key Points:

Motor vehicles provide essential transportation for both personal and commercial insureds. They also cause the death and disability of thousands of people each year. Therefore, an underwriter must carefully analyze several factors when considering auto insurance policies.

A. Personal Auto Underwriting Considerations

The desirability of individual personal auto policyholders is usually determined by specific characteristics of the individual drivers. The insurer's underwriting guidelines reflect management's evaluation of the factors related to the driver, most of which are also used to classify and rate the application. The major underwriting factors that are considered in most private passenger auto underwriting guidelines include these:

1. Age of operator

  a. Vehicle operator age is an important determinant of the likelihood of auto losses, because a disproportionate number of young drivers are involved in motor vehicle accidents relative to the driving population as a whole.

  b. Rating plans in virtually all states consider the age of the operator and charge considerably higher rates for young drivers.

  c. The ability of older drivers to drive safely may be compromised by age-related physical and mental impairments.

2. Age and type of auto

  a. The age of an auto generally indicates its mechanical condition.

  b. The loss experience for specific types of autos in areas such as bumper-impact results, damageability, repairability, and likelihood of vehicle theft are considered when underwriting or pricing an account.

3. Vehicle use

  a. A long commuting distance or business use of an auto would affect rates because those factors increase loss potential. Rates reflect these classifications of auto use:

  • Cars driven for pleasure use only

  • Cars driven to work in a carpool in which drivers rotate driving responsibility

- Cars driven to work more than three miles but fewer than ten miles one way
- Cars driven to work more than ten miles one way
- Cars driven for business use

   b. Underwriters must determine whether the driving mileage indicated is excessive in view of the rate that applies and should consider this when pricing the policy.

4. Driving record

   a. Underwriters evaluate a driver's prior accidents and prior moving violations.

   b. The driver's prior loss history may indicate poor driving habits, recklessness, or simply a lack of skill.

   c. The applicant or insured, index bureaus, and motor vehicle records are sources of underwriting information, although these sources often provide incomplete information.

5. Territory

   a. Liability and physical damage losses vary based on the driver's principal garaging location and where the vehicle is used.

   b. Theft and vandalism occur more frequently in congested urban areas. Drivers are more likely to be involved in auto accidents in urban areas but more likely to be involved in fatal accidents in rural areas.

   c. Other territorial considerations are unrelated to population density. An example is weather conditions.

6. Gender and marital status

   a. More men than women die in motor vehicle accidents probably due to the greater number of miles men drive and the greater likelihood that they will engage in risky behavior such as speeding and driving under the influence of alcohol.

   b. The marital status of younger drivers is both a rating and an underwriting factor, and it relates directly to stability.

   c. Some states regulate the use of gender and marital status for underwriting purposes. A few states prohibit price discrimination based on gender or marital status.

7. Occupation

   a. Occupation is rarely used overtly in evaluating personal auto exposures, but it is sometimes a factor in making an underwriting decision on a particular submission.

   b. Some insurers make accommodations for vehicles used in such occupations by rating them as personal autos with a surcharge to reflect the additional exposures.

    c. Some insurers require such accounts to be submitted under their commercial auto programs.

  8. Personal characteristics

    a. Underwriters often order consumer investigation reports to provide information on the personal characteristics of applicants and other drivers.

    b. Many insurers use credit scoring to evaluate the stability of insurance applicants.

  9. Physical condition of driver

    a. Physical impairments may be a problem if allowances for the impairment have not been made.

    b. Auto modifications made to accommodate a driver with physical impairments and the driver's demonstrated driving mastery usually make the applicant acceptable.

  10. Safety equipment

    a. Many new cars come equipped with advanced safety systems, and these are considered in pricing and evaluating an account.

    b. Vehicles that incorporate global positioning system technology and wireless communication technology for safety purposes have also earned rate credits from some insurers.

B. Commercial Auto Underwriting Considerations

The analysis of a commercial auto risk should closely follow the characteristics used in rating the policy. Factors that underwriters consider for commercial vehicle drivers include their motor vehicle record, especially if it indicates any violations; accident history; and experience with operating commercial motor vehicles. Underwriters also consider factors relating to the vehicle. Commercial auto policies are class rated. Trucks, tractors, and trailers, as well as truckers hauling exclusively for one concern, are classified and rated using these four factors:

  1. Vehicle weight and type

    a. The damage resulting from an auto accident is related to the size, weight, and speed of the vehicles involved.

    b. Commercial tractor-trailer rigs are more likely than others to cause severe damage when an accident occurs. Large trucks are also difficult to maneuver.

  2. Vehicle use

    a. Some vehicles may be used almost continually to haul goods, while others may be used only to travel to and from job sites, remaining parked most of the time.

b. The ISO *Commercial Lines Manual (CLM)* classifies trucks, tractors, and trailers into these classifications:

- Service use applies to vehicles that are used principally to transport personnel or material to job sites. Because they are used to the least extent, service vehicles receive the lowest rate.

- Retail use means that the vehicle is used primarily for deliveries to and pickups from households. This use class receives the highest rate.

- Commercial use applies to any vehicle that does not fall into one of the preceding two classes.

c. The underwriter verifies that vehicles are properly classified to ensure that sufficient premium is charged for the loss exposure.

d. The *CLM* also provides classifications for public use vehicles.

3. Radius of operation

a. Radius of operation is another measure of road exposure. The distance traveled, as well as the nature of that travel, can affect accident frequency.

b. Trucks operated over long distances may be more likely to have more severe accidents than those operated locally.

4. Special industry classifications

a. Special industry classifications, or secondary classifications, consist of eight major industry classifications, each of which is further divided into subclassifications.

- Truckers—Vehicles used to transport the goods or materials of others; this does not include moving household goods, office furniture, or fixtures and supplies.

- Food delivery—Vehicles that wholesale food distributors and food manufacturers use to transport raw and finished products.

- Specialized delivery—Delivery vehicles such as armored cars or autos for delivering film, magazines or newspapers, mail and parcel post, and similar items.

- Waste disposal—Vehicles transporting waste material for disposal or resale.

- Farmers—Vehicles owned by farmers and used in farming operations.

- Dump and transit mix trucks and trailers—Vehicles that have no other appropriate classification and that have an incidental dumping operation.

- Contractors—All vehicles used by contractors, other than dump trucks.

- Not otherwise specified—Vehicles that cannot be classified into any other group.

   b. From an underwriting perspective, trucks, tractors, or trailers with special industry classifications can present additional concerns and require the underwriter to gather more information.

C. Underwriting Use of Risk Control Services

An insurer's risk control activities are important to achieving and maintaining the underwriting profitability of an account.

   1. Risk control reports

      a. Risk control reports are a first-hand evaluation of an account by the insurer's risk control representative.

      b. Risk control reports confirm and supplement information on the application, such as determining how well the insured adheres to its fleet safety program.

      c. Some insurers rely on the expertise of their risk control representatives to provide services to their commercial auto accounts.

      d. Many insurers involve risk control representatives in analyzing claim information to determine whether underlying conditions exist that could be corrected to reduce future losses.

      e. A risk control representative who is familiar with many commercial auto accounts will likely be able to share risk prevention and risk reduction measures with accounts that demonstrate a need.

   2. Fleet safety programs

      a. A fleet safety program consists of the written policy and procedures that an account uses in the management of its drivers and vehicles.

      b. For accounts in the transportation business, a fleet safety program is essential and is usually a significant part of their overall operational guidelines.

      c. A fleet safety program generally indicates that the account's management understands the value of risk management and is working to prevent and control losses.

      d. Although the content of fleet safety programs varies, most programs include provisions specifying vehicle use, driver selection, vehicle maintenance, and accident reporting.

- Copies of the fleet safety program are usually given to employees who have permission to operate company-owned vehicles.

- Good fleet safety programs are clear, concise, and written at a level appropriate for the program user.

Educational Objective 8
Describe the underwriting considerations for workers compensation insurance.

Key Points:

Underwriting workers compensation insurance is similar to underwriting general liability insurance because general liability and workers compensation insurance, to a large extent, present many of the same hazards. The difference, however, is that general liability underwriting concerns itself with injuries to the general public while workers compensation underwriting focuses on injuries to the insured's employees.

A. Underwriting Guidelines for Individual Classes and Applicants
  1. Not all insurers offer workers compensation insurance coverage, and of those that do, many insurers have fairly strict underwriting guidelines to the classifications approved by underwriting management.
  2. If an applicant is in a classification written by the insurer, specific underwriting criteria are used to evaluate the acceptability.
    a. The primary underwriting consideration is the existence or nonexistence of on-premises and off-premises hazards.
    b. The underwriters may decide to investigate an applicant further based on certain factors.
  3. Experience modification factor
    a. The experience modification factor serves as an index of the account's desirability within a particular class.
    b. If an experience-rated policy develops adverse results during the year, the experience rating mechanism ensures that the policyholder will be penalized in future policy periods.
    c. Experience rating provides an accurate method to capture statistics about an applicant.
    d. National Council on Compensation Insurance (NCCI's) experience rating plan is used in the majority of states.
  4. Temporary and seasonal employees
    a. These employees are generally not as well trained as full-time employees and, therefore, have a greater risk of being injured.
    b. An important consideration for an underwriter regarding leased employees relates to whether the company that leases workers is considered the employer for workers compensation purposes or the organization that hires them.

    c. NCCI has developed several endorsements for use with workers compensation policies covering leased workers.

5. Subcontractors

    a. Most workers compensation laws hold a contractor responsible for workers compensation benefits to employees of its uninsured subcontractors.

    b. The policyholder must either prove that the loss exposure has been insured by the subcontractor or pay a premium based on the subcontractor's payroll as well as the insured's own payroll.

6. Maritime occupations

    a. Maritime loss exposures are those related to occupations involving work on vessels while at sea or in close proximity to bodies of water, such as on docks, on piers, or in terminals.

    b. The principal federal laws covering on-the-job injuries for maritime occupations are the United States Longshore and Harbor Workers' (USL&HW) Compensation Act and the Merchant Marine Act.

    c. The latter is more commonly known as the Jones Act and is intended to cover masters and crew members of vessels.

    d. Maritime loss exposures can be overlooked when certain occupations or employees conduct occasional tasks that fall outside their regular duties, creating a "gray area" for coverage.

    e. Underwriters must always be alert to the existence of potential maritime loss exposures.

    f. Maritime loss exposures can be assessed by reviewing certificates of insurance, the type of equipment owned, a list of jobs in progress, and previous loss experience.

    g. An underwriter can discover USL&HW Act exposures in many typical construction and erection operations.

7. Relative premium size

Even otherwise acceptable applicants may be rejected if the workers compensation premium is too high relative to other coverages.

8. Employee concentration

    a. Workers compensation underwriters have placed more emphasis on the concentration hazard since the terrorist attacks of September 11, 2001, which demonstrated that an employer with a large number of employees at a single location faces the possibility that a single incident could result in many injuries or deaths.

B. Management Attitude and Capability

  1. In evaluating management of an insured, the underwriter should consider the willingness and ability of management to minimize hazards and reduce losses.

  2. Employee morale and claim consciousness often reflect management attitude toward workers compensation and industrial safety.

  3. When assessing management, underwriters also should perform a wage analysis, which could reveal whether its salaries are attracting high-quality employees and minimizing turnover. They also should consider whether management provides healthcare benefits for its employees.

C. On-Premises Hazards

A variety of on-premises hazards affect workers compensation loss experience. On-premises hazards relating to housekeeping and maintenance are found in almost all occupations, while special hazards of the class are related to a particular operation or industry.

  1. Housekeeping

    From an underwriting standpoint, housekeeping refers to a workplace's physical layout, its cleanliness, and its operating efficiency.

  2. Maintenance

    a. Poorly maintained machinery presents an inherent danger.

    b. Specific hazards might be present as a result of the type of machines, equipment, materials, and processes used in a particular firm's operation.

    c. Specific hazards vary widely but can be placed in these categories:

      • Machinery and equipment

      • Material-handling

      • Electrical

      • Occupational

      • Fire and explosion

      • Slips, falls, and poor working conditions

      • Dangerous processes, resulting in burns from heat and chemicals

      • Flying and falling material, resulting in eye and head injuries

      • Miscellaneous hazards, resulting in cuts, punctures, bumps, bruises, and abrasions

  3. Occupational disease

    a. Workers compensation laws provide benefits for some diseases in addition to injuries from accidents on the job.

    b. The definition varies by state, but an occupational disease is generally one resulting from causes the worker faces on the job and to which the general public is not exposed.

    c. Some of the occupational diseases covered by the various state workers compensation laws are silicosis, asbestosis, radiation, tuberculosis, pneumoconiosis, and heart or lung disease.

    d. Exposure to unfavorable conditions at work does not always cause occupational disease.

    e. In an industrial setting, hazard analysis also includes monitoring the work environment for the presence of industrial poisons that can enter the body by ingestion, inhalation, or skin absorption.

4. Cumulative trauma injuries

    a. Cumulative trauma disorders, sometimes referred to as repetitive strain injuries (RSI), arise from a series of minor stresses over a period of time.

    b. These relatively minor injuries accumulate until they require medical treatment and can result in a disability.

5. Analysis of on-premises hazards

Most accidents occur as a result of either an unsafe act or an unsafe condition.

    a. Unsafe acts or practices on the part of employees include failing to use the proper personal protective equipment.

    • Management can influence employee behavior through its hiring policy, safety program, and enforcement of safety rules.

    • Premises inspections can indicate the extent to which the insured tolerates unsafe actions.

    b. Unsafe conditions are generally easier to identify than unsafe acts. Routine practices that usually are safe can become unsafe in particular circumstances, creating more likely hazards than those that are more apparent.

    c. The loss history of the policyholder and others in the same industry provides information on the types of losses that might occur.

    d. Advisory loss costs or rates take into account the difference in relative hazards among occupational classes.

D. Off-Premises Hazards

Employees in some organizations fulfill all their employment duties on the premises, while employees in other organizations have a great deal of travel or off-premises work.

1. Three aspects should be considered when evaluating off-premises hazards:
   a. The duration of travel
   b. The mode of transportation
   c. The hazards at remote job sites
2. The same techniques for evaluating on-premises hazards can be used for off-premises hazards.

Educational Objective 9

Describe the underwriting considerations for umbrella and excess liability insurance.

Key Points:

Because they are designed to cover large, infrequent losses, umbrella and excess liability insurance policies entail unique underwriting considerations.

A. Umbrella and Excess Liability Insurance
1. Umbrella liability insurance, both personal and commercial, is designed to cover large, low-frequency losses.
   a. Most umbrella policies have a deductible or self-insured retention that the policyholder must pay.
   b. Umbrella policies are not standardized.
2. Most umbrella policies are designed to serve three functions:
   a. Provide excess liability limits above all specified underlying policies
   b. Provide coverage when the aggregate limits of the underlying policies have been exhausted
   c. Provide coverage for gaps in the underlying policies
3. An umbrella policy requires that liability insurance with agreed limits of liability be maintained on the underlying policies.
4. Excess liability insurance increases the limits of liability on one or more underlying policies but does not generally broaden coverage. Excess policies are frequently written on a layered basis, with several policies providing successively higher limits.

B. Underwriting the Risk
1. For umbrella and excess liability policies, loss severity, as opposed to loss frequency, is the primary underwriting concern.
2. Because these types of policies usually have a long tail, the underwriter must approach loss severity by using a longer and broader underwriting perspective.
3. The underwriter should also consider any catastrophe loss exposures issues that could affect liability claims in the future.
4. Underwriting acceptability is a more important issue if the potential for significant drop-down coverage is present.

C. Underwriting the Underlying Policies
1. Underwriting umbrella or excess policies requires a careful analysis of the same loss exposures covered by the underlying policies, as well as additional loss exposures covered by the umbrella (and in some cases excess) policies but not by underlying coverage.
2. These elements of the underlying insurance can affect underwriting:
   a. Type of insurance
   b. Name of insurer
   c. Applicable limits and deductibles
   d. Premium for bodily injury liability coverages
   e. Premium for property damage liability coverages
   f. Details of extensions of coverage beyond standard policy provisions

D. Underwriting the Insurer
1. Because the umbrella or excess insurer must assume defense of a claim if the underlying insurer cannot, underwriters should consider the underlying insurer's financial condition.
2. An insurer's solvency may be assessed based on the rating it receives from a recognized service such as A.M. Best or Standard & Poor's.

Key Words and Phrases:

Key Words

Frame construction
A class of construction that has load-bearing components made of wood or other combustible materials such as brick or stone veneer.

Joisted masonry construction
A class of construction that has load-bearing exterior walls made of brick, adobe, concrete, gypsum, stone, tile, or similar materials; that has floors and roofs of combustible materials; and that has a fire-resistance rating of at least one hour.

Mill construction
A subclassification of joisted masonry construction that uses heavy timber for columns, beams, supports, and ties; has a minimum two-hour fire-resistance rating on bearing walls; and has an absence of floor joists.

Noncombustible construction
A class of construction in which the exterior walls, floor, and roof of a building are constructed of, and supported by, metal, gypsum, or other noncombustible materials.

Masonry noncombustible construction
Masonry construction or construction that includes exterior walls of fire-resistive construction with a fire-resistance rating of not less than one hour.

Modified fire-resistive construction
A class of construction that has exterior walls, floors, and roofs of masonry or other fire-resistive materials with a fire-resistance rating of one to two hours.

Fire-resistive construction
A class of construction that has exterior walls, floors, and roofs of masonry or other fire-resistive material with a fire-resistance rating of at least two hours.

Fuel load (fire load)
The expected maximum amount of combustible material in a given area of a building, including both structural elements and contents, commonly expressed in terms of weight of combustibles per square foot.

Fire division
A section of a structure so well protected that fire cannot spread from that section to another, or vice versa.

Fire wall
A floor-to-roof wall made of noncombustible materials and having no open doors, windows, or other spaces through which fire can pass.

Parapet
A vertical extension of a fire wall that extends above a roofline.

Building codes
Local ordinances or state statutes that regulate the construction of buildings within a municipality, county, or state.

Occupancy
The type or character of use of the property in question.

Special hazards of the class
A characteristic typical of all occupancies in a given class that can cause or aggravate a loss. An example is the hazard of cooking, common to the restaurant class.

Special hazards of the risk
A condition that can cause a loss but that is not typical of an occupancy. An example is the use of a welding torch in an auto repair shop.

Protection
Measures taken to prevent or reduce the damage done by fire.

Public fire protection
Fire protection equipment and services made available through governmental authority to all properties within a defined area.

Local fire alarm system
A detection system, triggered by smoke or heat, that sounds a bell, siren, or another audible alert at the premises only.

Central station system
A private detection service that monitors the systems of multiple businesses and/or residences and that calls appropriate authorities or dispatches its own personnel when an alarm is activated.

Wet pipe sprinkler systems
Automatic fire sprinkler systems with pipes that always contain water under pressure, which is released immediately when a sprinkler head opens.

Dry pipe sprinkler systems
Automatic fire sprinkler systems with pipes that contain compressed air or another inert gas that holds a valve in the water line shut until an open sprinkler head releases the gas and allows water to flow through the previously dry pipe to the sprinkler head.

Pre-action sprinkler systems
Automatic fire sprinkler systems with automatic valves controlled by smoke or heat detectors.

Deluge sprinkler system
A type of sprinkler system in which all the heads remain permanently open; when activated by a detection system, a deluge valve allows water into the system.

Fire brigade
A fire service in which building personnel in establishments located far from municipal fire services respond to fire situations.

External exposure
A loss exposure outside the area owned or controlled by the insured.

Replacement cost
The cost to repair or replace property using new materials of like kind and quality with no deduction for depreciation.

Actual cash value
A method in valuing property which is calculated as the cost to replace or repair property minus depreciation, the fair market value, or a valuation determined by the broad evidence rule.

Coinsurance clause
A clause that requires the insured to carry insurance equal to at least a specified percentage of the insured property's value.

COPE
Four interdependent elements that are analyzed by commercial property underwriters when evaluating submissions for property insurance; construction, occupancy, protection, and external exposures.

Vicarious liability
A legal responsibility that occurs when one party is held liable for the actions of a subordinate or associate because of the relationship between the two parties.

Breach of warranty
The failure to meet the terms of a promise or an agreement associated with a product.

Implied warranty of merchantability
An implied warranty that a product is fit for the ordinary purpose for which it is used.

Implied warranty of fitness for a particular purpose
An implied warranty that a product is fit for a particular purpose; applies if the seller knows about the buyer's purpose for the product.

Negligence
The failure to exercise the degree of care that a reasonable person in a similar situation would exercise to avoid harming others.

Strict liability (absolute liability)
Liability imposed by a court or by a statute in the absence of fault when harm results from activities or conditions that are extremely dangerous, unnatural, ultrahazardous, extraordinary, abnormal, or inappropriate.

Credit scoring
A decision-making tool that uses credit report information to develop a predictive score on the creditworthiness of an applicant for additional credit.

Class rate
A type of insurance rate that applies to all insureds in the same rating category or rating class.

Experience modification factor
A factor that tailors manual rates to an insured's experience based on the insured's payroll and loss record of certain prior years.

Umbrella liability insurance
Liability insurance that provides excess coverage above underlying policies and may also provide coverage not available in the underlying policies, subject to a self-insured retention.

Excess liability insurance
Insurance coverage for losses that exceed the limits of underlying insurance coverage or a retention amount.

Drop-down coverage
Coverage provided by many umbrella liability policies for (1) claims not covered at all by the underlying policies and (2) claims that are not covered by an underlying policy only because the underlying policy's aggregate limits have been depleted.

Risk Control and Premium Auditing

6

Educational Objective 1
Describe the goals of insurer risk control activities.

Key Points:

Insurers conduct risk control activities to achieve several goals:

Study Tips

Read actively, and use the review questions to reinforce your learning.

A. Earn a Profit

Risk control activities can help insurers to reach their profit goals in several ways:

1. Improving underwriting decisions

    By inspecting the premises and operations of insurance applicants, risk control representatives can improve the information on which the underwriting department bases its decisions about which applicants to accept and how to price coverage.

2. Improving premium volume

    a. Risk control personnel often recommend risk control measures that can change a marginal account to an acceptable account, thereby increasing the insurer's premium volume while meeting underwriting guidelines.

    b. Risk control personnel and the services they offer can be instrumental in winning new business by helping producers demonstrate added value to their prospective clients.

3. Encouraging insureds to improve risk control

    Risk control representatives can influence insureds to implement more effective risk control initiatives by working with them to identify risk control opportunities and safety improvements.

4. Reducing insureds' losses

    Risk control representatives can reduce losses that the insurer must pay, thereby helping keep the insurer's book of business profitable.

5. Providing an additional revenue source

   Many insurers sell unbundled risk control services to firms that have chosen to retain, or self-insure, their losses. Some insurers also provide their insureds with supplemental risk control services for a fee in addition to the policy premium. Several major insurers offer access to a variety of experts.

6. Reducing errors and omissions claims against the insurer

   Competent risk control service reduces the possibility of errors and omissions claims by insureds or others alleging injury because of the insurer's negligence.

B. Meet Customer Needs

1. By exercising sound risk control, organizations make their accounts more attractive to underwriters (especially during a hard market); help control their insurance premiums and possibly even lower them; reduce disruption to operations following accidents; remain socially responsible; comply with occupational safety and health standards; comply with local, state, and federal laws; and improve their financial performance.

2. Insurers who rely on the independent agency system to market their products often provide risk control services to help agents develop their relationships with insureds and potential accounts.

C. Comply With Legal Requirements

1. Some states require insurers to provide a minimum level of risk control service to commercial insureds.

2. Some insurers charge an additional fee for providing risk control services that exceed what the law requires.

D. Fulfill Duty to Society

1. Insurers benefit society by providing financial resources to help individuals and businesses recover from accidental losses. However, preventing accidental losses is clearly preferable.

2. Insurers have an ethical obligation to use their expertise wisely. By assisting insureds in preventing or reducing accidental losses, insurers pursue humanitarian goals and benefit society.

Educational Objective 2
Describe the risk control services provided by insurers.

Key Points:

Insurers provide these types of risk control services: conducting physical surveys, performing risk analysis and improvement, and developing safety management programs.

A. Conducting Physical Surveys

    1. This consists mainly of collecting underwriting information on a customer's loss exposures.

    2. In addition to evaluating loss exposures and physical hazards, the risk control representative evaluates management's commitment to risk control and employee attitudes about safety-conscious behavior.

    3. In connection with a physical survey, risk control representatives also make written recommendations that can help the customer eliminate or control risk exposures.

    4. Physical surveys provide benefits to both the underwriter and the insured:

        a. The survey report helps the underwriter gain a better understanding of the loss exposures being insured.

        b. The insured can gain a better understanding of its loss exposures.

        c. The insured can be more confident of an adequate recovery in the event of a total loss and is less likely to incur a coinsurance penalty in the event of a partial loss.

B. Performing Risk Analysis and Improvement

    1. The insurer's risk control representative might analyze the customer's loss history (risk analysis) and submit written recommendations (improvements) to the business owner or manager about how to reduce hazards that have previously led to losses.

    2. The insurer's risk control representatives can provide training, informational, or counseling services.

    3. Many insurers also serve as a convenient source of technical risk control information.

4. Some risk control departments enter into service contracts with their insureds or other clients to provide periodic testing and maintenance for fire protection (and detection) systems, which must be tested regularly to ascertain their reliability during emergencies.

5. A pre-construction review by the insurer of the drawings and specifications allows the policyholder to see how insurance rates and underwriting acceptability will be affected by the new construction.

C. Developing Safety Management Programs

1. Developing safety management programs begins with a complete evaluation of the insured's operations, just as in risk analysis and improvement risk control services.

2. After reviewing the evaluation, risk control consultants assist the insured in establishing risk control goals, selecting appropriate risk control measures, organizing the resources necessary to implement the chosen risk control measures, and establishing procedures to monitor the program.

3. The insured is ordinarily responsible for implementing the program without direct assistance from the risk control consultant.

4. After being implemented, the program must be monitored to determine whether adjustments are needed. The consultant can provide a great deal of technical assistance in the monitoring phase of the program.

D. Factors Affecting Service Levels

Every insurer must decide what levels of risk control service to provide and to which insureds. Several factors influence insurers' decisions.

1. Line of insurance

a. An insurer that writes only personal insurance is unlikely to provide extensive risk control services.

b. When insuring exceptionally high-valued property, such as a mansion or a yacht, the insurer might use specifically trained risk control representatives to develop underwriting information or recommendations for reducing physical hazards.

2. Commercial insured size

a. The large premiums generated by commercial insureds and the increased values at risk often make it economically feasible to provide such insureds with risk control services.

b. Insurers may provide options for insureds to purchase supplemental risk control services. By not including the cost for such supplemental services in the premium, insurers allow insureds who do not want or need these additional services to avoid subsidizing the costs associated with them.

3. Types of loss exposures insured

The risk control services an insurer provides depend to some degree on the types of loss exposures the insurer is willing to cover.

a. An insurer that covers large and complex industrial firms needs skilled personnel and sophisticated equipment to meet the risk control requirements of such firms.

b. An insurer that deals primarily with habitational, mercantile, and small manufacturing loss exposures may be able to maintain a less-sophisticated risk control department.

4. Potential legal liability

a. The threat of being named in a lawsuit for negligence in providing risk control services may lead some insurers to choose not to offer risk control services at all or to limit their risk control activities in order to avoid or minimize their exposure.

b. Some states have enacted statutes that protect insurers by preventing insureds, their employees, and third parties (including applicants) from bringing suit against an insurer for injuries or damages sustained as a result of providing, or failing to provide, risk control services.

c. If an insurer's underwriting department chooses to require certain controls as a prerequisite to providing coverage, such controls should be expressed as conditions of the insurance quote and the subsequent insurance agreement.

Educational Objective 3
Explain how risk control cooperates with other insurer functions.

Key Points:

An insurer's risk control efforts are most effective when they complement the activities of its other departments and various external organizations. These are the principal opportunities for risk control cooperation:

A. Underwriting

   1. The risk control function provides information to underwriters that enables them to make better underwriting decisions. This information consists primarily of field inspection reports.
   2. An insurer's risk control department can provide technical support to its underwriting department in many areas, such as fire hazards of new building materials.
   3. The risk control function can also help underwriters modify a new applicant's loss exposures to meet eligibility requirements, help insureds qualify for policy renewal, and help "rehabilitate" marginal accounts.

B. Marketing and Sales

   The risk control function also can be instrumental in helping the insurer's marketing and sales staff meet its goals. The risk control representative's evaluation can make the difference between an applicant's acceptance or rejection.

   1. By making marginal accounts acceptable, risk control helps marketing reach its sales goals.
   2. Risk control can also help marketing by proving to applicants and insureds that the insurer understands their business operations and associated hazards.
   3. Risk control can play a key role in retaining insureds as customers.
   4. Through their direct contact with insureds, risk control representatives can learn the insurance coverages or services insureds need or want.

C. Premium Auditing

   1. Risk control representatives typically visit the insured at the beginning of the policy period and as needed throughout the policy period, while premium auditors visit at the end of the policy period.

2. Risk control personnel can use the opportunity provided by their own inspections, as well as information from recent premium audits, to help improve insured documentation and the accuracy of premium audits.

D. Claims

The risk control department needs claim experience information to direct risk control resources and efforts to crucial areas.

1. The claims department relies on risk control for loss exposure data and background information that can support the loss adjusting process.

2. Regarding individual accidents, particularly in the workers compensation area, risk control can also benefit from information about the accident.

3. Risk control representatives are usually well informed in engineering, mechanical, and technological areas with which claims personnel might be unfamiliar.

4. Risk control representatives can also support the claims function by reviewing and emphasizing the importance of thorough loss documentation and proper claim reporting procedures.

E. Producers

1. Traditionally, producers encouraged the insured's risk control activities and coordinated the efforts of the insurer's risk control representatives with the insured.

2. Many large agencies and brokerages maintain their own risk control departments.

3. If an insured is receiving risk control services from both the insurer and its producer, the risk control entities of both organizations should strive to coordinate their efforts for the mutual benefit of all parties involved, particularly the insured.

Educational Objective 4
Explain why premium audits are conducted.

Key Points:

A premium audit is a methodical examination of a policyholder's operations, records, and books of account to determine the actual exposure units and premium for insurance coverages already provided. Insurers conduct premium audits for these reasons:

A. Determine Correct Premiums

1. The primary reason for premium auditing is to determine the correct premium for the policy period.

   a. Unless premiums are sufficient for the loss exposures covered, the insurer cannot operate profitably.

   b. If the insurer overcharges the insured, it will certainly encounter negative reactions when the error is discovered and will probably lose the business.

2. When a policy is written subject to audit, the actual premium can be calculated only after the end of the policy period when the exact exposure units or premium bases during the policy period are known.

3. A skilled premium auditor, employed by the insurer, usually assembles the information needed to determine the premium base, and determines the actual earned premium.

4. A premium audit is also important to provide the insurer with current and accurate information to determine whether the renewal premium estimate is in line with the audited exposures.

B. Collect Ratemaking Data

1. Insurance advisory organizations collect ratemaking data and, in most cases, project the costs of future losses, or loss costs.

2. A detailed class-by-class breakdown of exposure units obtained by a premium audit is necessary for the insurer's statistical report to the advisory rating organizations (rating bureaus), as well as for billing purposes.

   a. When an advisory organization has credible statistics showing premium volume, loss experience, and total insured exposure units for each rating class, its actuaries can calculate appropriate loss costs that are used to establish rates.

b. These data usually must be filed with state regulators to support rate increases or other rate filings.

C. Meet Regulatory Requirements
1. Although requirements vary by state, premium audits are often required to meet workers compensation insurance regulations.
2. By requiring workers compensation coverage, the state also assumes an obligation to ensure that such coverage is provided fairly and equitably.
3. Uniform workers compensation rules and rates are usually prescribed even in states allowing open competition on other types of insurance.

D. Deter and Detect Fraud
Insureds are less likely to submit false or misleading information when they know the information might be checked and independently verified by a premium auditor.

E. Reinforce Confidence of Insureds
1. A premium computed from a meticulous audit has credibility when the policyholder knows the auditor exercised due care in collecting and verifying the data.
2. The benefits of a competent audit include retaining insureds, improved record keeping on the part of insureds, and insureds being more receptive to risk control advice.

F. Obtain Additional Information
1. A premium audit might generate additional underwriting information about the policyholder, such as an incorrect classification or a new loss exposure that the underwriter had not previously identified. Such information can be useful to the underwriter in determining whether to renew a policy.
2. Premium audit information can also identify marketing opportunities and assist the claim department in adjusting certain types of losses.
3. Finally, a premium audit is a source of feedback on the insurer's image and effectiveness.

Educational Objective 5
Describe the premium auditing process.

Key Points:

These stages in the premium auditing process provide a framework for organizing the countless decisions auditors must make:

A. Planning

Because insurers cannot afford the expense of auditing every auditable policy every year, they must decide which policies to audit.

1. A voluntary report (also called a policyholder's report) is a form the insured completes and returns to the insurer's premium audit department. Once the insurer receives the voluntary audit report, it might choose to accept it, to perform a two-year audit at the end of the next policy period, or to initiate an immediate field audit to confirm the voluntary report.

2. Field audits (also called physical audits) consist of examinations of the insured's books and records at the insured's premises. For each audit, auditors must anticipate the classification and loss exposure concerns and determine the premium base and any necessary allocations. They must then plan how to approach the audit, what records to use, where the records are located, whom to contact, and which questions to ask.

3. The decision about whether to conduct a field audit is influenced by legal requirements, premium size, the insured's operations, prior audit experience, nature of the policy, cost of auditing, geographic factors, and staffing requirements.

4. Some audit teams use predictive modeling in planning both mandatory and discretionary audits.

B. Reviewing Operations

Before they look at the books, skilled premium auditors determine the nature of the operations insured.

1. Auditors observe the nature of the operation and compare it to similar businesses, looking for classifications that might not be shown on the policy; assess management quality and cooperation to determine how to proceed with the audit; and report any significant information to the underwriting department.

2. Auditors note organizational changes and new loss exposures and are always alert to other clues about the nature and direction of the insured's business.

3. A premium underwriter should supply underwriting with details about ownership and operations that are sufficient for rating purposes. The auditor should also indicate the proper classifications for any new loss exposures, the experience of the new operation's management, the financing of the operation, the marketing of its product(s), the derivation of its income, and any information about unusual hazards.

C. Determining Employment Relationships

After analyzing the insured's operations, premium auditors must determine those employees covered by the types of insurance for which premiums are based on payroll.

1. The premium basis of workers compensation policies includes the payroll of every person considered an employee under workers compensation laws. Therefore, the premium auditor must distinguish between employees and independent contractors.

2. Moreover, applicable workers compensation laws vary by state. Many policyholders do not realize that they must obtain certificates of insurance from their subcontractors; otherwise, premium auditors must include the subcontractors' payroll in the premium base.

3. Each state also has regulations regarding workers compensation for corporate officers, sole proprietors, and partners.

4. Many of the state workers compensation Test Audit programs also review the claims filed under workers compensation policies to verify that the injured employees were valid employees or under the insured's direction and control, subject to coverage, and that the employee's class assignment is proper.

D. Finding and Evaluating Books or Records

Premium auditors can examine all books or records of the policyholder related to insurance premiums. They must evaluate the accounting system to determine record accuracy and to identify any alternative sources to confirm the data.

1. In addition to meeting accounting standards, insureds should set up their records to take full advantage of insurance rules and requirements.

2. For large accounts, auditors frequently visit a prospective policyholder before the insurer accepts the account or shortly after acceptance. During this pre-audit survey, the premium auditor confirms the information on the application. Often, the auditor can also assist in setting up appropriate bookkeeping procedures.

E. Auditing the Books and Records

The premium auditor's expertise with classification questions can help underwriters to maintain the proper classifications of the insured's operations and align the deposit premium with the loss exposures covered by the policy. Proper classifications are important for these two reasons:

1. If the classification is incorrect and the rate on the policy is too high, the insured is being overcharged and consequently might be placed at a competitive disadvantage when bidding for jobs or pricing products. Such a situation could have serious legal ramifications if the insurer has acted negligently.

2. If the classification is incorrect and the rate on the policy is too low, an account is less likely to be profitable for the insurer. Premiums might decrease, but claims and expenses do not decrease when an insured is classified incorrectly.

F. Analyzing and Verifying Premium-Related Data

Once premium auditors have obtained the data necessary for calculating the premium, they must decide whether the data are reasonable.

1. These are some of the questions the premium auditor might ask:
   a. Are the data logical?
   b. Do the data seem complete?
   c. Do the data reflect enough detail for the insured's operations?
   d. Are the data consistent with industry averages?
   e. Can deviations from expected amounts be explained?

2. Premium auditors should verify premium-related data against the general accounting records and reconcile any discrepancies.

3. If a risk is misclassified, the auditor should attempt to correct the error and notify the underwriter as soon as possible when the error involves a lower-rated class.

G. Reporting the Findings

No premium audit is complete until the results are submitted. The premium-related data should be recorded and the billing information clearly summarized so that the audit can be processed and billed immediately.

1. Premium auditors must show in their reports how they obtained the data to enable others to retrace their audit steps.

2. The premium auditor should succinctly describe the insured's operations and explain any deviations from the usual operations for that type of business.

Educational Objective 6
Explain why premium audits must be accurate.

Key Points:

The insurance mechanism relies on each insurer to measure and classify loss exposures correctly. Premium audit errors can distort the insurer's rating structure and cause significant problems for both the insured and the insurer.

A. Importance for the Insured

1. If audit errors occur, insureds may end up paying the wrong premium for their insurance.
2. An experience rating bases an insured's current premium on the insured's past experience (exposure units and losses). When data on those exposure units and losses are incorrect, the experience modification is incorrect, resulting in the insured paying inaccurate future premiums.

B. Importance for the Insurer

1. Financial position

    A prompt and accurate premium audit can benefit the insurer's financial position in three ways:

    a. Accurate classification of loss exposures is important to ensure equitable and accurate insurance rates.

    b. Timely premium audits directly affect an insurer's cash flow management.

    c. Premium that has been developed by audit is fully earned and, consequently, has an immediate effect on profit and policyholders' surplus.

2. Customer retention

    Undetected premium audit errors can cause some insureds that are overcharged to switch to another insurer to obtain coverage at a lower premium. Insureds that are undercharged are likely to remain with their insurers. Consequently, the insurer loses premium volume, and underwriting results deteriorate.

3. Goodwill

    When policyholders are informed of errors in the premium audit, the insurer's image suffers.

    a. This could cause insureds to switch to other insurers, and insureds who do not switch might be less cooperative.

      b. Perhaps the biggest cost, however, is the marketing and underwriting effort expended to replace business that is lost because of premium audit errors.

  4. Efficiency

    Unless premium audits are complete and correct, additional work is generated for both the premium audit department and the insurer's other departments.

  5. Collections

    Insureds are not likely to pay premium bills they suspect to be incorrect. Even when the problem is eventually resolved, the insurer's cash flow suffers as a result of any delay.

C. Importance for Insurance Rates

Premium audits affect the equity and accuracy of class rates in two ways:

  1. Consistency and accuracy of classification determinations

    Premium auditors can assist the claim department in accurately classifying losses as well as loss exposures.

  2. Measurement of the exposure unit base

    An audit error, not in classification but in determining the exposure units, also distorts the rate structure. Either underreporting or overreporting the exposure units affects the rate for that class.

Educational Objective 7
Explain how premium auditing contributes to other insurer functions.

Key Points:

Effective insurer management capitalizes on the opportunities for premium auditing to contribute to other insurer functions.

A. Underwriting

Premium audit reports constitute a valuable source of information for underwriters, and effective cooperation between underwriters and premium auditors is essential to ensuring that existing accounts remain profitable.

1. A crucial responsibility of the premium auditing function is to classify insured exposures correctly. Premium auditors notify underwriting of any discrepancies between the classifications on the policy and those classifications that are proper for the operation.

2. Another important contribution of the premium auditing function to underwriting is the identification of inadequate exposure estimates.

3. A premium audit report can also provide a comparison of anticipated loss exposures to actual loss exposures.

4. For large accounts, advance audits—or pre-audit surveys—can be used to support underwriting decisions by ensuring that insurers issue policies based on correct business classifications and exposure bases.

5. Premium auditing can assist underwriting by identifying new exposures during review of the insured's operations.

6. Premium auditors are also in a position (from visiting the insured's premises) to provide underwriting with information on the desirability of an account.

7. While on the insured's premises, a premium auditor can become aware of physical, moral, and morale hazards.

   a. Examples of physical hazards include construction, hazardous materials, and poor safety or hygiene practices.

   b. Moral hazards can be indicated by questionable business practices or a failing business.

   c. Indicators of morale hazards include indifference to proper maintenance or poor financial records.

B. Marketing and Sales

1. It is important that premium audits be conducted in a timely manner. A delay of a return premium due to an insured could adversely affect the insurer's future marketing efforts.

2. The auditor's professional conduct and skill are also important factors in retaining an account.

3. If an insured is planning on expanding operations, an auditor may have the opportunity to refer the insured to marketing or sales.

4. Advance audits or pre-audit surveys can have significant public relations value. Insureds appreciate visits prior to the actual audit, especially if the auditor can help the insured with recordkeeping to take advantage of manual rules that might save the insured money.

C. Claims

1. Claims information can be valuable to premium auditing in the verification of employment classifications. However, premium auditing provides an even more valuable contribution to the claims function by verifying or correcting the classification codes assigned to an insured's claims.

2. Premium auditors can also verify that injured employees in workers compensation claims were employees of the insured when their injuries occurred. If there are any discrepancies in employment dates or wages, the premium auditor can notify claims.

3. Premium auditors can provide values of inventories, contractors' equipment lists and values, automotive equipment values, and other facts that are important to the claims function.

D. Risk Control

1. Since risk control representatives cannot visit every insured, the premium auditor can serve as a source of information for risk control.

2. The premium auditing process can contribute information about unsafe procedures or working conditions, observations of insureds' vehicles, and any hazards that provide opportunities for further risk control investigation and recommendations.

Key Words and Phrases:

Key Words

Moral hazard
A condition that increases the likelihood that a person will intentionally cause or exaggerate a loss.

Morale hazard (attitudinal hazard)
A condition of carelessness or indifference that increases the frequency or severity of loss.

Premium audit
Methodical examination of a policyholder's operations, records, and books of account to determine the actual exposure units and premium for insurance coverages already provided.

Exposure unit (unit of exposure)
The unit of measure (for example, area, gross receipts, payroll) used to determine an insurance policy premium.

Loss costs
The portion of the rate that covers projected claim payments and loss adjusting expenses.

Test Audit
An audit conducted by an insurance advisory organization or bureau to check the accuracy of insurers' premium audits.

Premium pay (shift differential)
A payroll system that increases the regular hourly wage rate for the night shift or other special conditions.

Deposit premium
The amount the primary insurer pays the reinsurer pending the determination of the actual reinsurance premium owed.

Experience modification
A rate multiplier derived from the experience rating computation.

Overview of the Claim Function

7

Educational Objective 1
Identify the goals of the claim function, the users of claim information, and the parties with whom claim personnel interact.

Key Points:

An insurer's claim function must fulfill its responsibility to the insured and pay covered claims, while also supporting an insurer's financial goals.

Study Tips

Rewriting key concepts in your own words can improve retention.

A. Claim Function Goals

The claim function has these two primary goals:

1. Complying with the contractual promise

   a. The first goal of the claim function is to satisfy the insurer's obligations to the insured as set forth in the insurance policy.

   b. The insurer fulfills this promise by providing fair, prompt, and equitable service to the insured, either directly or indirectly.

2. Supporting the insurer's financial goals

   a. By managing all claim function expenses, setting appropriate spending policies, and using appropriately priced providers and services, claim managers help maintain an insurer's underwriting profits.

   b. By overcompensating an insured or claimant, the insurer unnecessarily raises the cost of insurance for all its policyholders. Overpaid claims can lower profits, so the claim function should not overpay claims.

   c. Underpaid claims can result in dissatisfied insureds, litigation, or regulatory oversight, so the claim function should not underpay claims

   d. An insurer's success in achieving its financial goals is reflected in its reputation for providing the service promised.

B. Claim Information Users

The three primary recipients of claim information are the marketing, underwriting, and actuarial departments.

1. Marketing

    a. The marketing department needs information about customer satisfaction, timeliness of settlements, and other variables that assist in marketing the insurance product.

    b. The claim handling process can be a source of new coverage ideas and product innovations for niche marketers.

2. Underwriting

    a. Proper, consistent, and efficient claim handling enables underwriters to evaluate, select, and appropriately price loss exposures based on consistent claim costs.

    b. Claim representatives can report loss exposure characteristics they observe to underwriters.

3. Actuarial

    a. Actuaries need accurate information not only on losses that have been paid, but also on losses that have occurred and are reserved for payment to report appropriate reserves in the insurer's financial statements.

    b. In addition to incurred loss information, actuaries need accurate information on loss adjusting expenses and recoverable amounts associated with claims, such as salvage and subrogation, any ceded reinsurance recoverable, and deductibles, for financial statement reserves.

C. Claim Department Contacts

The claim department must interact effectively with outside contacts, such as these:

1. The public

The insurer's public image is determined largely by the claim department's behavior. Technological improvements have improved the quality and speed of claim service and communication.

2. Lawyers

    a. Even if litigation ensues, claim representatives should continue to interact in a cordial, professional manner with claimants' lawyers.

    b. When an insurer needs a lawyer either to defend the insured or to defend itself, claim representatives will assist the insurer's lawyer as needed by sharing claim details and assembling information that supports the insurer's legal position.

3. State regulators

    a. Regulators exercise controls by licensing claim representatives, investigating consumer complaints, performing market conduct investigations, and enforcing the Unfair Claims Settlement Practices Act or similar legislation.

    b. Not all states currently license adjusters, and no standard procedure or uniform regulation exists for those that do.

    c. State insurance regulators also handle customer complaints made against an insurer.

    d. Insurance regulators periodically perform market conduct investigations that include claim practices.

Educational Objective 2

Describe the claim department structure, types and functions of claim personnel, and claim personnel performance measures.

Key Points:

Claim departments can be found in insurance companies, in large business entities that self-insure, in third-party administrators (TPAs), and in agents' or brokers' offices.

A. Claim Department Structure

An insurer's claim department can be organized in several different ways. Various claim positions within a claim department can include these:

1. A senior claim officer heads the claim organization and reports to the chief executive officer, the chief financial officer, or the chief underwriting officer.

2. The senior claim officer may have a staff located in the same office. This staff is often called the home-office claim department.

3. The senior claim officer may have several claim offices or branches countrywide or worldwide.

   a. Remote offices may all report directly into the home-office claim department or to regional/divisional claim offices.

   b. Regional claim officers may have one or more branch offices reporting to them.

   c. Each branch office may have a claim manager, one or more claim supervisors, and a staff of claim representatives.

B. Claim Personnel

A claim representative (a generic title that refers to all who adjust claims, except for public adjusters) fulfills the promise to pay the insured or to pay on behalf of the insured by handling a claim when a loss occurs.

1. Staff claim representatives

   a. Staff claim representatives are employees of an insurer, and they handle most claims.

   b. They may include inside claim representatives, who handle claims exclusively from inside an insurer's office, and field claim representatives, who handle claims both inside and outside the office.

2. Independent adjusters
   a. Certain insurers may not find it economically feasible to set up claim offices in every state where insureds are located. In this case, insurers may contract with independent adjusters to handle claims in strategic locations.
   b. Some insurers use independent adjusters when their staff claim representatives are too busy to handle all claims themselves, such as when disaster strikes.
3. Third-party administrators
   Businesses that choose not to purchase insurance but to self-insure can contract with TPAs who handle claims, keep claim records, and perform statistical analyses.
4. Producers
   a. The term "producer" is used to describe anyone who sells insurance.
   b. Insurers may give some producers the authority to pay claims up to a certain amount. Those producers can issue claim payments, called drafts, directly to insureds for covered claims, thus reducing the time an insured waits for payment.
5. Public adjusters
   a. A public adjuster is an organization or a person hired by an insured to represent the insured in a claim in exchange for a fee.
   b. In general, the public adjuster prepares the insured's claim and negotiates the settlement with the staff claim representative or independent adjuster.

C. Claim Performance Measures
The quality of a claim department's performance can be measured using best practices, claim audits, and customer satisfaction.
1. Profitability measures
   a. The insurer's loss ratio is one of the most commonly used measures of evaluating the insurer's financial well-being.
   b. The loss ratio is an insurer's incurred losses (including loss adjustment expenses) for a given period divided by its earned premiums for the same period.
   c. The expense ratio is developed using underwriting expenses plus other, nonclaim-related expenses divided by the written premium.
   d. The loss ratio plus the expense ratio equal the combined ratio, which represents an insurer's underwriting profitability.

e. Because claims usually do not occur immediately after a policy is issued and because they take some time to be paid, insurers can invest premiums to generate additional income until the premiums are needed to pay claims. They seek to earn the highest possible return from investments while making sure that funds are available to meet their financial obligations.

f. When an insurer's loss ratio and combined ratio increase, the claim department, along with other functions, is pressured to reduce expenses.

2. Quality measures

   a. Best practices

   In the context of a claim department, best practices usually refers to a system of identified internal practices that produce superior performance.

   • Claim department best practices are often based on legal requirements specified by regulators, legislators, and courts.

   • Other best practices may relate to timely responses and payments.

   b. Claim audits

   Insurers use claim audits to ensure compliance with best practices and to gather statistical information on claims.

   • A claim audit is performed by reviewing a number of open and closed claim files and evaluating the information contained in those files.

   • Claim audits can be performed by the claim staff who work on the files (called a self-audit), or they can be performed by claim representatives from other offices or by a team from the home-office.

   • Claim audits evaluate both quantitative and qualitative factors.

   c. Customer satisfaction

   • While compliments are usually acknowledged, supervisors or managers must respond to complaints, and most claim departments have procedures for doing so.

   • However received, complaints must be investigated by management and responded to in a timely manner.

Educational Objective 3

Describe the following activities in the claim handling process:

- Acknowledging and assigning the claim

- Identifying the policy and setting reserves

- Contacting the insured or the insured's representative

- Investigating the claim

- Documenting the claim

- Determining the cause of loss, liability, and the loss amount

- Concluding the claim

Key Points:

The claim representative is responsible for thoroughly investigating a claim to determine how coverage applies. However, investigation is only one activity in the claim handling process. To ensure that every claim is handled in good faith from beginning to end, the claim representative must follow a systematic claim handling process.

A. Acknowledging and Assigning the Claim

Generally, the first activity of the insurer in the claim handling process involves these two functions:

1. Acknowledging receipt of the claim

    a. The purpose of the acknowledgment is to advise the insured that the claim has been received.

    b. Some insurers acknowledge claims immediately upon receiving the loss notice by contacting the insured. Others acknowledge the claim after it has been assigned to a claim representative.

2. Assigning the claim to a claim representative who has the appropriate skills to handle it

    a. Many insurers transfer claim files to a claim manager for assignment to a claim representative.

    b. Some insurers assign claims based on territory, type of claim, extent of damage, workload, or other criteria contained in the insurer's claim information system.

    c. State licensing requirements must be considered when assigning a claim to a claim representative.

    d. After receiving the claim assignment, the claim representative contacts the insured, and possibly the claimant (if it is a third-party claim), to acknowledge the claim assignment, explain the claim process, and make appropriate arrangements for damaged and undamaged property or get information on any injury.

B. Identifying the Policy and Setting Reserves
    1. Identifying the policy
        a. The claim representative must thoroughly read the policy, using the framework for coverage analysis, to determine what types of coverage apply to the loss.
        b. If it is apparent from the loss notice that coverage may not be available for the loss, the claim representative must notify the insured of this concern through a nonwaiver agreement or a reservation of rights letter to reserve the insurer's rights under the policy.
    2. Setting reserves
        a. Claim representatives will establish claim or case (loss) reserves, often in conjunction with identifying the policy.
        b. The insurer's claim information system often determines the types of reserves that are established.
          • There may be one reserve for property damage and another for bodily injury.
          • Some systems require separate reserves for each claimant in a claim.
        c. Insurers can use different methods of setting reserves, including these six common methods:
          • Under the individual case method, claim representatives set an individual or a case reserve for each claim or cause of loss based on the claim representative's expectation of what the insurer will pay.
          • Using the roundtable method, a consensus reserve figure from claim personnel may be reached, or an average of all the figures may be calculated.
          • The average value method is useful when there are small variations in loss size for a particular type of claim and when claims can be concluded quickly. These values are usually based on data from past claims and adjusted to reflect current conditions.
          • Under the formula method, a formula may be developed based on the assumption that a certain ratio exists between certain costs, such as the medical cost and the indemnity (or wage loss) in a workers compensation claim.

- Under the expert system method, the details of a particular claim are entered into the computer, and the program applies the appropriate rules to suggest reserves for the loss.
- The loss ratio method is used to suggest standard reserves for similar types of claims or for a class of loss exposures. The actuarial department uses this method when other methods of establishing claim reserves are inadequate.

  d. Insurers are required by law and accounting practices to establish reserves for losses that have been incurred but not reported (IBNR).

3. Causes of reserve errors

   a. Consistently inaccurate or inadequate reserves on thousands of claims can distort the ratemaking process. This may eventually affect an insurer's ability to write business competitively and ultimately affect solvency.

   b. Reserving errors can be caused in several ways:
      - Initial reserves may be inaccurate because they are determined based on limited information.
      - Reserve inaccuracy can also be the result of the claim representative's poor planning, lack of expertise in estimating claim severity, or unwillingness to re-evaluate the facts. When a claim representative makes incremental increases in claim reserves without any significant change in the facts, it is called stairstepping.
      - Claim representatives may not anticipate inflation and the ultimate cost of a claim that takes years to settle.
      - Claim representatives may underestimate the future settlement value of a claim if they are overconfident of their ability to conclude the claim for a lesser amount.

   c. Some inadvertent errors in setting reserves can be detected by using computer software that stores claim information.

   d. Claim representatives should increase or decrease the reserve amounts to reflect new factual information received.

C. Contacting the Insured or the Insured's Representative

   1. The initial contact with the insured reassures the insured that the claim will be investigated and provides the claim representative with an opportunity to explain the claim process and begin the claim investigation.

   2. Generally, the claim representative reviews the initial loss report and policy and then contacts the insured and schedules a time to speak with the insured or a party representing the insured about the facts of the loss.

3. If the loss involves a third-party claimant, then the claim representative also contacts the claimant and schedules a meeting with the claimant or a party representing the claimant to discuss the facts of the loss.

4. Before making initial contact with any of the parties, the claim representative should prepare a list of questions for the insured or claimant and a set of instructions on how the claim will be handled and on any actions the insured or claimant will have to complete.

5. The claim representative must be prepared to explain the policy terms and their meanings in relation to the loss and must be careful not to give the insured or claimant the impression that a claim will be paid if possible grounds exist to deny a claim.

6. Once contact is made, the claim representative should take these actions:

    a. Tell the insured what is required to protect damaged property and document the claim. Be specific about what the insured must do, and provide deadlines.

    b. Describe the inspection, appraisal, and investigation the claim representative will be conducting.

    c. Tell the insured what additional investigation is needed to resolve potential coverage issues.

    d. Explain potential coverage questions or policy limitations or exclusions, and obtain a nonwaiver agreement when necessary.

    e. If medical and wage loss information is part of the claim, obtain the necessary authorizations.

    f. Explain the amount of time it will take to process and conclude the claim.

    g. Supply the insured with a blank proof of loss form for property damage and any necessary written instructions so that the insured can document the claim.

7. Claim representatives must be aware of the legal implications of their words and actions when communicating with insureds.

    a. Good faith

        When conducting a good-faith investigation, a claim representative must attempt to correctly and promptly resolve coverage issues. Many situations that present coverage issues require further investigation to determine whether the claim should be paid or denied.

b. Waiver and estoppel
  - Waiver is the voluntary or intentional relinquishment of a known contractual right, such as one contained in a policy condition or exclusion.
  - Estoppel is a legal bar to asserting certain contractual conditions because of a party's previous actions or words to the contrary. Estoppel results when one party's action causes another party to rely on that behavior or those words with detrimental results.

c. Nonwaiver agreements and reservation of rights letters
  - A nonwaiver agreement, which must be signed by both parties, protects the insurer from estoppel by reserving the right to deny coverage based on information developed during the investigation. It also alerts the insured to a potential coverage problem.
  - A reservation of rights letter serves the same purpose as a nonwaiver agreement but is in letter form, and it is a unilateral document; it does not require the insured to sign or agree to the contents of the letter.

D. Investigating the Claim

Investigation can take many different forms, and all aspects of it must be documented to create a complete claim file. Information that will only be available for a short time must be investigated first, and third-party claimants should be contacted early.

1. Claim investigations

These examples are common to many types of claims:

a. Claimant investigation

Claim representatives usually take a claimant's statement to help determine the value of the injury or damage, how it was caused, and who is responsible. The claimant may or may not be the insured.

b. Insured/witness investigation

Claim representatives often take statements (either written or recorded) from the insured and witnesses because they can provide valuable information about the circumstances surrounding the loss.

c. Accident scene investigation

The accident scene offers crucial clues in automobile, third-party liability, and workers compensation claims.

d. Property damage investigation

In automobile and property damage claims, this investigation confirms the cause of the loss and the extent of damage. For business income claims, a property damage investigation is useful for determining lost profits or loss of business use resulting from covered property damage. It also helps confirm a need to temporarily move operations and use rental equipment.

e. Medical investigation

Claim representatives conduct medical investigations in all bodily injury claims to determine the costs of the medical treatment, the expected duration of medical treatment and disability, the need for rehabilitation, the suitability of medical care for the type of injuries the claimant suffered, and the pain and suffering that result from the accident.

f. Prior claim investigation

Claim representatives conduct prior claim investigations on all claims to avoid paying for property damage or bodily injury that has been paid through prior claims by the same insurer or by other insurers.

2. Subrogation investigation and recovery

When an insurer pays a claim to an insured for a loss caused by a negligent third party, the insurer can recover that payment amount from the negligent third party through the right of subrogation.

a. When claim representatives investigate any loss, they must be alert to any subrogation possibilities; they should look for ways to recover any money paid out on the claim.

b. The subrogation clauses in most insurance policies require the insured to cooperate with the insurer by assigning the rights of subrogation to the insurer through a subrogation agreement.

c. If an insured breaches the subrogation agreement, the insurer has the right to collect from the insured the amount that could have been recovered from the responsible third party.

d. The insurer has no right of recovery for losses that the insured has absorbed because of lack of coverage, exclusions, or coverage limitations under the policy. Therefore, both the insurer and the insured may have rights to recover from the responsible third party.

e. Claim representatives must consider the costs required to pursue subrogation as well as the likelihood of success. They must also be alert for any contract that may deny the right of subrogation (such as a lease agreement). The insurer's decision does not affect the insured's right to pursue payment.

f. When the two insurers cannot agree on liability, they can agree to arbitrate the dispute, often through intercompany arbitration.

E. Documenting the Claim

   1. Diary systems

   a. Because claim representatives simultaneously handle many claims, they must have a system for working on and reviewing each claim.

   b. A diary system allows the claim representative to work on a claim one day and then diary it or calendar it for review.

   c. Diary systems are usually maintained by the insurer's claim processing system.

   - This may automatically set diary dates for the file based on the type of claim.
   - Claim representatives who set dates manually must ensure that their handling of the file meets the requirements of any applicable unfair claims practices acts.

   2. File status notes

   a. File status notes (or an activity log) must accurately reflect and document investigations, evaluations of claims, decisions to decline coverage, or decisions to settle the claims.

   b. Because lawyers and state regulators can obtain copies of claim files, the file status notes and other file documentation must reflect these elements:

   - Clear, concise, and accurate information
   - Timely claim handling
   - A fair and balanced investigation considering the insured's and the insurer's interests
   - Objective comments about the insurer, insured, or other parties associated with the claim
   - A thorough good-faith investigation

   3. File reports

   Internal and external reports to various parties are developed by claim representatives to document claim activity.

   a. Preliminary reports

   An insurer may require preliminary reports within the first twenty-four hours, within seven days of the claim assignment, or only if the file remains open after thirty days. Preliminary reports acknowledge that the claim representative received the assignment, inform the insurer about initial activity on the claim, suggest reserves, note coverage issues, and request assistance, if needed.

   b. Status reports

   Status reports tell the insurer how the claim is progressing on a periodic basis, generally every fifteen to thirty days. In these reports, claim representatives record the progress of the claim, recommend reserve changes, and request assistance and settlement authority when the amount payable exceeds their authority.

   c. Summarized reports

   Summarized reports are often detailed narratives that follow an established format with captioned headings that give them structure. Claim representatives usually file a summarized report within thirty days of the assignment date. Insurers may require summarized reports for specific claims that require review by managers at regional or home offices.

   d. External reports

   External claim reports inform interested parties about the claim and notify the public of the insurer's financial standing. These reports are prepared for producers, some states' advisory organizations, and others who have an interest in the claim to provide details about the losses, such as the amount paid and outstanding reserves.

F. Determining the Cause of Loss, Liability, and the Loss Amount

   1. The facts of the case determine the cause of loss and the liability for the loss.

   2. Concurrent to the determination of the cause of the loss and the liability for the loss, the claim representative may determine the amount of the loss.

      a. For a property claim, the claim representative investigates the amount of damage to the property and the cost to repair or replace it, and may also investigate the amount of business income lost.

      b. To determine a loss amount in a bodily injury claim, the claim representative investigates the extent of the injury, the residual and lasting effects of the injury, and the amount of pain and suffering the individual has endured.

G. Concluding the Claim

When the investigation has been completed and all documentation has been received, the claim representative must decide whether to pay the claim or deny it.

1. Payments

   a. When a covered claim is concluded through negotiation or other means, the claim representative or claim personnel must issue a claim payment. Claim payments can be made by check, draft, or electronic transfer of funds.

   b. When issuing claim payments, claim personnel must ensure that the proper parties are paid.

   c. Claim representatives must check databases to ensure that the claim payment complies with federal and state laws.

   - The Office of Foreign Asset Control, an agency of the United States Department of the Treasury, requires all claim payors to check the master list of potential terrorists and drug traffickers before making a claim payment.

   - Many states have statutes that require a claim representative to check a database to determine whether a claimant or beneficiary owes unpaid child support. If child support is owed, the claim representative must follow specific procedures when issuing the payment because the unpaid child support has priority.

2. Claim denial

   a. When claim investigations reveal that a policy does not provide coverage for a loss or when an insured fails to meet a policy condition, the claim representative must make a timely claim denial.

   b. Insurers often have strict guidelines that claim representatives must follow when denying claims, and some insurers require a claim manager's approval to issue a claim denial.

   c. Before denying a claim, the claim representative must analyze the coverage carefully, investigate the loss thoroughly, and evaluate the claim fairly and objectively. Courts often favor insureds when a claim denial fails to meet these requirements and may assess penalties against the insurer.

   d. The claim representative must prepare a denial letter as soon as possible. Some denial letters are drafted by lawyers to ensure that they comply with the jurisdiction's legal requirements.

   - An insured who disagrees with the denial should be invited to submit additional information that would give the insurer cause to re-evaluate the claim.

- Insurers usually send denial letters by certified mail with a return receipt requested to be signed by the addressee.

3. Alternative dispute resolution (ADR)

If an insurer and an insured or a claimant cannot agree on the claim value or claim coverage, they may resolve the disagreement in court. ADR refers to methods for settling disputes outside the traditional court system that are less expensive and time consuming than litigation. These are the most common ADR methods:

a. Mediation

Using this method, a neutral outside mediator examines the disputing parties' issues, points out weakness, proposes solutions, and helps the participants reach a mutually agreeable settlement.

b. Arbitration

Using this method, the disputing parties use a neutral outside party to examine the issues and develop a settlement. The advantage of arbitration is that someone other than the insurer and the claimant decides the case.

- Under binding arbitration (required by some states' laws for arbitrated claim disputes), the parties must accept the arbitrator's decision.
- Under nonbinding arbitration, neither party is forced to accept the arbitrator's decision. However, the decision provides the "winner" with leverage for future negotiations.

c. Appraisals

The appraisal provision is included in property insurance policies as a form of ADR used to settle disputes between insurers and their insureds over the amount owed on a covered loss before litigation.

d. Mini-trials

A mini-trial enables parties to test the validity of their positions and continue negotiations. Parties can terminate the process at any time. The parties agree not to disclose in future litigation anything that occurs during the mini-trial, to preserve their rights in litigation if the negotiation fails. This allows claimants and insurers to learn the likely outcome of their cases without the delays in the legal system.

    e. Summary jury trials

    A summary jury trial offers a forum for deciding the merits of cases for court proceedings. It may also assist in negotiations. A summary jury trial is staged much like a regular jury trial, except that only a few witnesses are used to present the case and lawyers present summarized information.

4. Litigation

    a. Litigation can occur at almost any point during the life of a claim. However, it occurs most often when the parties to the claim are unable to reach an agreement by negotiation or ADR, or when a claim is denied.

    b. Many insurance policies require insurers to defend their insureds at trial. The duty to defend usually ends when the amount the insurer has paid in settlements or judgments on the claim reaches the insurer's limit of liability.

    c. Claim representatives participate in developing a litigation strategy for the insured's defense and for litigation expense control.

5. Closing reports

    a. When a claim is resolved, the claim representative may complete a closing or final report, which can include the claim representative's recommendations on subrogation, advice to underwriters, and other suggestions.

    b. These reports can be used to evaluate the likelihood of a successful subrogation action, to audit the claim representative's performance, and to be submitted to reinsurers for reimbursement of loss payment.

Educational Objective 4

Explain how the law of bad faith relates to an insurer's duty of good faith and fair dealing and how the legal environment affects the law of bad faith.

Key Points:

To avoid bad-faith allegations, claim representatives must understand the law of bad-faith claims. Bad-faith law evolved from the special relationship between insurers and insureds based on the implied duty of good faith and fair dealing.

A. Development of the Law of Bad Faith

Some courts decided that insurers have an implied duty of good faith and fair dealing when settling claims, requiring insurers to value their insureds' interests at least as much as their own. The standard of conduct for proving bad faith continues to evolve.

B. Duty of Good Faith and Fair Dealing

Bad-faith claims have developed to such an extent in insurance for these reasons:

1. It is in the public interest to ensure that insurers have the financial resources to pay claims.

2. Because of the unequal bargaining power of the parties to the insurance contract, the insurer is held to a higher standard of conduct than are parties of other contracts. The insurer not only dictates the terms of the contract but usually controls the claim investigation, evaluation, negotiation, and settlement.

   a. Some courts use a negligence (sometimes called due care) standard in determining whether a claim representative's (and, by extension, the insurer's) actions constitute bad faith.

   b. When applying a gross misconduct standard, courts have historically looked for signs of a dishonest purpose or conscious wrongdoing.

C. Legal Environment of Bad Faith

Bad-faith litigation is becoming more common, and the bases on which bad-faith claims can be brought are expanding. Even unfounded charges of bad faith can drain insurer resources.

1. Although most bad-faith law is case law, some states have passed laws relating to bad faith.

2. Claim representatives must be aware of the bad-faith law in every state in which they handle claims.

Educational Objective 5
Describe the elements of good-faith claim handling.

Key Points:

To use the defenses to bad-faith claims, the insurer and the claim representative must be able to show they acted in good faith. The definition of good faith allows courts great leeway in deciding what constitutes good faith in a given situation. As a result, common sense and good judgment must underlie all claim handling. Good-faith claim handling involves these elements:

A. Thorough, Timely, and Unbiased Investigation

    1. Claim representatives should thoroughly investigate claims, collect all relevant and necessary evidence, and be alert for new information that may change the course of the claim.

    2. An insured who makes a claim expects prompt contact from the claim representative. Timely contact with the parties to the claim benefits the insurer in several ways.

        a. Parties are more likely to remember the details of the loss accurately.

        b. The parties are more likely to share information if contacted promptly; prompt contact reassures insureds and claimants that their claims are important and makes them less likely to accept the advice of others who may encourage them to retain a lawyer or pursue unnecessary litigation.

    3. When investigating claims, claim representatives should pursue all relevant evidence, especially evidence that establishes the claim's legitimacy, without bias.

B. Federal Statutes

    Claim representatives must also comply with state unfair claim practices acts and with federal statutes designed to ensure the privacy of confidential information.

    1. Health Insurance Portability and Accountability Act (HIPAA)

    This act addresses the use and disclosure of individual health information and applies to health plans, healthcare clearing houses (that process health information), and healthcare providers.

   2. Gramm-Leach-Bliley Act (GLB)

     This act protects the security and confidentiality of customers of financial institutions and sets forth requirements for protecting and using customer information. The act protects both current and prior customers of financial institutions such as banks, securities firms, and insurers.

   3. Sarbanes-Oxley Act

     This act requires publicly traded companies to meet and certify certain financial disclosure requirements. It requires commercial insureds and many insurers to conduct more extensive reporting of claim information, provide greater accuracy in setting claim reserves, and conduct more extensive audits of claims and claim files.

   4. Fair Credit Reporting Act

     This act promotes the accuracy and privacy of personal information assembled by credit reporting agencies, including credit reports, consumer investigation reports, and employment background checks.

C. Complete and Accurate Documentation

   A claim file must provide a complete and accurate account of all the activities and actions taken by the claim representative.

D. Fair Evaluation

   A fair approach to evaluating liability claims is to evaluate them as if no coverage limit existed. Claim representatives can perform a fair evaluation if they have conducted a thorough, timely, unbiased investigation and understand the jurisdiction of the claim.

   1. A crucial element of fair claim evaluation is a prompt evaluation.

   2. Fair evaluations are based on facts, not opinions.

E. Good-Faith Negotiation

   Good-faith negotiations flow naturally from thorough, timely, unbiased investigations and prompt, fair evaluations.

   1. Claim representatives should take the initiative in making realistic offers when doing so is likely to promote a settlement.

   2. Claim representatives should not trade unrealistic offers and demands with lawyers. They should respond to such demands by offering a settlement that is consistent with the evidence and documentation in the claim file.

   3. Claim representatives should use policy provisions, such as arbitration clauses, when applicable, to resolve disputes over the settlement amount.

F. Regular and Prompt Communication

Communicating with all parties to a claim (for example, the insured, the defense attorney, and the excess insurer) is a crucial aspect of good-faith claim handling and resolving claims.

1. Insureds

Keeping insureds informed is especially important because they expect it, they are most likely to make a bad-faith claim, and they may have the most important information about an accident.

2. Defense attorney

The defense attorney should regularly and promptly inform the insured of all major events in the defense. If attorneys fail to communicate promptly and regularly, claim representatives should contact them to solicit information and correct any misunderstandings.

3. Excess insurer

If the insured has excess insurance, the claim representative should notify the excess insurer of the claim and provide the insured with copies of all communications.

G. Competent Legal Advice

Following the advice of competent lawyers can be considered evidence that an insurer acted in good faith. Lawyers have an ethical obligation to be loyal to the insured first and the insurer second, because the insured is the lawyer's client. When resolving a coverage question, insurers should avoid conflicts of interest by using lawyers other than the defense lawyers hired to defend an insured.

H. Effective Claim Management

An insurer's claim management directly affects a claim representative's ability to handle claims in good faith. Claim management involves many duties, including these three, which are crucial to good-faith claim handling:

1. Consistent supervision

Supervisors and managers should work with claim representatives frequently and consistently to ensure that claims are investigated, evaluated, and resolved promptly and accurately.

2. Thorough training

Insurers should provide continuous and consistent training for claim representatives relating to all necessary claim handling procedures and best practices as well as to good-faith claim handling.

3. Manageable caseloads

Supervisors and managers must monitor the number of claims assigned to a claim representative (referred to as caseload or pending) to ensure that the work is manageable.

Key Words and Phrases:

Key Words

Third-party administrator (TPA)
An organization that provides administrative services associated with risk financing and insurance.

Independent adjuster
An independent claim representative who handles claims for insurers for a fee.

Loss ratio
A ratio that measures losses and loss adjustment expenses against earned premiums and that reflects the percentage of premiums being consumed by losses.

Incurred losses
The losses that have occurred during a specific period, no matter when claims resulting from the losses are paid.

Earned premiums
The portion of written premiums that corresponds to coverage that has already been provided.

Expense ratio
An insurer's incurred underwriting expenses for a given period divided by its written premiums for the same period.

Nonwaiver agreement
A signed agreement indicating that during the course of investigation, neither the insurer nor the insured waives rights under the policy.

Reservation of rights letter
An insurer's letter that specifies coverage issues and informs the insured that the insurer is handling a claim with the understanding that the insurer may later deny coverage should the facts warrant it.

Individual case method
A method of setting reserves based on the claim's circumstances and the claim representative's experience in handling similar claims.

Roundtable method
A method of setting reserves by using the consensus of two or more claim personnel who have independently evaluated the claim file.

Average value method
A case reserving method that establishes a predetermined dollar amount of reserve for each claim as it is reported.

Formula method
A method of setting claim reserves by using a mathematical formula.

Expert system method
A method of setting reserves with a software application that estimates losses and loss adjustment expenses.

Loss ratio method
A loss reserving method that establishes aggregate reserves for all claims for a type of insurance.

Stairstepping
Incremental increases in claim reserves by the claim representative without any significant change in the facts of the claim.

Subrogation
The process by which an insurer can, after it has paid a loss under the policy, recover the amount paid from any party (other than the insured) who caused the loss or is otherwise legally liable for the loss.

Mediation
An alternative dispute resolution (ADR) method by which disputing parties use a neutral outside party to examine the issues and develop a mutually agreeable settlement.

Arbitration
An alternative dispute resolution (ADR) method by which disputing parties use a neutral outside party to examine the issues and develop a settlement, which can be final and binding.

Mini-trial
An alternative dispute resolution method by which a case undergoes an abbreviated version of a trial before a panel or an adviser who poses questions and offers opinions on the outcome of a trial, based on the evidence presented.

Summary jury trial
An alternative dispute resolution method by which disputing parties participate in an abbreviated trial, presenting the evidence of a few witnesses to a panel of mock jurors who decide the case.

Breach of contract
The failure, without legal excuse, to fulfill a contractual promise.

Adjusting Property and Liability Claims

8

Educational Objective 1

Explain how and why the activities in the framework for handling property claims are accomplished.

Key Points:

Claim representatives must answer these general questions as part of the property claim handling process. The answers to these questions are determined by applying the insurance policy provisions to the specific facts of loss.

Study Tips

Remember to register for your exam by calling The Institutes at (800) 644-2101.

A. Who Has an Insurable Interest? Who Is an insured?

  1. Interests in property

    Generally, anyone who would be financially harmed by the destruction of property has an insurable interest in that property.

    a. A sole owner has complete interest in a property.

    b. Under joint ownership, two or more owners each have a complete, indivisible interest in a property.

    c. Ownership in common involves two or more owners, each with an identifiable fractional financial interest in the property.

    d. Security interests are created by contractual agreement or by law. The secured party is generally a creditor of the property owner.

  2. Policy requirements for an insurable interest

    a. Rather than listing the existence of an insurable interest as a precondition to coverage, insurance policies simply limit payment on any claim to the extent of the insured's interest.

    b. Whenever there are multiple insurable interests in property, each party may have its own insurance protecting its own interest.

      • Parties with different interests who commonly have separate insurance policies are landlords and tenants, bailors and bailees, and mortgagors and mortgagees.

      • Claim representatives must identify all insurable interests in damaged property.

3. Identification of insureds

    a. Claim representatives must deal with the right parties to avoid paying the claim to the wrong person and to avoid invalidating any legal notices the insurer has given.

    b. Claim representatives can determine which parties to deal with because the policy declarations identify the named insureds. The policy also indicates who can make claims and who must perform the insured's duties in the event of loss.

B. What Property Is Insured? Where Is It Insured? When Is It Insured?

    1. Property type and location

        a. As part of determining what property is covered, claim representatives must understand the difference between real and personal property.

- Real property is land and everything attached to it, such as buildings.
- Personal property is everything not considered real property.

        b. Claim representatives can determine whether fixtures are real property by asking these three questions:

- How permanently attached to the real property is the fixture?
- Is the fixture well adapted to the real property?
- What was the intent of the owner?

    2. Policy period

    All property policy conditions state that coverage applies only during the policy period stated on the declarations page.

C. What Are the Covered Causes of Loss?

    1. Direct and indirect loss

        a. Direct loss concerns the amount of financial loss that is covered by the policy. Direct loss is damage to property caused by a covered cause of loss with no intervening cause.

        b. The most important type of indirect loss is loss of use of property.

    2. Physical and nonphysical loss to property

        a. Physical loss to property occurs when the property can no longer be used for its intended purpose because it has been destroyed or damaged, or has disappeared. Physical loss is tangible.

        b. Nonphysical loss is intangible and includes loss of value to property not caused by physical damage or destruction.

3. Exclusions and verification of causes of loss

Verification of some causes of loss can be complicated by several exclusions, including these:

   a. Gradual causes of loss

   b. Ordinance or law

   c. Faulty design, construction, or material

   d. Intentional acts of the insured

D. What Is the Dollar Amount of Loss?

   1. Replacement cost

      a. Replacement cost settlement provisions spare claim representatives the difficulties of determining actual cash value and convincing the insured to agree with that value.

      b. The claim representative and the insured must identify the property precisely using these details:

         • For personal property, the manufacturer's name, product description, and exact model or style numbers must be determined.

         • For real property, the exact measurements and descriptions and an exact specification of the type and quality of materials are necessary.

      c. Once the property has been fully identified and described, the claim representative must determine the cost to replace it at the time of loss.

      d. If the exact type of property damaged or destroyed is no longer available, the claim representative can make a settlement based on property of like kind and quality.

      e. Determining replacement cost for building damage requires construction estimates. Proper estimates are based on these factors:

         • Specifications

         • Materials

         • Labor

         • Overhead

         • Profit

      f. The claim representative will do one of these:

         • Release an actual cash value settlement to the insured, with the balance paid on complete repair or replacement

         • Parcel out a replacement cost settlement as repair or replacement is gradually accomplished

2. Actual cash value
   a. Claim representatives applying the actual cash value formula must have a sophisticated understanding of depreciation.
   b. Depreciation represents loss of value. Aside from physical wear and tear, obsolescence is the main cause of depreciation.
   c. Some courts have defined actual cash value to mean fair market value.
   d. Other courts have required adjusters to consider all pertinent factors, including physical wear and tear, obsolescence, market value, and any other relevant factors. This approach is known as the broad evidence rule.

3. Deductibles
   a. Applying a deductible is a simple matter when a loss is otherwise fully covered. Applying deductibles to a loss that is not fully covered is more difficult.
   b. When a coinsurance penalty reduces the recoverable amount of loss, the insured benefits by having the deductible applied first. Some policies explicitly state not to.

4. Stated values and agreed amounts
   a. A stated amount is typically determined by appraising the insured's property or by reviewing a sales receipt for the property in question. In the event of a loss, the insured is entitled to no more than the least amount of these:
      • The property's actual cash value
      • The cost to repair or replace
      • The applicable amount of insurance
   b. On an agreed-amount basis, the insurer agrees to restore the property to its condition before the loss or to pay the agreed amount.

5. Repair or replace option
   Claim representatives choose the repair or replace option whenever it is significantly less expensive to do so.

6. Appraisal clause
   The appraisal clause found in every property insurance policy is used solely to settle disputes over the value of the property or the amount of loss. In the appraisal procedure, both the claim representative and the insured obtain estimates and other supporting documentation from contractors. Either these two parties or their contractors negotiate the differences and usually reach an agreement.

E. What Are the Insured's Duties After a Loss?

   1. Provide prompt notice

     a. Although policies do not require the insured to give notice in any particular form, they do require that the notice be "prompt."

     b. In case of loss by theft, the insured is required to notify the police. In cases of lost or stolen credit cards, the insured must notify the credit card or funds transfer card company.

   2. Protect property

   The insured is required to protect the property from further loss by making emergency repairs and by implementing emergency safeguards.

   3. Assist with the loss adjustment process

   As part of assisting with the loss adjustment process, insureds must inventory all damaged property and, under certain policies, all undamaged property as well.

     a. The inventory must include quantities, values, and amounts of loss and might be required as part of, or independently of, the proof of loss.

     b. The insured must show the damaged property to the adjuster.

     c. The insured must allow books and other records to be inspected.

     d. Some insurance policies require the insured to cooperate. The absence of such a duty in other policies means that the insured has no general duty of cooperation.

   4. Provide proof of loss

     a. The proof of loss is the insured's official version of the loss.

     b. In a proof of loss, the insured is typically required to specify the time, place, and cause of loss; the interests in the property; any other insurance on the property; and detailed estimates, inventories, bills, and other documentation that prove the loss.

     c. Many states have laws specifying the number of days following receipt of a proof of loss that a claim representative has to either accept or reject the proof of loss or to tell the insured specifically what is further required.

     d. Many insurers routinely waive the proof of loss.

   5. Submit to examination under oath

     a. The examination under oath is a policy condition that the insured must fulfill, if required by the insurer.

     b. An examination under oath is usually conducted after the insured completes and submits a proof of loss.

F. What Procedures Are Used to Conclude a Claim?

    1. Determining the cause of loss

        a. A claim representative may accept the insured's word and settle the claim accordingly if there were no extenuating circumstances, there was no question that the said loss occurred and that fraud was not a factor, and the loss was properly documented.

        b. When circumstances dictate, the claim representative might hire an expert to complete the claim investigation.

        c. A claim representative may personally investigate the cause of a loss by inspecting the damaged property, taking the insured's statement, or both.

    2. Determining the amount of loss

        a. A claim representative who personally determines the amount of a loss must take careful, detailed inventories of personal property to specify the exact quantities and types of property, and must prepare estimates for losses to buildings.

        b. Most claim representatives leave the item-by-item preparation of a personal property inventory to the insured, and the claim representative performs a spot check.

        c. A claim representative who prepares estimates must have extensive knowledge of construction practices, material prices, and labor allowances.

    3. Documenting the cause and amount of loss

        When claim representatives investigate and gather the information necessary to determine the amount of settlement checks, they should simultaneously create files that enable others to understand the claim. Insurers, state insurance regulators, and reinsurers require complete and accurate claim files.

    4. Determining salvage value and subrogation rights

        a. Whenever an insurer pays the insured the full value of personal property that has suffered a loss, the insurer is entitled to take ownership of the property and can subsequently resell it. Ordinarily, claim representatives either sell or consign the property to professional salvage companies.

        b. An insurer might have subrogation rights when a party other than the insured is responsible for causing the loss.

            • When handling a claim involving potential subrogation, the claim representative must be especially thorough in establishing and documenting the cause of loss and may notify the responsible party of the liability claim.

- When an insurer obtains a recovery through subrogation efforts, it must first pay the attorneys' fees and other expenses of subrogation, and then reimburse the insured for any deductible or any other amount of loss not covered. The insurer receives the remaining recovery amount.

Educational Objective 2

Describe the challenges of adjusting the following types of property claims:

- **Residential dwelling claims**

- **Residential personal property claims**

- **Commercial structure claims**

- **Business income claims**

- **Merchandise claims**

- **Transportation and bailment claims**

- **Catastrophe claims**

Key Points:

Specific types of property loss claims raise specific issues.

A. Residential Dwelling Claims

Claim representatives handling losses to homes have two goals: (1) to address the insured's concerns and (2) to enforce policy provisions and protect the insurer's rights.

1. Insured's concerns

For insureds, the emotional trauma of seeing their home damaged is compounded by uncertainty and anxiety about their insurance and the claim handling process.

2. Additional living expense

a. The claim representative should explain the scope of additional living expense and emphasize to insureds that they must obtain and keep receipts and that compensation is only for additional living expense.

b. The insured's residence must be uninhabitable (because of a covered loss) before additional living expense coverage is available.

3. Contractors

The insurance policy obligates the insured to provide proof of damages. Some insurers allow claim representatives to recommend contractors to insureds.

a. The insured might interpret the claim representative's recommendation as a guarantee that the contractor's estimate will be accepted or that its work will be of good quality.

      b. Some insurers fear that allowing claim representatives to make recommendations might lead to the claim representatives' receiving kickbacks and gratuities from contractors.

   4. Restoration and cleaning services

   The claim representative must quickly become involved in hiring a professional cleaning and restoration service when necessary.

B. Residential Personal Property Claims

Claims for loss to residential personal property present claim representatives with some difficult challenges.

   1. Inventory

      a. Damaged personal property is usually available for the claim representative's inspection unless fire or theft caused the loss.

      b. Even when personal property is burned beyond recognition or is stolen, the insured must prepare an inventory.

   2. Depreciation

      a. Homeowners generally can produce no better evidence of their property's depreciation than of its existence.

      b. In the absence of specific evidence of the age or condition of property, certain assumptions can be made.

   3. Sublimits

   The claim representative should explain the rationale of sublimits: some property is especially vulnerable to theft (for example, cash, jewelry, and firearms), and large coverage limits for such property would greatly increase the exposure to loss and the insurance premium.

   4. Scheduled property

      a. Individual property usually gets scheduled coverage because it is valuable. Scheduled coverage usually identifies the property precisely.

      b. The claim representative can contact merchants and appraisers who specialize in such property to determine whether it can be repaired, whether it can be replaced through a secondary market, how much its value has decreased because of a loss, and whether the insurer can buy replacements at a discount.

C. Commercial Structure Claims

Handling claims for losses to commercial structures is usually limited to highly skilled and experienced claim representatives because the value of commercial structures can easily reach millions of dollars.

1. Architects and contractors

   The claim representative may have to employ an architect to review building specifications; identify changes in building codes or suggest alternatives to obsolete construction features and building techniques; and to identify contractors that are responsible, capable, and reasonably priced.

2. Property's actual cash value

   The value of commercial structures is more variable than that of residences. Commercial structures are more likely than residences to significantly depreciate because of factors other than wear and tear.

   a. The principle of supply and demand determines the value of a commercial structure.

   b. The demand for commercial structures fluctuates with the overall economy and with business conditions in particular industries.

   c. The supply of commercial structures is characterized by frequent shortages and oversupplies.

   d. A claim representative evaluating the actual cash value at the time of loss of a commercial structure must consider market conditions.

   e. Commercial structures are more susceptible than residences to economic and technological obsolescence.

3. Problems with mortgageholders

   Commercial mortgage agreements usually make the mortgage amount completely due and payable upon the destruction of the structure.

   a. The mortgageholder might ignore the owner's desire to rebuild the structure and want to be paid in full.

   b. The claim representative cannot resolve this problem because it is between the structure's owner and the mortgageholder.

4. Contamination and pollution cleanup

   Serious losses at commercial structures might result in contamination and pollution.

   a. The claim representative's own health and safety might be at risk from exposure to pollutants at the loss site.

   b. The coverage for pollution cleanup is extremely limited in most policies.

   c. The claim representative should have contacts with specialized technical services that can help the insured to decontaminate a site.

5. Arson investigation

The claim representative must prove these three things to establish arson of an insured structure and can engage an origin-and-cause expert and a special investigative unit (SIU) to assist:

a. Incendiary fire

b. Motive

c. Opportunity

D. Business Income Claims

Proper settlement of business income claims requires detailed analysis of financial records.

1. Identifying the best loss settlement approach

Business income claims can be settled prospectively or retrospectively.

a. Prospective settlements are those made before the property has been repaired.

b. Retrospective settlements are those made after the property has been repaired and the insured has resumed operations.

2. Determining business income loss

The business should complete a work sheet to determine the likely amount of income loss. This amount can be understood as either (1) revenue minus cost of goods sold minus discontinued operating expenses or as (2) net profit (or loss) plus operating expenses that continue.

3. Determining the period of restoration

The period of restoration is the time starting seventy-two hours after the loss and ending when the repairs should be complete.

4. Determining extra expense amounts

For extra expenses to be covered, they must be incurred to avoid or minimize the suspension of business.

5. Consulting accountants to determine amounts

Probably no type of claim requires as much use of accounting assistance as business income claims.

E. Merchandise Claims

The valuation of merchandise that the insured holds for sale raises unique issues; it offers the best opportunities for salvage and use of salvor services, and its claims must be settled in special ways.

1. Merchandise valuation

The replacement cost of merchandise is the insured's cost to replace that merchandise.

a. Actual cash value standards can be difficult to apply to merchandise.

    b. Merchandise is subject to significant depreciation caused by obsolescence.

  2. Salvage

    a. Proceeds from the sale of damaged merchandise can be significant.

    b. Professional salvage firms can act quickly to protect goods from further damage, inventory and separate goods, and give advice to claim representatives about the likely amount of residual value in damaged goods.

  3. Reporting form losses

    Inventories of merchandise are often insured under reporting form policies that require the insured to submit regular reports of value.

    a. The claim representative must determine the value of the insured's inventory as of the date of the last report.

    b. If the insured underreported its inventory's value, the insured cannot recover the full loss amount.

    c. If the insured fails to submit a report when due, then the loss adjustment is based on the last report submitted.

  4. Importance of negotiation

    Under a percentage of value settlement, the merchant keeps the merchandise and is reimbursed for its decreased value.

F. Transportation and Bailment Claims

  Property is frequently in the possession of someone other than its owner. Losses to such property create complicated legal and insurance policy coverage issues.

  1. Insurance coverages

    a. Claim representatives handling transportation and bailment claims must orient themselves to the applicable insurance policy.

    b. Policies for carriers and bailees typically protect the interests of both the owner and the carrier/bailee.

      • A carrier/bailee's insurance policy that extends to liability for the owner's property requires the claim representative working for the carrier/bailee's insurer to settle the owner's claim.

      • Some carrier/bailee policies protect the owner regardless of the carrier/bailee's legal liability.

  2. Legal liability

    The terms of the contract between the carrier and the bailee affect legal liability between them. In absence of an agreement to the contrary, the law makes common carriers liable for damage to an owner's goods, with few exceptions.

a. Carriers usually specify the dollar amount of their liability in their bill of lading, which is a receipt for the goods and a contract for transportation.

b. An owner or a shipper with a large loss exposure can use a released bill of lading to avoid paying high insurance rates for the carrier's increased liability.

G. Catastrophe Claims

Property claim representatives response to catastrophes includes pre-loss and post-loss planning.

1. Pre-loss planning

Claim departments must have a sufficient number of claim representatives in potential disaster areas while maintaining acceptable service throughout the rest of the country.

a. Claim offices in areas likely to "host" disaster recovery teams should prepare kits that include everything a visiting claim representative needs to operate in a disaster area.

b. Every claim representative who is likely to be called into an area should be licensed.

2. Post-loss planning

a. Catastrophes cause the claim representatives to modify normal claim handling procedures.

b. Local agents should be familiar with the insurer's claim practices so they can advise insureds on how to begin loss recovery.

c. Contractors' services might be at a premium after a catastrophe. Because contractors from around the country flock to disaster areas to help mitigate the shortage, insureds should be advised to be very careful about paying advanced fees to unknown contractors.

Educational Objective 3

Explain how and why the activities in the framework for handling a liability claim are accomplished.

Key Points:

Liability insurance policies protect the insured against the financial consequences of legal liability. Therefore, liability claim representatives spend most of their time and effort investigating and evaluating the legal aspects of liability and damages in relatively less time than property claim representatives enforcing and evaluating insurance policy terms. The party making a liability claim against the insured is the claimant (also referred to as the third party). The insurer has no contract with, and the liability claim representative has no contractual obligations to, the third-party claimant. Liability claims include both property damage and bodily injury liability. Handling a liability claim entails four steps, which are not necessarily completed sequentially:

A. Determining Coverage

The first step in the liability claim adjusting process is determining coverage. The essential coverage clause of most liability insurance policies is simple. When determining coverage, claim representatives are primarily concerned with the possible application of exclusions.

1. The claimant's allegations determine coverage, even if those allegations are disputed and even if they are eventually proved untrue.

2. Whenever coverage is doubtful or not applicable to part of a claim, the claim representative must explain to the insured clearly, in writing, why this is so and what both the claim representative and the insured must do.

3. Liability insurance policies apply to claims for bodily injury, property damage, and personal injury coverage under the CGL.

4. Liability insurance policies generally exclude coverage for the insured's intentional acts. Claim representatives must answer several questions to apply this exclusion.

    a. Did the insured intend the result of his or her action or merely intend to commit the action without contemplating the injurious outcome?

    b. Can intentional acts be excluded when the claimant also alleges negligence or strict liability on the insured's part?

    c. Is the insured liable for the intentional acts of an agent or a servant, if the insured is vicariously liable?

  5. Generally, liability insurance does not guarantee that insureds will perform their contractual agreements. However, the consequences of a breach of contract might be covered even if the breach itself is not.

  6. Claims for property damage to another's property that has been damaged while in the insured's care, custody, or control or while the insured was working on it are clearly excluded from coverage by the typical liability insurance policy.

B. Determining Legal Liability

The second step in the liability claim adjusting process is determining legal liability. Proper investigation is essential in determining legal liability. The claim representative's investigation is guided by the facts that must be established to determine legal liability.

  1. The claim representative organizes the investigation according to what information is needed and what is most important. Getting the insured's account of the accident, taking statements from witnesses, and collecting all relevant evidence are important aspects of the investigation.

  2. Negligence is the usual basis of tort liability. A cause of action in negligence requires a legal duty owed to the claimant, a breach of that duty that causes harm, a causal connection between the breach and the harm, and actual bodily injury or damage on the claimant's part.

    a. When a person has failed to behave carefully and prudently, that person has likely breached a duty of care.

    b. Proximate (or legal) cause requires that an unbroken chain of events must link the "cause" and the injurious "event."

    c. Unless negligent behavior causes bodily injury or property damage to another party, the wrongdoer escapes any legal consequences.

    d. Torts can also be based on strict liability (or "absolute liability"), which is liability that exists regardless of whether the insured was negligent.

  3. Criminals are legally liable in civil courts to their victims. A claim representative handling a claim filed against a convicted criminal must often concede liability, but not necessarily coverage.

4. A party who breaches a contract is legally liable to the other party to the contract.

    a. The claim representative must investigate all potential contractual defenses.

        - Did the claimant breach the contract first, thereby excusing further performance by the insured?

        - Did a precondition for the insured's contractual obligations not occur or fail to be met?

        - Did the insured and the claimant substitute a new contract for a previous one?

    b. In cases of contractual hold-harmless agreements and assumptions of risk clauses, the claim representative must scrutinize the contract to determine whether it applies to the situation in question.

5. A claim representative handling a case involving an alleged statute violation must determine what the statute requires, what the insured did, and whether any insurance policy exclusion applies.

6. Vicarious liability is liability imposed on a party because of that party's relationship to a wrongdoer. Most claims against commercial insureds involve vicarious liability because corporations are legal entities that act through their employees.

7. As claim representatives investigate liability, they also investigate possible defenses.

    a. Absence of any one of the elements necessary to prove negligence also serves as a type of defense.

    b. Comparative or contributory negligence exists whenever a claimant's own fault contributes to causing his or her bodily injury.

        - Under comparative negligence laws, the claimant's recovery may be reduced in proportion to the claimant's share of fault. Two primary forms of comparative negligence are the "pure" form and the "modified" form.

        - In the few states that recognize contributory negligence, any fault on the claimant's part completely bars the claimant from recovery.

    c. The assumption of risk defense applies whenever a claimant knows of a risk and voluntarily assumes it anyway.

    d. Each state has statutes of limitations—statutory time limitations on the right to file lawsuits. Failure to file a lawsuit within the allotted time waives any obligation on the tortfeasor's part so that an expired statute of limitations can serve as an absolute defense.

  e. Claimants often assert claims believing that the mere occurrence of the accident entitles them to compensation, but many accidents occur through no one's fault. The absence of negligence defense applies in such cases.

C. Determining Damages

 The third step in the liability claim adjusting process is determining damages.

 1. For bodily injury claims, damages can be classified as either special damages or general damages. Special damages are established for losses that can be quantified. General damages are for intangible losses.

  a. Medical expenses must be related to the bodily injury, necessary to heal the bodily injury, and reasonable in amount.

  b. Any amount that a claimant would have earned during a disability period is recoverable. Lost wages are established by verifying the extent and period of disability and the claimant's earnings.

  c. Pain and suffering is an intangible factor in every bodily injury case. It includes inconvenience, anxiety, and other types of distress.

  d. Claimants sometimes suffer scarring or loss of bodily function that might not cause pain but that reduces the quality of life.

  e. Loss of consortium is an element of damages that generally belongs to the injured party's spouse. Consortium traditionally consists of sex, society, and services.

  f. Any of the previous elements of damages that can be expected to continue into the future should be included in a settlement or jury verdict.

  g. Future damages should be adjusted to their present value.

 2. In some respects, determining damages in third-party property damage liability claims is easier than in first-party property damage claims. The claim representative need not worry about deductibles, special sublimits, coinsurance, or damages caused by both covered and noncovered causes.

  a. In third-party claims, the law allows a deduction for depreciation from replacement cost.

  b. The property owner's own negligence can be a major factor in settling third-party claims.

  c. Many property damage liability claims first appear as subrogation claims from other insurers.

D. Negotiating and Settling Claims

The fourth step in the liability claim adjusting process is negotiating and settling claims.

1. Settling liability claims is the most valuable service that liability claim representatives perform for insureds, claimants, insurers, and society.

2. Negotiating to settle claims is a key responsibility of claim representatives. Negotiation involves discussing all issues and arriving at a mutually satisfactory disposition of the claim.

   a. Liability insurance policies usually give insurers the right to settle claims, but they do not impose a duty to settle because insurers might want to litigate a claim.

   b. The insurer must have the right to litigate to protect itself against frivolous, fraudulent, or unfounded claims.

   c. When the value of a claim approaches or exceeds the insured's policy limit, making settlement becomes a legal obligation and is no longer just good judgment.

3. Most claims are settled using a general release, in which the claimant releases the insured of all liability for the claim and the insurer agrees to pay the claimant the agreed settlement amount.

4. Liability claims are usually settled with a lump-sum payment. Sometimes, the settlement requires a structured settlement, which includes both a lump-sum payment at the time of settlement and a series of payments into the future.

5. Many insurers also use advance payments to discourage claimants from hiring lawyers, and some practice walk-away settlements.

E. Litigation Process

1. Although the majority of claims are settled before suit is filed and the majority of suits are settled before trial, courts play an essential role in settling claims.

   a. Courts are not fast, inexpensive, or predictable. Claimants who might otherwise rely on courts to determine their rights against insureds have an incentive to negotiate.

   b. The values that lawyers and claim representatives place on claims are derived from actual results of claims litigated to conclusion.

2. In addition to paying amounts for which the insured is legally liable (up to policy limits), insurers are also obligated to defend their insureds against lawsuits.

   a. The insurer can select the defense lawyer, and the insured is then obligated to cooperate with that chosen lawyer. As long as it is solely liable for the claim, the insurer can dictate defense strategy. The insurer can unilaterally decide to settle or to continue a claim's defense.

   b. Generally, an insurer must defend an entire claim whenever a plaintiff's allegations for any part of the claim are covered. Coverage applies according to the plaintiff's allegations, not according to the claim's merits.

   c. When plaintiffs assert claims that are not clearly covered in the same lawsuit as covered claims or are not covered at all, the insured has the right to involve a lawyer of the insured's choosing at the insured's expense. The insurer's lawyer still has the right to control the case as long as the insurer's money is at stake.

Educational Objective 4

Describe the challenges of handling each of the following types of claims:

- **Auto bodily injury liability claims**

- **Auto property damage claims**

- **Premises liability claims**

- **Operations liability claims**

- **Products liability claims**

- **Workers compensation claims**

- **Professional liability claims**

Key Points:

The claim representative's general duties to determine coverage, legal liability, and damages, and to negotiate and settle claims, exist in all liability claims. The challenges of performing these duties vary by claim.

A. Auto Bodily Injury Liability Claims

Auto claims can be complicated regarding coverage determination; accident reconstruction; and coordination with no-fault, workers compensation, and uninsured or underinsured motorists claims.

1. Coverage determination is simple only when the accident involves the named insured as the driver and a vehicle specifically listed on the policy. Situations in which the named insured, or another insured, has coverage while driving a vehicle not listed on the policy or when someone other than the named insured is using a covered vehicle are more complicated.

2. Whenever the parties disagree about what happened, claim representatives or accident reconstruction experts might be able to determine the facts. Accident reconstruction experts are most helpful in determining vehicle speed and what a driver should have been able to at the time of an accident.

3. A claim representative handling auto liability claims must frequently deal with other insurers that provide auto no-fault or workers compensation benefits to an injured claimant. Difficulties can arise between the claim representative and the other insurer whenever subrogation rights do not exist or comparative negligence is a crucial issue.

4. Under uninsured motorists (UM) coverage, the insured becomes the claimant. A person who drives without insurance or who causes hit-and-run accidents is usually not a credible witness and uninsured motorists are often unavailable and uncooperative; consequently, with no favorable witness, UM claims are extremely difficult for insurers to defend.

   a. The claim representative has limited powers to defend UM claims. In the event of any disagreement over the settlement amount, the insured can require arbitration.

   b. Fraud and exaggeration can be at least as common in UM claims as they are in third-party liability claims.

5. Underinsured motorists (UIM) coverage varies by state and by UIM endorsement.

   a. In states that apply a limits trigger, the UIM endorsement applies when the negligent driver carries liability insurance limits that are lower than the limits provided by the injured party's UIM coverage.

   b. In states that apply a damages trigger, the UIM endorsement applies when the negligent driver carries liability insurance limits that are lower than the insured party's damages.

   c. Another variation among states' UIM laws relates to stacking limits, which is the application of two or more limits to a single auto accident.

      • Interpolicy stacking involves two or more separate policies.

      • Intrapolicy stacking occurs when a single policy covers more than one vehicle.

B. Auto Property Damage Claims

   Auto accidents can result in the insured's becoming legally liable for damage to property such as buildings, appurtenant structures, landscaping, contents of over-the-road shipments, or other vehicles.

   1. When the cost to repair a vehicle plus its remaining salvage value equals or exceeds the vehicle's pre-loss value, the vehicle is a constructive total loss.

      a. By paying the vehicle's pre-loss value and taking the salvage, the insurer pays less overall.

      b. Should the insured want to keep the auto, the claim representative is entitled to pay the claim based on the actual cash value (ACV), adjusted for salvage value.

2. If a vehicle can be repaired, the claim representative should obtain an agreed repair price from the body shop selected by the insured or claimant.

   a. This agreement demonstrates that the claim representative's evaluation of the loss is legitimate and prevents disputes between the insurer and the claimant or between the auto owner and the body shop.

   b. Although the claim representative should try to agree on a repair price, the choice of a body shop should be left to the claimant.

C. Premises Liability Claims

Claim representatives handling premises liability claims must establish good rapport with the claimant, both to establish the cause of the accident and to determine comparative negligence. Witnesses and employees of the insured can often help the claim representative in these efforts.

1. Legal liability in premises liability claims is determined by negligence theories.

   a. The standard of care for property owners is traditionally qualified by the claimant's status on the premises.

   - An owner owes only a slight level of care toward a trespasser, primarily a duty not to inflict intentional injury.

   - An intermediate level of care is owed to licensees, a group that includes social guests, letter carriers, and solicitors.

   - A property owner owes a high level of care to business invitees, those who are on the premises at the owner's invitation to do business with the owner.

   b. When investigating premises liability claims, claim representatives should solicit statements from the claimant and all witnesses who can testify about either the accident or the condition of the accident scene.

   c. The claim representative should determine the insured's cleaning, maintenance, and inspection practices and should obtain copies of any logs or other records of such activities.

2. Unless their accidents were caused by a hidden hazard, claimants usually provide one of three reasons for the accident.

   a. They had no idea what caused their accident. Regarding liability, this reason amounts to no negligence on the insured's part.

   b. They knew of the causes but failed to observe and avoid them. Regarding liability, comparative negligence exists on the claimant's part.

c. They were aware of and observed the causes before the accidents but encountered them anyway. Regarding liability, this reason amounts to assumption of the risk by the claimant.

D. Operations Liability Claims

Claims arising out of an insured's operations are similar to premises claims with regard to liability theories and applicable defenses. The primary difference is that operations liability claims usually focus on an unsafe act rather than an unsafe condition.

1. An insured's operations are alleged to be responsible for an accident whenever the accident results from an unsafe or improper act by the insured or the insured's employees, whenever the insured fails to provide proper supervision of another party for whom it is responsible, or whenever the insured has contractually assumed liability.

2. When investigating operations liability claims, the claim representative should begin by investigating exactly how the claimant's accident occurred. Questions to resolve include these:

a. Exactly where did the accident occur?

b. What workers were in the vicinity?

c. Who employs and supervises these workers?

d. Exactly what were these workers doing at the time of the accident?

e. What equipment were the workers operating?

f. What did each worker see?

3. Contractor-insureds are often liable for the property damage and bodily injury caused by others because they have assumed contractual liability.

a. Generally, courts recognize contractual assumptions of liability as valid but interpret them narrowly.

b. A claim representative examining an assumption of liability clause must determine whether it requires defense and indemnity or just indemnity.

c. Insurance coverage for contractual assumptions of liability varies.

4. The claim representative should immediately try to preserve the accident scene through photos, diagrams, and detailed measurements. Construction sites change rapidly, and witnesses' memories can become confused and vague.

E. Products Liability Claims

Any party that manufactures or sells a product that harms another can be liable for that harm.

1. In addition to traditional negligence theories, products liability can be based on breach of warranty or strict liability in tort.

   a. A warranty is any contractual promise about the product that accompanies the sale.

   b. An express warranty is an explicit statement about a product that accompanies the sale.

   c. Under strict liability, the nature of the product is the issue, not the defendant's behavior. The issue is whether the product is defective in a way that makes it unreasonably dangerous.

2. The product in question must be carefully identified for subsequent identification of the manufacturer.

   a. If a wholesaler or retailer resells a product in the same condition in which it left the manufacturer, the manufacturer is responsible for indemnifying the wholesaler or retailer from any products liability claims.

   b. A wholesaler or retailer is liable as far as the public is concerned.

3. Determining liability in products claims often involves redesigning the product after an accident. The feasibility of redesign can be determined only through expert opinion.

4. Often, the product itself cannot realistically be redesigned, so the plaintiff alleges that the warnings and instructions that accompanied the product were inadequate and that the product was defective.

   a. The claim representative should determine whether the warnings and instructions provided, if followed, would have prevented the claimant's accident.

   b. The claim representative should also investigate whether the claimant read the instructions.

5. Claimants are often injured while using products in ways that are not intended or foreseeable. Claim representatives who suspect improper use should obtain detailed statements from the claimants.

F. Workers Compensation Claims

   1. The majority of work-related bodily injury claims are covered under Part One of the Workers Compensation and Employers Liability Insurance Policy, which theoretically provides the exclusive remedy for bodily injury claims caused or aggravated by conditions of employment regardless of fault and usually without judicial intervention.

2. A small percentage of bodily injury claims fall under Part Two, the Employers Liability coverage part. Employers liability is a liability-based third-party coverage under which the employee must prove negligence.

   a. Employers liability coverage applies to employees who are excluded from workers compensation laws by employment exemptions, such as agricultural workers.

   b. Employers liability also provides coverage for care and loss of services to a spouse and to family members of an injured employee who suffer bodily injury as a consequence of the employee's bodily injury.

   c. Third-party-over claims and dual capacity claims would also not be covered under workers compensation coverage, but would be covered under employers liability coverage.

   d. The claim handling process used for employers liability is similar to the process used for other third-party claims.

3. Workers compensation claims that involve only medical expenses are usually processed with no investigation. Should an accident involve lost time from work, the claim representative is likely to conduct an investigation.

4. The law requires the employer (or its insurer) to pay all necessary and reasonable medical expenses related to the bodily injury sustained on the job. Consequently, workers compensation policies have no policy limits.

   a. To control medical expenses, some workers compensation insurers have entered into agreements with preferred provider organizations (PPOs), through which the insurer receives a discount on the usual medical expenses in exchange for a volume of referrals.

   b. Insurers control workers compensation medical expenses by conducting medical bill audits.

   c. Utilization review services are another valuable tool to control medical expenses by determining whether medical treatment is necessary.

   d. Medical management controls medical expenses on the small percentage of claims that involve high medical expenses. It ensures that the claimant receives care in appropriate facilities with appropriate specialists.

5. Controlling disability expenses is probably the foremost challenge for workers compensation claim representatives.

   a. Once a claim has been initially accepted as compensable, the insurer can end disability payments only by agreement with the claimant or by order of the compensation commission.

b. Claim representatives can control disability expenses by insisting that the treating physician explain why the claimant cannot perform his or her job responsibilities.

c. A claim representative can also work with the employer to modify the employee's job by removing its most physically demanding parts.

G. Professional Liability Claims

Liability claims for professional malpractice are generally handled by specialized insurers and claim representatives. Because of the importance of these claims to the insured's professional reputation, the insured is usually involved in his or her own defense, and these claims are likely to be litigated to verdict rather than settled.

1. Professionals are required to exercise the standard of care accepted in their profession.

a. Malpractice claims are usually proved by experts who testify that the defendant should have behaved or decided differently, given the facts and circumstances when the professional services were rendered.

b. Many physicians are found at fault for failing to obtain a patient's informed consent.

2. Damages in medical malpractice claims are similar to those in other bodily injury cases, except that the physician is not liable for the underlying condition that initially prompted treatment.

3. For alleged attorney malpractice, the underlying legal matter from which the malpractice claim arose must be relitigated or reconsidered in the professional liability claim.

4. Generally, malpractice claims are litigated by only the most sophisticated plaintiff and defense attorneys. The insured is also likely to be heavily involved in the claim's defense.

a. Many professional malpractice insurance policies require the insured's consent to settle.

b. A claim representative involved in a professional malpractice claim must investigate any possible defenses.

Educational Objective 5

Given a claim, determine coverage for a loss using the framework for coverage analysis and the activities in the claim handling process.

Key Points:

In order to successfully complete this case study, students should use the claim handling process and apply the framework for coverage analysis. Students should have a thorough understanding of these activities:

- Acknowledging and assigning the claim
- Identifying the policy and setting reserves
- Contacting the insured or the insured's representatives
- Investigating the claim
- Documenting the claim
- Determining the cause of loss, liability, and the loss amount
- Concluding the claim

Key Words and Phrases:

Key Words

Depreciation
The reduction in value caused by the physical wear and tear or technological or economic obsolescence of property.

Broad evidence rule
A court ruling explicitly requiring that all relevant factors be considered in determining actual cash value.

Agreed amount
A method of valuing property in which the insurer and the insured agree on the property's value at the time the policy is written and that states the amount in the policy declarations as the amount the insurer will pay in the event of a total loss to the property.

Sublimit
A policy provision that imposes smaller limits for certain kinds of property or lines of insurance.

Prospective settlements
Settlements made before property has been repaired.

Retrospective settlements
Settlements made after property has been repaired and the policyholder has resumed operations.

Business income
Sum of (1) net profit or loss that would have been earned or incurred if the suspension had not occurred and (2) normal operating expenses, including payroll, that continue during the suspension.

Period of restoration
The period during which business income loss is covered under the BIC forms; it begins seventy-two hours after the physical loss occurs and ends when the property is (or should have been) restored to use with reasonable speed. (With regard to extra expense coverage, it begins immediately after the physical loss occurs.)

Bill of lading
A document acknowledging receipt of goods from the shipper, given by the carrier which includes the terms of the contract of carriage for the goods.

Released bill of lading
A bill of lading that limits the carrier's liability for cargo loss in return for charging a lower freight rate than would be charged for carrying the cargo subject to full valuation.

Proximate cause
A cause that, in a natural and continuous sequence unbroken by any new and independent cause, produces an event and without which the event would not have happened.

Hold-harmless agreement (or indemnity agreement)
A contractual provision that obligates one of the parties to assume the legal liability of another party.

Assumption of risk
A defense to negligence that bars a plaintiff's recovery for harm caused by the defendant's negligence if the plaintiff voluntarily incurred the risk of harm.

Comparative negligence
A common-law principle that requires both parties to a loss to share the financial burden of the bodily injury or property damage according to their respective degrees of fault.

Contributory negligence
A common-law principle that prevents a person who has been harmed from recovering damages if that person's own negligence contributed in any way to the harm.

Pain and suffering
Compensable injuries that are difficult to measure, such as physical and mental distress and inconvenience associated with a physical injury.

Bad-faith claim
A claim that implies or involves actual or constructive fraud, a design to mislead or deceive another, or a neglect or refusal to fulfill some good-faith duty or some contractual good-faith obligation.

Structured settlement
An agreement in settlement of a claim involving specific payments made over a period of time.

Advance payment
A payment made to a claimant following a loss to cover the immediate expenses resulting from that loss.

Walk-away settlement
A settlement that involves lump-sum payments made by insurers to settle claims and that does not require a release from the claimant.

Constructive total loss
A loss that occurs when the cost to repair damaged property plus its remaining salvage value equals or exceeds the property's pre-loss value.

Warranty
A written or oral statement in a contract that certain facts are true.

Express warranty
An explicit statement about a product by the seller that the buyer or other user may rely on and that provides a remedy in the event the product does not perform as claimed.

Preferred provider organization (PPO)
An administrative organization that meets the common needs of healthcare providers and clients and that identifies networks of providers and contracts for their medical services at discounted rates.

Medical management
A medical expense control measure that involves directing and coordinating efforts of healthcare providers to meet patient and insurer needs.

Actuarial Operations

9

Educational Objective 1

Describe the actuarial function in insurer operations and the actuarial services required by insurers.

Key Points:

The actuarial function is responsible for ensuring that the insurer operate effectively and conducts its operations on a financially sound basis.

Study Tips

Pace your study. Don't cram.

A. What Is an Actuary?

   1. Actuaries are professionals who evaluate the financial consequences of future events.; they have a formal educational process, a set of standards for performance, and a code of conduct.

   2. Actuaries often rely heavily on mathematical models and statistical techniques, but their examination process also covers insurance operations, accounting, insurance law, and financial analysis.

B. Actuarial Functions

   1. One of the major functions of actuaries is to direct insurer ratemaking operations.

   2. Actuaries also develop factors that are applied to loss costs in order to reflect individual insurer experience and expenses.

   3. Another major function of an actuary involves the estimation of an insurer's unpaid liabilities and adequacy of its loss reserves. Insurers are required by both accounting standards and law to set aside funds for the future payments on claims for which they are liable.

   4. Actuaries are also instrumental in developing insurer's predictive models using data mining tools.

5. Because of their quantitative background and familiarity in dealing with uncertain events, actuaries often perform other tasks, primarily related to assessment of insurer risks, including these:

   a. Analyzing reinsurance needs to determine the level and concentration of risk the insurer can retain versus the cost of reinsurance

   b. Estimating future cash flows so that assets will be available when claims are to be paid

   c. Assessing corporate risk by testing the adequacy of surplus under potential adverse conditions (catastrophe, sudden change in asset values, soft pricing, and inflation, for example)

   d. Providing financial and statistical information to regulators and applicable statistical agents (with accounting and finance areas)

   e. Participating in corporate planning and budgeting

C. Actuarial Services

   1. Many large insurers employ a number of actuaries. Although small insurers may have a few actuaries on staff, most tend to rely on actuarial consultants.

   2. Insurers that employ staff actuaries may also retain actuarial consultants. Outside actuaries can supplement staff knowledge with specialized expertise, provide independent opinion when needed, and ease workload peaks.

   3. Insurers with limited data for ratemaking rely on rates or loss costs prepared by actuaries at advisory organizations, such as Insurance Services Office (ISO), American Association of Insurance Services (AAIS), or the National Council on Compensation Insurance (NCCI).

Educational Objective 2

Describe the insurer goals of ratemaking and the ideal characteristics of rates.

Key Points:

Insurance ratemaking is challenging, because when rates are developed, the amounts of fortuitous future losses and their associated expenses are unknown. In light of this uncertainty, insurers try to develop rates that meet their goals.

A. Ratemaking Goals

   1. From the insurer's perspective, the primary goal of ratemaking is to develop a rate structure that enables the insurer to compete effectively while earning a reasonable profit on its operations.

   2. The rates must result in premiums that adequately cover all losses and expenses and that leave a reasonable amount for profits and contingencies.

   3. To be profitable, the insurer must have adequate rates. However, to maintain its book of business, the insurer's rates must be competitive.

   4. To be approved, rates must comply with applicable regulations. Rate regulation is generally based on having rates that are adequate, not excessive, and not unfairly discriminatory.

B. Ideal Characteristics of Rates

   Ideally, rates should have these five characteristics:

   1. Stable

   Stable rates are highly desirable because changing rates is expensive. Rates should also be stable because sudden large rate changes cause dissatisfaction among customers and sometimes lead to regulatory or legislative actions.

   2. Responsive

   Rates should include the best possible estimates of losses and expenses that will arise from the coverage.

   3. Provide for contingencies

   Rates should provide for contingencies, such as unexpected variations in losses and expenses.

   4. Promote risk control

   Ratemaking systems help to promote risk control by providing lower rates for policyholders who exercise sound risk control.

5. Reflect differences in risk exposure

   A rate is a charge for the exposure to risk. If insureds have attributes that make them more or less susceptible to a risk, using a flat rate means that some will be overcharged and others will be undercharged.

Educational Objective 3
Describe the components of an insurance rate and common ratemaking terms.

Key Points:

A rate is the basis for the premium charged by an insurer. To understand why a certain premium or rate is charged, the components that make up a rate must be understood. Knowledge of the components and terminology used in ratemaking will serve as a foundation to understanding the ratemaking process.

A. Rate Components

    1. An insurance rate consists of three components:

        a. An amount needed to pay future claims and loss adjustment expenses (prospective loss costs)

        b. An amount needed to pay future expenses, such as acquisition expenses, overhead, and premium taxes (expense provision)

        c. An amount for profit and contingencies (profit and contingencies factor)

    2. Once the insurance rate is calculated, it is multiplied by the appropriate number of exposure units to produce a premium.

B. Ratemaking Terms

These are common terms used in the ratemaking process:

    1. Exposure base (sometimes just exposure) is a variable that approximates the loss potential of a type of insurance.

    2. Earned exposure unit is the exposure unit for which the insurer has provided a full period of coverage. The periods are typically measured in years.

    3. Pure premium is the amount included in the rate per exposure unit required to pay losses. This component is also sometimes called the loss cost.

    4. Expense provision is the amount added to the pure premium required to pay expenses. This component is sometimes referred to as underwriting expenses.

    5. Loss adjustment expenses (LAE) are the expenses associated with adjusting claims. These expenses are often split into either allocated or unallocated LAE.

6. Insurers add a loading for profit and contingencies. This loading protects the insurer against the possibility that actual losses and expenses will exceed the projected losses and expenses included in the insurance rate.

C. Investment Income

    1. A property-casualty insurer performs two distinct operations:

        a. The insurance operations write policies, collect premiums, and pay losses. The result is called underwriting profit.

        b. The investment operations use the funds generated by the insurance operations to buy or sell bonds, stocks, and other investments to earn an investment profit.

    2. Insurers commonly consider investment results explicitly in their rate calculations.

    3. The investment return earned by an insurer depends largely on the types of insurance written, the loss reserves, and associated unearned premium reserves.

    4. An insurer's loss reserves for liability insurance are usually much greater than its loss reserves for an equivalent amount of property insurance.

Educational Objective 4

Explain how the following factors can affect ratemaking:

- **Estimation of losses**

- **Delays in data collection and use**

- **Change in the cost of claims**

- **Insurer's projected expenses**

- **Target level of profit and contingencies**

Key Points:

Estimating future events and costs in the real world is subject to uncertainty.

A. Estimation of Losses

   1. The key to developing insurance rates that are adequate to pay future claims is estimating the amount of losses for those claims.

      a. Past loss experience is generally used as a starting point to estimate future losses.

      b. Ratemaking is based on estimating losses from past coverage periods and then adjusting those losses for future conditions.

      c. Past loss experience may not be completely known because not all covered losses are paid immediately.

      d. The difference between the estimated amount that will ultimately be paid for claims and the actual loss amount paid to date is the loss reserves.

   2. Insurance rates are based partly on incurred losses. Incurred losses include both paid losses and outstanding loss reserves.

   3. Loss reserves are estimates of future payments for covered claims that have already occurred.

      a. Insurers are legally required to set aside funds for these future payments; these are shown as liabilities on their balance sheets.

      b. If loss reserve estimates are too low, rates will probably be too low. If loss reserves are too high, rates will probably be too high.

B. Delays in Data Collection and Use

   1. Because conditions are constantly changing, any delay between when data are collected and when they are used tends to reduce rate accuracy.

      a. A delay inevitably occurs between when losses are incurred and when they are reflected in rates charged to customers.

      b. During the delay period, economic or other factors can increase or decrease the rates the insurer should charge if the premium is to reflect the expected losses.

   2. The delay in reflecting loss experience in rates stems from several sources, including these:

      a. Delays by insureds in reporting losses to insurers

      b. Time required to analyze data and prepare a rate filing

      c. Delays in obtaining state approval of filed rates

      d. Time required to implement new rates

      e. Time period during which rates are in effect, usually a full year

C. Change in Cost of Claims

   1. Both loss severity and loss frequency affect an insurer's loss experience during any given period.

   2. Economic inflation or deflation during the inevitable delay also affects the average cost of a loss (severity).

   3. Legislative or regulatory changes such as modification in rules governing claim settlement can affect the number of losses (frequency).

   4. Some factors that affect the size and frequency of losses cannot be identified or measured directly, but their aggregate effect on losses can be determined with reasonable accuracy by trending.

D. Insurer's Projected Expenses

   1. Expenses can change over time, and any projected changes must be considered in the ratemaking process.

   2. Rather than past expenses, it is sometimes more relevant to use judgment or budgeted expenses, especially when conditions change dramatically.

   3. Ratemakers are challenged to allocate general administrative expenses properly among different types of insurance.

E. Target Level of Profit and Contingencies

The insurer must decide what provision for profit and contingencies should be included in the rate. Consideration is given to the overall desired rate of return, including likely returns from investment income versus underwriting profit, respectively.

Educational Objective 5

Describe the following ratemaking methods:

- Pure premium

- Loss ratio

- Judgment

Key Points:

Insurers commonly use three ratemaking methods:

A. Pure Premium Ratemaking Method

1. This method uses loss per exposure based on past experience as the basis for the rate.

2. The pure premium method has four steps.

   a. The first step is to calculate the pure premium.

   b. The second step is to estimate expenses per exposure unit based on the insurer's past expenses.

   - Whatever loss adjustment expenses are included in the pure premium are excluded from the expenses.

   - Investment expenses are not directly reflected in rate calculations.

   c. The third step is to determine the profit and contingencies factor.

   d. The final step is to add the pure premium and the expense provision and divide by one minus the profit and contingencies factor.

3. Fixed and variable expenses

   a. Some insurers separate their expenses into two components:

   b. Fixed expenses are stated as a dollar amount per exposure unit.

   c. Variable expenses are stated as a percentage of the rate.

B. Loss Ratio Ratemaking Method

1. The loss ratio method uses two loss ratios—the actual loss ratio and the expected loss ratio of the insurer during the selected experience period.

2. The expected loss ratio plus the provision for expenses, profit, and contingencies always add up to 100 percent.

3. For a new type of insurance, either the pure premium method or the judgment method must be used.

C. Judgment Ratemaking Method
1. This method is still used for some types of insurance, such as ocean marine insurance, some inland marine classes, aviation insurance, and situations when limited data are available, as with terrorism coverage.
2. Although the judgment ratemaking method might use limited or no loss experience data, an experienced underwriter or actuary generally has a sense of what rates have produced desired results in the past.

Educational Objective 6

Describe each of the following steps in the ratemaking process:

- **Collect data**

- **Adjust data**

- **Calculate the indicated overall rate change**

- **Determine territorial and class relativities**

- **Prepare and submit rate filings to regulatory authorities as required**

Key Points:

Ratemaking can involve a number of complex technical issues. An understanding of the process involved reveals the importance and contribution of each of the four steps in the ratemaking process.

A. Collect Data

1. To obtain and maintain usable data, each insurer must code data when transactions occur.

2. Claim data are collected when claims are reported, reserves are established or changed, checks or drafts are issued, or claims are closed.

3. Before collecting ratemaking data, the insurer must determine the kinds of data needed. The data fall into three general categories:

   a. Losses, both paid and incurred (including any loss adjustment expenses to be included in the pure premium)

   b. Earned premium and/or exposure information

   c. Expenses, including a profit and contingencies factor

4. If rates are to vary by rating class and/or territory, data must be identified for each class and territory.

5. Different aggregations of data may be used, depending on the line of business.

   a. The calendar-year method is unsuitable for collecting ratemaking data for liability and workers compensation insurance. Either the policy-year method or accident-year method should be used.

   b. The calendar-year method may be satisfactory for ratemaking data collection for fire, inland marine, and auto physical damage insurance.

B. Adjust Data

After data have been collected, they must be adjusted. Actuaries use several ways of adjusting premium and loss data:

1. Adjust premiums to current rate level

    a. If rates charged in the experience period were written at different rate levels, premiums will need to be adjusted to the current level.

    b. The ideal way to adjust premiums to current rate level is to calculate the premium for each policy in the experience period at current rate level.

    c. Premiums may also have to be adjusted for different levels of coverage purchased.

2. Adjust historic experience for future development

    a. When policy-year or accident-year experience is used to predict future results, one must remember that the experience might not be complete.

    b. The insurer must estimate the values of future payments for open claims and add it to the payments to date in order to estimate the ultimate losses of each period.

    c. The future development of the losses can be estimated by several actuarial methods.

    -   The most common method used is applying loss development factors to the current experience.
    -   With any method, the goal is to estimate the final, total cost to pay all the claims within each year.

3. Apply trending to losses and premium

    a. Trending is the review of historic environmental changes and projecting such changes into the future.

    b. Trend adjustments can come from various sources. The most frequently used source of trends is historical experience.

    c. Exponential trending assumes that data being projected will increase or decrease by a fixed percentage each year as compared with the previous year.

    d. Losses may need to be adjusted to current conditions if other significant external changes have affected loss payouts in recent years. Premiums may also need to be trended to reflect changing conditions.

C. Calculate Indicated Overall Rate Change

1. The purpose of adjustments, development, and trending is to bring prior experience to a level comparable to the future rate's policy period.

2. Based on the adjusted experience, an overall rate indication is calculated.

3. Several different methods, such as the loss ratio method and the pure premium method, can be used to produce an indication.

D. Determine Territorial and Class Relativities

1. If rates vary by territory and/or class, they are reviewed after the calculation of the overall rate change.

2. Relativities reflect the extent to which various subsets of insureds in a state deserve rates that are higher or lower than the statewide average rate.

3. Territorial relativities can be determined by comparing the estimated loss ratio (or pure premium) for each geographic territory to the statewide average loss ratio (or pure premium).

   a. If a given territory has limited experience, its territorial loss ratios are likely to vary widely.

   b. Differences from the overall average rate must be supported by credible experience.

4. Class relativities are used to develop rates for each rating class. Class relativities are determined similarly to territorial relativities.

E. Prepare and Submit Rate Filings

1. A rate filing is a document submitted to state regulatory authorities. The form for and the amount of information required in a filing vary by state.

2. Generally, the filing must include at least these seven items:

   a. Schedule of the proposed new rates

   b. Statement about the percentage change, either an increase or a decrease, in the statewide average rate

   c. Explanation of differences between the overall statewide change in rate and the percentage change of the rates for individual territories and/or rating classes (if any)

   d. Data to support the proposed rate changes, including territorial and class relativities

   e. Expense provision data

   f. Target profit provision included in the rates, if applicable, and any supporting calculations

   g. Explanatory material to enable state insurance regulators to understand and evaluate the filing

3. In some states, approval must be obtained before the rates are used. In other states, formal approval is not required by law.

4. If an advisory organization files rates or loss costs on behalf of an insurer, it handles any follow-up or negotiations.

5. When loss costs are filed by an advisory organization, the insurer is responsible for filing its expense provisions, which would yield its final rates.

Educational Objective 7

Describe the policy-year, calendar-year, accident-year, and report-year data aggregation methods.

Key Points:

Insurers and rating organizations collect information about every premium and loss transaction. For ratemaking, reserving, and reporting purposes, the transactions during a specific period are compiled into useful aggregations that attempt to match losses with the premiums from the underlying coverage.

A. Policy-Year Method

    1. The policy-year method of aggregating data involves analyzing earned premiums, exposure units, and incurred losses associated with a particular group of policies that were issued during a specific twelve-month period.

    2. For year-long policies, the coverage period for this group spans two years because policies issued on 12/31/X1 expire one year later, on 12/31/X2.

    3. The policy-year method is the only ratemaking data collection method that exactly matches losses, premiums, and exposure units to a specific group of insureds.

    Two major disadvantages apply to the policy-year ratemaking data collection method:

      a. It takes longer to gather data for this method than for the other methods.

      b. There is additional expense to gather data by policy year. The data used in the other methods are gathered in part as a byproduct of the insurer's accounting operations. Although this additional expense was once considered a major disadvantage of the policy-year method, automated recordkeeping has reduced the extra cost of compiling policy-year statistics.

B. Calendar-Year Method

    1. The calendar-year method involves aggregating data from accounting records to estimate earned premiums and incurred losses.

    2. Earned premiums for the calendar period must be calculated from the written premiums and unearned premium reserves.

3. Earned premiums equal written premiums for the year plus the difference between unearned premiums at the beginning of the year and unearned premiums at the end of the year. This formula provides a reasonably accurate estimate of the premiums earned from the coverage provided during the period.

4. Under the calendar-year method of ratemaking data aggregation, incurred losses must also be estimated.

   a. Incurred losses equal losses paid during the year plus the difference between loss reserves at the end of the year and loss reserves at the beginning of the year.

   b. The incurred loss formula sometimes results in inaccuracies.

5. Calendar-year data reflect how insurers must report their income on their financial statements.

6. Insurer accounting records usually do not contain exposure unit data. Consequently, calendar-year data cannot be used alone in the pure premium ratemaking method unless exposure unit information is also collected separately.

7. Calendar year losses can arise due to changes in reserves for losses that occurred in previous years, and so might not reflect current experience alone. Therefore, the calendar-year method is the least accurate ratemaking data collection method.

C. Accident-Year Method

1. The accident-year method uses the earned premium for the calendar period being reviewed, but calculates incurred losses for the given period using all losses and claims arising from insured events occurring during that period.

2. Since accident-year losses arise only from insured events that occur during the period, they are not affected by changes in reserves for events that occurred in other periods.

3. The accident-year method achieves much of the accuracy of the policy-year method while preserving most of the economy and speed of the calendar-year method.

4. Because accident-year data are relatively easy to compile, and it is useful as a basis of projecting ultimate losses, it is required to be reported by line of business in the Schedule P of each company's Annual Statement.

D. Report-Year Method

1. The report-year method is similar to the accident-year method, except that claims are aggregated by when the claim was reported rather than when it occurred.

2. Some insurance lines of business, such as medical malpractice and general liability, provide claims-made coverage.

    a. Aggregating by report year for these coverages has the same benefits accident-year aggregation has for standard coverages; it is available faster than policy year experience, and can be much more accurate than calendar year experience.

    b. Report-year data are also used in analyzing known (reported) claim experience separately from incurred but not reported (IBNR) experience.

3. Report-year collection is the least common of the four loss aggregation methods.

Educational Objective 8

Explain how the following ratemaking factors vary by type of insurance:

- **Experience period**
- **Trending**
- **Large loss limitations**
- **Credibility**
- **Increased limits factors**

Key Points:

Major differences between ratemaking for different lines of business can be found in five instances.

A. Experience Period

    1. Using an experience period of one to three years is common for auto insurance and other types of liability insurance.

    2. The experience period used for other property causes of loss, such as wind, is even longer—frequently twenty years or more.

    3. Three factors can be considered in determining the appropriate experience period:

        a. Legal requirements

        b. The variability of losses over time

        c. The credibility of the resulting ratemaking data

B. Trending

    1. Trending may be based on experience or external indices.

    2. For property insurance, loss claim frequency is low and generally stable, so trending may be restricted to claim severity.

    3. Economic inflation or deflation over the course of payments can affect the average cost of a claim (severity).

    4. In some lines, such as fire insurance, trending both losses and premiums is necessary.

        a. Losses are trended partly to reflect any effects of inflation on claim costs.

        b. Premiums are also trended in other types of insurance for which the exposure units are affected by inflation.

5. A special trending problem exists in workers compensation insurance. Because the benefits for such insurance are established by statute, legislation or a court decision can change the benefits unexpectedly.

6. For equipment breakdown insurance, trending is applied to the risk control expenses because they constitute such a large portion of the rate.

C. Large Loss Limitations

Unusual rate fluctuations could result from occasional large losses, whether from large individual losses or from an accumulation of smaller losses from a single event, such as a hurricane.

1. In liability insurance, these fluctuations are controlled by using only basic limit losses in calculating incurred losses. Basic limit losses are losses capped at some predetermined amount.

2. A similar practice is followed in workers compensation insurance ratemaking. Individual claims are limited to a specified amount for ratemaking purposes. Another limitation applies to multiple claims arising from a single event. Both limitations vary over time and by state.

3. Loss limitations also apply in ratemaking for property insurance. For example, when a large single loss occurs in fire insurance, only part of it is included in ratemaking calculations in the state in which it occurred. The balance is spread over the rates of all the states.

4. Most losses from catastrophic events, such as hurricanes, are excluded from ratemaking data and replaced by a flat catastrophe charge in the rates. A catastrophe model, which incorporates past experience with scientific theory, is often used to calculate an appropriate charge for these potential losses.

D. Credibility

Credibility is a measure of the predictive ability of data.

1. Fully credible ratemaking data have sufficient volume to provide an accurate estimate of the expected losses for the line, state, territory, and/or class being reviewed.

2. Credibility assumptions vary by type of insurance.

   a. In auto insurance, advisory organizations and some larger insurers consider the statewide loss data to be fully credible.

   b. For property insurance, advisory organizations might determine that even the statewide loss data are not fully credible. A three-part weighted average could be used, combining the state loss data for the rating class, regional (multi-state) loss data of the rating class, and state loss data for a major group encompassing several rating classes.

3. The credibility factor is used as the weight in the weighted average.

   a. It indicates the amount of weight to give to the actual loss experience for the territory or class as compared with an alternative source.

   b. A credibility factor is a number between 0 (no credibility) and 1 (full confidence).

4. The pure premiums for workers compensation insurance developed by the National Council on Compensation Insurance (NCCI) are composed of pure premium charges for medical and indemnity costs.

E. Increased Limits Factors

1. Actuaries use a number of ratemaking techniques for pricing coverage amounts in excess of the basic limit.

2. The most common approach to establishing rates for coverage greater than the basic limit is to develop increased limits factors.

3. Charges to increase liability limits can, and frequently do, exceed 100 percent of the charge for basic coverage limits. Several reasons exist for the large increased limits factors for several lines of business:

   a. The additional coverage purchased by the customer can be much higher than the basic limit.

   b. Higher limits can also require a portion of the coverage to be reinsured, with the additional expense of reinsurance included in the rate.

   c. Because large losses occur less frequently than small losses and take longer to settle, the variability of losses in higher coverage layers is greater than for the basic limit losses, and the credibility is lower.

Educational Objective 9

Describe the purpose and types of loss reserves, the importance of accurate estimation of loss reserves, and techniques used by actuaries in their analysis.

Key Points:

A matter of critical concern to an insurer is the holding of the appropriate amount of loss reserves.

A. Purpose of Loss Reserves

    1. Insurers are required by law and good accounting practice to establish reserves for losses that reasonably can be assumed to have been incurred.

    2. Loss reserves are also needed to provide a complete picture of an insurer's financial status.

    3. Insurers do not completely know their costs of doing business in advance of the sale of the product.

    4. The liability carried on an insurer's books for future payments on incurred claims is commonly called loss reserve.

        a. The liability is not just for payments of claimants' losses; the insurer is also responsible for future loss adjustment expenses (LAE).

        b. Such expenses include both allocated loss adjustment expenses (ALAE) and unallocated loss adjustment expenses (ULAE).

B. Types of Loss Reserves

    The principal types of loss reserves established by insurers are case reserves and bulk reserves.

    1. Case reserves are amounts that represent the estimated loss value of each individual claim.

        a. Case reserves are set according to the specific characteristics of each claim.

        b. The claim department is responsible for setting case reserves on each of the individual claims.

    2. Insurers make general provision for additional reserves, called bulk reserves. The bulk (or aggregate) reserves can have three components:

        a. Incurred but not reported (IBNR) reserves

        b. Reserves for losses that have been reported but for which the established case reserves are inadequate (sometimes called IBNER [incurred but not enough recorded] reserves)

      c. Reserves for claims that have been settled and then reopened

C. Importance of Accurate Loss Reserves

  1. The purpose of loss reserve analysis is to determine whether the carried loss and loss adjustment expense reserves can be expected to adequately cover the losses that have been incurred but not yet been paid.

  2. Analysis might be undertaken by a number of parties for various reasons:

      a. Management, as part of its analysis of costs of doing business

      b. The insurer's auditors, to determine whether the insurer's financial statements accurately indicate its financial condition and performance

      c. Rating agencies (such as A. M. Best or Standard & Poor's), on behalf of potential investors or creditors

      d. Regulators (on behalf of policyholders), to assure that claims will be paid

  3. The effect of inaccurate loss reserves can be substantial. Loss reserves (including LAE reserves) often exceed the total surplus for an insurer and are usually a considerable multiple of the earnings in a year.

      a. An overestimation of loss reserves (higher than ultimately paid) can lower an insurer's financial strength ratings, reduce statutory limits on premiums that can be written, or lead to dissolution of an insurer.

      b. If loss reserves are underestimated, the insurer can become insolvent when it becomes apparent that the future payments will exceed the reserve level.

D. Analysis of Loss Reserves

  1. The analysis is usually done by an actuary, using a variety of methods and techniques.

  2. In most cases, estimates are made of the ultimate losses to be paid on the exposures to date; the loss reserve is then estimated by subtracting payments to date. Sometimes, separate projections of the reserve are required for known claims and for IBNR claims, and those results are added together.

3. Among the most common methods used to estimate ultimate losses are these:

   a. The expected loss ratio method uses a prior estimate of ultimate losses rather than current experience. It is often used when current experience is limited or of little predictive value, and in fact, the method ignores the experience to date.

   b. The loss development method assumes that future changes in the loss will occur in a similar manner as in the past. This method assumes that the experience to date is an indicator of what future payments will be.

   c. The Bornhuetter-Ferguson method uses parts of the other two methods. It accepts the experience to date (unlike the expected loss ratio method), but assumes that future results are independent of the current experience. The ultimate projection from this method is the sum of actual results to date plus expected future results.

4. The selection of the appropriate method to be used depends on the data available, timing, and other characteristics of the experience reviewed.

E. Loss Development—a Closer Look

   1. Most commonly used to project losses (both paid and reported) to ultimate values, the loss development method is also used to project allocated loss adjustment expenses, claim counts, and even premiums.

   2. The loss development method involves four steps.

      a. Compile the experience into a loss development triangle— The loss development triangle is a table showing values for a specific group of claims at different points in time. The table is arranged so that it is easy to see values and changes of different groups at similar ages of development.

      b. Calculate the age-to-age factors—The calculation is based on the information presented in the loss development triangle. The triangle provides an overview of how each accident year's losses develop over time.

      c. Select the loss development factors.

      d. Apply factors to experience to make projections—Immature loss data is projected to full maturity. The respective factors multiply the losses to produce a projected ultimate loss.

   3. The loss development method does have limitations.

      a. Any changes in business practices or external conditions could affect the usefulness of this method.

b. Large one-time events such as catastrophes would disrupt the historical pattern of development.

Key Words and Phrases:

Key Words

Data mining
The process of extracting hidden patterns from data that is used in a wide range of applications for research and fraud detection.

Ratemaking
The process insurers use to calculate insurance rates, which are a premium component.

Rate
The price per exposure unit for insurance coverage.

Premium
The price of the insurance coverage provided for a specified period.

Pure premium
The average amount of money an insurer must charge per exposure unit in order to be able to cover the total anticipated losses for that line of business.

Expense provision
The amount that is included in an insurance rate to cover the insurer's expenses and that might include loss adjustment expenses but that excludes investment expenses.

Underwriting expenses
Costs incurred by an insurer for operations, taxes, fees, and the acquisition of new policies.

Loss adjustment expense (LAE)
The expense that an insurer incurs to investigate, defend, and settle claims according to the terms specified in the insurance policy.

Allocated loss adjustment expenses (ALAE)
The expenses an insurer incurs to investigate, defend, and settle claims that are associated with a specific claim.

Unallocated loss adjustment expenses (ULAE)
Loss adjustment expenses that cannot be readily associated with a specific claim.

Underwriting profit
Income an insurer earns from premiums paid by policyholders minus incurred losses and underwriting expenses.

Ultimate loss
The final paid amount for all losses in an accident year.

Experience period
The period for which all pertinent statistics are collected and analyzed in the ratemaking process.

Investment income
Interest, dividends, and net capital gains received by an insurer from the insurer's financial assets, minus its investment expenses.

Pure premium method
A method for calculating insurance rates using estimates of future losses and expenses, including a profit and contingencies factor.

Loss ratio method
A method for determining insurance rates based on a comparison of actual and expected loss ratios.

Judgment ratemaking method
A method for determining insurance rates that relies heavily on the experience and knowledge of an actuary or an underwriter who makes little or no use of loss experience data.

Loss cost multiplier
A factor that provides for differences in expected loss, individual company expenses, underwriting profit and contingencies; when multiplied with a loss cost, it produces a rate.

Calendar-year method
A method of collecting ratemaking data that estimates both earned premiums and incurred losses by formulas from accounting records.

Policy-year method
A method of collecting ratemaking data that analyzes all policies issued in a given twelve-month period and that links all losses, premiums, and exposure units to the policy to which they are related.

Accident-year method
A method of organizing ratemaking statistics that uses incurred losses for an accident year, which consist of all losses related to claims arising from accidents that occur during the year, and that estimates earned premiums by formulas from accounting records.

On-level factor
A factor that is used to adjust historical premiums to the current rate level.

Loss development factor
An actuarial means for adjusting losses to reflect future growth in claims due to both increases in the incurred amount for reported losses and incurred but not reported (IBNR) losses.

Exponential trending
A method of loss trending that assumes a fixed percentage increase or decrease for each time period.

Written premiums
The total premium on all policies written (put into effect) during a particular period.

Unearned premiums
The portion of written premiums that corresponds to coverage that has not yet been provided.

Bulk reserves
Reserves set aside for future expected claim payments but not associated with any specific claim; include a provision for incurred but not reported (IBNR) claims, future development of known claims (beyond the carried case reserves), and potential reopening of claims that have been settled.

Schedule P
The NAIC Annual Statement Schedule that shows detailed historical information on paid and reserved losses and LAE.

Claims-made coverage
Coverage that is triggered by a claim alleging bodily injury or property damage that is made during the policy period, even if the claim arises from an event that happened before policy inception.

Basic limit
The minimum amount of coverage for which a policy can be written; usually found in liability lines.

Catastrophe model
A type of computer program that estimates losses from future potential catastrophic events.

Credibility
The level of confidence an actuary has in projected losses; increases as the number of exposure units increases.

Credibility factor
The factor applied in ratemaking to adjust for the predictive value of loss data and used to minimize the variations in the rates that result from purely chance variations in losses.

Increased limit factor
A factor applied to the rates for basic limits to arrive at an appropriate rate for higher limits.

Risk charge
An amount over and above the expected loss component of the premium to compensate the insurer for taking the risk that losses may be higher than expected.

Incurred but not reported (IBNR) reserves
A reserve established for losses that reasonably can be assumed to
have been incurred but not yet reported.

Actuary
A person who uses mathematical methods to analyze loss data and
develop insurance rates.

Reinsurance

10

Educational Objective 1
Describe reinsurance and its principal functions.

Key Points:

Reinsurance is one way insurers protect themselves from the financial consequences of insuring others.

A. Basic Terms and Concepts

    1. Reinsurance is the transfer from one insurer (the primary insurer) to another (the reinsurer) of some or all of the financial consequences of certain loss exposures covered by the primary insurer's policies.

    2. Reinsurance is transacted through a reinsurance agreement, which specifies the terms under which the reinsurance is provided.

    3. The reinsurer typically does not assume all of the primary insurer's insurance risk. The reinsurance agreement usually requires the primary insurer to retain part of its original liability. This retention can be expressed as a percentage of the original amount of insurance or as a dollar amount of loss.

    4. In reinsurance, the term risk often refers to the subject of insurance, such as a building, a policy, a group of policies, or a class of business.

    5. The primary insurer pays a reinsurance premium for the protection provided just as any insured pays a premium for insurance coverage, but, because the primary insurer incurs the expenses of issuing the underlying policy, the reinsurer might pay a ceding commission to the primary insurer.

    6. Under a retrocession, one reinsurer, the retrocedent, transfers all or part of the reinsurance risk that it has assumed or will assume to another reinsurer, the retrocessionaire.

B. Reinsurance Functions

    Although several of its uses overlap, reinsurance is a valuable tool that can perform six principal functions for primary insurers:

Study Tips

1. Increase large-line capacity
   a. Increasing allows a primary insurer to assume more significant risks than its financial condition and regulations would otherwise permit.
   b. The maximum amount (or line) of insurance that an underwriter is willing to accept on a single account is subject to these influences:
      • The maximum amount of insurance or limit of liability allowed by insurance regulations, which prohibit an insurer from retaining more than 10 percent of its policyholders' net worth on any one loss exposure
      • The size of a potential loss or losses that can safely be retained without impairing the insurer's earnings or policyholders' surplus
      • The specific characteristics of a particular loss exposure
      • The amount, types, and cost of available reinsurance

2. Provide catastrophe protection
   Without reinsurance, catastrophes could greatly reduce insurer earnings or even threaten insurer solvency when a large number of its insured loss exposures are concentrated in an area that experiences a catastrophe.

3. Stabilize loss experience
   a. Volatile loss experience can affect the stock value of a publicly traded insurer; alter an insurer's financial rating by independent rating agencies; cause abrupt changes in the approaches taken in managing the underwriting, claim, and marketing departments; or undermine the confidence of the sales force.
   b. In addition to aiding financial planning and supporting growth, this function of reinsurance encourages capital investment because investors are more likely to invest in companies whose financial results are stable.
   c. Reinsurance can be arranged to stabilize the loss experience of a line of insurance, a class of business, or a primary insurer's entire book of business.
   d. Reinsurance can limit a primary insurer's liability for loss exposures.

4. Provide surplus relief
   a. Many insurers use reinsurance to provide surplus relief, which satisfies insurance regulatory constraints on excess growth.

   b. State insurance regulators monitor several financial ratios as part of their solvency surveillance efforts, but the relationship of written premiums to policyholders' surplus is generally a key financial ratio and one considered to be out of bounds if it exceeds 3 to 1 or 300 percent.

   c. Some reinsurance agreements facilitate premium growth by allowing the primary insurer to deduct a ceding commission, an amount paid by the reinsurer to the primary insurer to cover part or all of a primary insurer's policy acquisition expenses.

   d. Because the ceding commission replenishes the primary insurer's policyholders' surplus, the surplus relief facilitates the primary insurer's premium growth and the increase in policyholders' surplus lowers its capacity ratio.

5. Facilitate withdrawal from a market segment

   a. A primary insurer may want to withdraw from a market segment that is unprofitable, undesirable, or incompatible with its strategic plan.

   b. One approach to withdrawal is for the primary insurer to transfer the liability for all outstanding policies to a reinsurer by purchasing portfolio reinsurance. The reinsurer accepts all the liability for certain loss exposures covered under the primary insurer's policies, but the primary insurer must continue to fulfill its obligations to its insureds.

   c. A novation completely eliminates the liabilities a primary insurer has assumed. It is not considered portfolio reinsurance because the substitute insurer assumes the direct obligations to insureds covered by the underlying insurance.

6. Provide underwriting guidance

   a. Reinsurers work with a wide variety of insurers in the domestic and global markets under many different circumstances and accumulate a great deal of underwriting expertise.

   b. Reinsurers that provide underwriting assistance to primary insurers must respect the confidentiality of their clients' proprietary information.

Educational Objective 2
Describe the three sources of reinsurance.

Key Points:

Reinsurance can be purchased from three sources:

- Professional reinsurers
- Reinsurance departments of primary insurers
- Reinsurance pools, syndicates, and associations

Additionally, the reinsurance business has several professional and trade associations that serve member companies and provide information to interested parties.

A. Professional Reinsurers

Professional reinsurers interact with other insurers either directly or through intermediaries as primary insurers do.

1. A reinsurer whose employees deal directly with primary insurers is called a direct writing reinsurer.

2. Reinsurance intermediaries generally represent a primary insurer and work with that insurer to develop a reinsurance program that is then placed with a reinsurer or reinsurers. The reinsurance intermediary receives a brokerage commission.

3. Some broad generalizations may be made about professional reinsurers:

    a. Primary insurers dealing with direct writing reinsurers often use fewer reinsurers in their reinsurance program.

    b. Reinsurance intermediaries often use more than one reinsurer to develop a reinsurance program for a primary insurer.

    c. Reinsurance intermediaries can often help secure high coverage limits and catastrophe coverage.

    d. Reinsurance intermediaries usually have access to various reinsurance solutions from both domestic and international markets.

    e. Reinsurance intermediaries can usually obtain reinsurance under favorable terms and at a competitive price because they can determine prevailing market conditions and work repeatedly in this market with many primary insurers.

4. Professional reinsurers evaluate the primary insurer before entering into a reinsurance agreement because the treaty reinsurer underwrites the primary insurer as well as the loss exposures being ceded.

   a. The reinsurer gathers information about the primary insurer's financial strength and also considers the primary insurer's experience, reputation, and management.

   b. The relationship between the primary insurer and the reinsurer is considered to be one of "utmost good faith," because each party is obligated to and relies on the other for full disclosure of material facts about the subject of the agreement.

5. The primary insurer should evaluate the reinsurer's claim-paying ability, reputation, and management competence before entering into the reinsurance agreement.

B. Reinsurance Departments of Primary Insurers

Some primary insurers also provide treaty and facultative reinsurance.

1. A primary insurer may offer reinsurance to affiliated insurers, regardless of whether it offers reinsurance to unaffiliated insurers.

2. To ensure that information from other insurers remains confidential, a primary insurer's reinsurance operations are usually separate from its primary insurance operations.

3. Many primary insurers are groups of commonly owned insurance companies. Intragroup reinsurance agreements are used to balance the financial results of all insurers in the group.

C. Reinsurance Pools, Syndicates, and Associations

These entities provide member companies the opportunity to participate in a line of insurance with a limited amount of capital—and a proportionate share of the administrative costs—without having to employ the specialists needed for such a venture.

1. Reinsurance pool

   Here, a policy for the full amount of insurance is issued by a member company and reinsured by the remainder of the pool members according to predetermined percentages.

   a. Pools are formed for any of these reasons:

      • Insurers' reinsurance needs are not adequately met in the regular marketplace.

      • Specialized insurance requires underwriting and claim expertise that the individual insurers do not have.

      • Reinsurance intermediaries form reinsurance pools to provide reinsurance to their clients.

   b. A reinsurance pool may accept loss exposures from non-member companies or offer reinsurance only to its member companies.

   c. Some reinsurance pools restrict their operations to narrowly defined classes of business while others reinsure most types of insurance.

2. Syndicate

   a. Each member shares the risk with other members by accepting a percentage of the risk. These members collectively constitute a single, separate entity under the syndicate name.

   b. Syndicates are a key component of Lloyd's, an association that provides the physical and procedural facilities for its members to write insurance.

3. Association

An association consists of member companies that use reinsurance and risk-sharing techniques.

   a. In many cases, the member companies issue their own policies; however, a reinsurance certificate is attached to each policy, under which each member company assumes a fixed percentage of the total amount of insurance.

   b. Organizations of this type allow members to share risks that require special coverages or special underwriting techniques, and can increase the primary insurer's capacity to insure extra-hazardous risks.

D. Reinsurance Professional and Trade Associations

Unlike many primary insurers, reinsurers do not use service organizations such as Insurance Services Office (ISO) and the American Association of Insurance Services (AAIS) to develop loss costs and draft contract wording. However, the reinsurance field has several associations that serve member companies and provide information to interested parties.

   1. Intermediaries and Reinsurance Underwriters Association (IRU)

   Founded in 1967 and composed of intermediaries and reinsurers that broker or assume non-life treaty reinsurance, IRU publishes the *Journal of Reinsurance*. IRU also conducts claim seminars, sponsors an internship program for college students, and holds conferences for members.

2. Brokers & Reinsurance Markets Association (BRMA)

   BRMA represents intermediaries and reinsurers that are predominately engaged in United States treaty reinsurance business obtained through reinsurance brokers. BRMA seeks to identify and address industry-wide operational issues and has compiled the *Contract Wording Reference Book.*

3. Reinsurance Association of America (RAA)

   RAA is a not-for-profit trade association of professional reinsurers and intermediaries. All members are domestic U.S. companies or U.S. branches of international reinsurers. In addition to member advocacy and lobbying at both the state and federal levels, the RAA analyzes aggregate data and conducts seminars countrywide.

Educational Objective 3
Describe treaty reinsurance and facultative reinsurance.

Key Points:

There are two types of reinsurance transactions:

A. Treaty Reinsurance

Treaty reinsurance uses one agreement for an entire class or portfolio of loss exposures, and is also referred to as obligatory reinsurance. The reinsurance agreement is typically called the treaty.

   1. Although some treaties allow the reinsurer limited discretion in reinsuring individual loss exposures, most treaties require that all loss exposures within the treaty's terms must be reinsured.

   2. Treaty reinsurance provides primary insurers with the certainty needed to formulate underwriting policy and develop underwriting guidelines.

   3. Treaty reinsurance agreements are tailored to fit the primary insurer's individual requirements. The price and terms of each reinsurance treaty are individually negotiated.

   4. Most, but not all, treaty reinsurance agreements require the primary insurer to cede all eligible loss exposures to the reinsurer, so that the reinsurer is not exposed to adverse selection.

B. Facultative Reinsurance

Facultative reinsurance uses a separate reinsurance agreement for each loss exposure it wants to reinsure, and is also referred to as non-obligatory reinsurance.

   1. The primary insurer is not obligated to purchase reinsurance, and the reinsurer is not obligated to reinsure loss exposures submitted to it.

   2. A facultative reinsurance agreement is written for a specified time period and cannot be canceled by either party unless contractual obligations, such as payment of premiums, are not met.

   3. The reinsurer issues a facultative certificate of reinsurance that is attached to the primary insurer's copy of the policy being reinsured.

   4. Facultative reinsurance serves four functions:

   a. Facultative reinsurance can provide large line capacity for loss exposures that exceed the limits of treaty reinsurance agreements.

    b. Facultative reinsurance can reduce the primary insurer's exposure in a given geographic area.

    c. Facultative reinsurance can insure a loss exposure with atypical hazard characteristics and thereby maintain the favorable loss experience of the primary insurer's treaty reinsurance and any associated profit-sharing arrangements.

    d. Facultative reinsurance can insure particular classes of loss exposures that are excluded under treaty reinsurance.

5. The expense of placing facultative reinsurance can be high for both the primary insurer and the reinsurer.

Educational Objective 4

Describe the types of pro rata reinsurance and excess of loss reinsurance and their uses.

Key Points:

Each reinsurance agreement negotiated between a primary insurer and reinsurer is unique because its terms reflect the primary insurer's needs and the willingness of reinsurers in the marketplace to meet those needs. Several forms of reinsurance have been developed to serve the functions of reinsurance and help insurers meet their goals.

A. Pro Rata Reinsurance

Under pro rata reinsurance, or proportional reinsurance, the primary insurer cedes a portion of the original insurance premiums to the reinsurer as a reinsurance premium. Pro rata reinsurance can be identified as either quota share or surplus share.

1. The reinsurer usually pays the primary insurer a ceding commission for the loss exposures ceded. The ceding commission reimburses the primary insurer for policy acquisition expenses incurred when the underlying policies were sold.

   a. When the ceding commission is a fixed percentage of the ceded premium with no adjustment for the primary insurer's loss experience, it is referred to as a flat commission.

   b. The reinsurance agreement may also include a profit-sharing commission, or profit commission, which is negotiated and paid to the primary insurer after the end of the treaty year if the reinsurer earns greater-than-expected profits on the reinsurance agreement.

   c. Sometimes, as an alternative to the flat commission and profit-sharing commission, the ceding commission initially paid to the primary insurer may be adjusted to reflect the actual profitability of the reinsurance agreement. This type of commission is called a sliding scale commission.

2. In addition to policy acquisition expenses, insurers incur loss adjustment expenses. Loss adjustment expenses that can be related to a specific loss are usually shared proportionately by the primary insurer and the reinsurer.

3. Pro rata reinsurance is generally chosen by newly incorporated insurers or insurers with limited capital because it is effective in providing surplus relief.

4. The distinguishing characteristic of quota share reinsurance is that the primary insurer and the reinsurer use a fixed percentage in sharing the amounts of insurance, policy premiums, and losses (including loss adjustment expenses).

  a. Quota share reinsurance can be used with both property insurance and liability insurance, but is more frequently used in property insurance.

  b. Most reinsurance agreements specify a maximum dollar limit above which responsibility for additional coverage limits or losses reverts to the primary insurer (or is taken by another reinsurer).

  c. In addition to a maximum coverage amount limitation, some pro rata reinsurance agreements include a per occurrence limit, which restricts the primary insurer's reinsurance recovery for losses originating from a single occurrence. This per occurrence limit may be stated as an aggregate dollar amount or as a loss ratio cap.

  d. Primary insurers exposed to catastrophic losses usually include catastrophe excess of loss reinsurance in their reinsurance programs.

  e. These observations can be made about quota share reinsurance:

  • Because the retention and cession amounts are each a fixed percentage, the dollar amount of the retention and the dollar amount of the cession change as the amount of insurance changes.

  • Because the primary insurer cedes a fixed percentage under a quota share treaty, even policies with low amounts of insurance that the primary insurer could safely retain are reinsured.

  • Quota share treaties are straightforward because of the fixed percentage used in sharing premiums and losses.

  • Because the primary insurer and the reinsurer share liability for every loss exposure subject to the quota share treaty, the reinsurer is usually not subject to adverse selection.

  f. A variable quota share treaty has the advantage of enabling a primary insurer to retain a larger proportion of the small loss exposures that are within its financial capability to absorb, while maintaining a safer and smaller retention on larger loss exposures.

5. The distinguishing characteristic of surplus share reinsurance is that when an underlying policy's total amount of insurance exceeds a stipulated dollar amount, or line, the reinsurer assumes the surplus share of the amount of insurance (the difference between the primary insurer's line and the total amount of insurance).

   a. These observations can be made about surplus share reinsurance:

   • The surplus share treaty does not cover policies with amounts of insurance that are less than the primary insurer's line. Many primary insurers use surplus share reinsurance instead of quota share reinsurance so that they do not have to cede any part of the liability for loss exposures that can be safely retained.

   • The amount of insurance for a large number of loss exposures may be too small to be ceded to the treaty but, in the aggregate, may cause the primary insurer to incur significant losses that are not reinsured.

   • Because the percentage of policy premiums and losses varies for each loss exposure ceded, surplus share treaties are more costly to administer than quota share treaties. Primary insurers must keep records and, in many cases, periodically provide the reinsurer with a report called a bordereau.

   • Surplus share treaties may provide surplus relief to the primary insurer because the reinsurer usually pays a ceding commission for those policies ceded.

   b. Many surplus share treaties allow the primary insurer to increase its line from a minimum amount to a maximum amount. The flexibility provided by the reinsurer in the surplus share treaty is usually communicated to the primary insurer's underwriters through a line guide, or line authorization guide.

   c. When the total underwriting capacity of the primary insurer's surplus share treaty (first surplus) is insufficient to meet its large line capacity needs, the primary insurer can arrange for additional surplus share reinsurance from another reinsurer.

B. Excess of Loss Reinsurance

In an excess of loss reinsurance agreement, also called "non-proportional reinsurance," the reinsurer responds to a loss only when the loss exceeds the primary insurer's retention, often referred to as the attachment point. The primary insurer fully retains losses that are less than the attachment point, and will sometimes be required by the reinsurer to also retain responsibility for a percentage of the losses that exceed the attachment point.

1. Excess of loss reinsurance premiums are negotiated based on the likelihood that losses will exceed the attachment point. The reinsurance premium for excess of loss reinsurance is usually stated as a percentage (often called a rate) of the policy premium charged by the primary insurer (often called the subject premium or underlying premium).

2. Generally, reinsurers do not pay ceding commissions, but the reinsurer may reward the primary insurer for favorable loss experience by paying a profit commission or reducing the rate used in calculating the reinsurance premium.

3. A working cover enables the primary insurer to spread its losses over several years.

   a. The primary insurer and the reinsurer anticipate that profitable years will offset unprofitable ones.

   b. Reinsurers typically require a working cover to contain an occurrence limitation of two or three times the reinsurance limit.

4. The purpose of a co-participation provision is to provide the primary insurer with a financial incentive to efficiently manage losses that exceed the attachment point.

5. In addition to indemnifying losses in a layer of coverage, the reinsurer's obligation may also extend to payment of loss adjustment expenses. These are the two most common approaches to handling loss adjustment expenses:

   a. Pro rata in addition

   Prorate the loss adjustment expenses between the primary insurer and the reinsurer based on the same percentage share that each is responsible for the loss.

   b. Loss adjustment expense included in the limit

   Add the loss adjustment expenses to the amount of the loss when applying the attachment point of the excess of loss reinsurance agreement.

6. There are five types of excess of loss reinsurance:

   a. Per risk excess of loss

   This is often referred to as property per risk excess of loss and is generally used with property insurance. It applies separately to each loss occurring to each risk, with the primary insurer usually determining what constitutes one risk (loss exposure).

   b. Catastrophe excess of loss

   This protects the primary insurer from an accumulation of retained losses that arise from a single catastrophic event. It may be purchased to protect the primary insurer and its reinsurers on a combined basis but is more frequently purchased to protect the primary insurer on a net basis after all other reinsurance recoveries are made.

   • Because the attachment point and reinsurance limit apply separately to each catastrophe occurring during a policy period, the catastrophe excess of loss reinsurance agreement defines the scope of a catastrophic occurrence through a loss occurrence clause.

   • Catastrophe excess of loss reinsurance agreements often include a provision requiring the primary insurer to pay an additional premium to reinstate the limits of the agreement after a loss.

   c. Per policy excess of loss

   This is used primarily with liability insurance and applies the attachment point and the reinsurance limit separately to each insurance policy issued by the primary insurer, regardless of the number of losses occurring under each policy.

   d. Per occurrence excess of loss

   This is usually used for liability insurance. It applies the attachment point and the reinsurance limit to the total losses arising from a single event affecting one or more of the primary insurer's policies.

   • It usually has an attachment point that is less than the highest liability policy limit offered by the primary insurer.

   • Cash cover can be provided for a combination of different types of liability insurance. It has an attachment point higher than any of the limits of the applicable underlying policies.

- Cash cover may be useful for types of liability insurance in which loss adjustment expenses are likely to be very high and the underlying per occurrence reinsurance limits include these expenses rather than pro rate them. Primary insurers also use clash cover when they want protection from extra-contractual damages and excess of policy limits losses.

e. Aggregate excess of loss

This type of excess of loss reinsurance can be used for property or liability insurance and covers aggregated losses that exceed the attachment point and occur over a stated period, usually one year.

- The attachment point in an aggregate excess of loss treaty can be stated as a dollar amount of loss or as a loss ratio. When the attachment point is stated as a loss ratio, the treaty is called "stop loss reinsurance."

- Aggregate excess of loss treaties are less common and can be more expensive than the other types of excess of loss reinsurance. The treaty usually specifies an attachment point and reinsurance limit that does not result in the primary insurer earning a profit on the reinsured policies when the policies were unprofitable overall.

Educational Objective 5

Describe finite risk reinsurance and other methods that rely on capital markets as alternatives to traditional and non-traditional reinsurance.

Key Points:

While the demand for traditional reinsurance continues to evolve as the industry adapts to new economic and regulatory pressures, alternatives to traditional reinsurance have emerged.

A. Finite Risk Reinsurance

Finite risk reinsurance is a nontraditional type of reinsurance in which the reinsurer's liability is limited (or "finite") and anticipated investment income is expressly acknowledged as an underwriting component.

1. Because this type of reinsurance transfers a limited amount of risk to the reinsurer with the objective of improving the primary insurer's financial result, it is often called financial reinsurance.

2. Finite risk reinsurance can be arranged to protect a primary insurer against the combination of a traditionally insurable loss exposure and a traditionally uninsurable loss exposure.

3. A finite risk reinsurance agreement typically has a multi-year term, which allows the risk and losses to be spread over several years, while being subject to an aggregate limit for the agreement's entire term.

4. The primary insurer can rely on long-term protection and a predictable reinsurance cost over the coverage period, while the reinsurer can rely on a continual flow of premiums.

5. Finite risk reinsurance premiums can be a substantial percentage of the reinsurance limit. This reduces the reinsurer's potential underwriting loss to a level that is much lower than that typically associated with traditional types of reinsurance.

6. Finite risk reinsurance is designed to cover high-severity losses. The reinsurer commonly shares profits with the primary insurer when it has favorable loss experience or has generated income by investing the prepaid premium.

B. Capital Market Alternatives to Traditional and Non-Traditional Reinsurance

Capital markets have emerged as tools that primary insurers can use to finance risk as an alternative to insurance. Instead of purchasing reinsurance to cover its potential liabilities, the primary insurer uses traded security instruments to finance insurance risk. These are among the methods most often used:

1. Catastrophe bond

This type of insurance-linked security is specifically designed to transfer insurable catastrophe risk to investors.

a. A bond is issued with a condition that if the issuer suffers a catastrophe loss greater than the specified amount, the obligation to pay interest and/or repay principle is deferred or forgiven.

b. As long as catastrophe-related losses do not exceed the specified amount, investors earn a relatively high interest rate and receive a return of their principal.

c. If catastrophe losses exceed the specified loss amount, the interest and/or principal forgone by bondholders is used to pay losses.

2. Catastrophe risk exchange

This is a means through which a primary insurer can exchange a portion of its insurance risk for another insurer's risk. A primary insurer with a geographic concentration of loss exposures can use a catastrophe risk exchange to reduce its losses from a single loss occurrence.

3. Contingent surplus note

A primary insurer designs this so that, at its option, it can immediately obtain funds by issuing notes at a pre-agreed rate of interest.

4. Industry loss warranty (ILW)

This is an insurance-linked security that covers the primary insurer in the event that the industry-wide loss from a particular catastrophic event exceeds a predetermined threshold. Its coverage is triggered only by industry losses.

5. Catastrophe option

This agreement gives the primary insurer the right to a cash payment from investors if a specified index of catastrophe losses reaches a specified level (the strike price).

6. Line of credit

This is an arrangement in which a bank or another financial institution agrees to provide a loan to a primary insurer in the event the primary insurer suffers a loss.

7. Sidecar

   This is a limited-existence special purpose vehicle (SPV) that provides a primary insurer additional capacity to write property catastrophe business or other short-tail lines through a quota share agreement with private investors.

   a. Investors in the SPV assume a proportion of the risk and earn a corresponding portion of the profit on the primary insurer's book of business.

   b. The primary insurer charges a ceding commission and may receive a profit commission if the book of business is profitable.

Educational Objective 6

Describe the factors that should be considered in the design of a reinsurance program.

Key Points:

Many kinds of reinsurance exist, and, with rare exceptions, any primary insurer can find a combination of reinsurance agreements that meet its needs. Designing an optimal reinsurance program requires careful analysis of a primary insurer's needs, retentions, and reinsurance limits. Assistance in this could come from reinsurers, reinsurance intermediaries, and consultants.

A. Factors Affecting Reinsurance Needs

Primary insurers consider several factors to determine their reinsurance needs, all of which interact to increase or decrease a primary insurer's need for reinsurance:

1. Growth plans

a. A primary insurer that expects rapid premium growth is likely to need more reinsurance than a primary insurer that expects premium volume to remain stable or to decrease.

b. There are three reasons for the need for additional reinsurance:

- Rapid growth can cause a drain on a primary insurer's policyholders' surplus.

- The loss ratio for a primary insurer's new business is likely to be less stable than the loss ratio for its established business, which has undergone renewal underwriting.

- Growth often entails expanding into markets with greater coverage requirements.

c. Pro rata reinsurance is the appropriate choice if a rapidly growing primary insurer needs only surplus relief.

d. If the major concern is loss ratio stability or large line capacity, excess of loss reinsurance may be an appropriate choice.

2. Types of insurance sold

a. Generally, primary insurers selling personal insurance need less reinsurance than those selling commercial insurance because personal insurance loss exposures need relatively lower coverage limits. Personal insurance loss exposures are also more homogeneous and subject to fewer severe hazards than commercial insurance loss exposures.

    b. Some types of insurance require a greater commitment of policyholders' surplus (capital) than do others. State insurance regulators use a risk-based capital system to establish an insurer's minimum capital requirements.

    c. A primary insurer that sells several types of insurance is more diversified and therefore more likely to have a stable loss ratio than a primary insurer selling only a few types of insurance.

3. Geographic spread of loss exposures

    a. A wide geographic spread may stabilize the insurer's loss ratio and minimize reinsurance needs, especially in property insurance. Poor loss experience in one area may be offset by good loss experience in another area during a given period.

    b. Insurance regulation, laws governing tort liability, law enforcement practices, and other factors affecting property or liability insurance losses vary by geographic area. Adverse changes in these factors in one geographic area may be offset by favorable developments in another if the loss exposures are geographically diverse.

4. Insurer size

    a. Typically, small primary insurers need proportionately more reinsurance to stabilize loss ratios than large primary insurers.

    b. According to the law of large numbers, actual losses tend to approach expected losses as the number of loss exposures increases.

5. Insurer structure

The legal form of a primary insurer may affect its reinsurance needs. For example, stock insurers have more access to capital markets than mutual and reciprocal insurers.

6. Insurer financial strength

    a. An insurer that is financially strong needs less reinsurance than a financially weaker one for two reasons:

- It does not need surplus relief to increase its premium capacity.
- It needs less reinsurance to stabilize its loss ratio.

    b. One aspect of evaluating an insurer's financial strength involves assessing the stability and liquidity of its invested assets. Policyholders' surplus must be invested in assets that are readily marketable and not subject to wide fluctuations in market price.

c. Because common stock may be marketable only at a substantial loss in an unfavorable market, a primary insurer that holds large amounts of it in an investment portfolio needs to be more heavily reinsured than one that holds short-term bonds.

d. A primary insurer that invests a large portion of its funds in wholly-owned subsidiaries needs to have a substantial reinsurance program because the stock of subsidiaries is not generally marketable.

7. Senior management's risk tolerance

a. Senior management must be comfortable with the insurance risk assumed, particularly when setting retentions or changing the reinsurance program.

b. Senior management must be confident that other stakeholders are comfortable with the adequacy of the primary insurer's reinsurance program.

c. The practical effect of any proposed reinsurance program changes on supervisors and underwriters must also be considered.

B. Factors Affecting Retention Selection

Although the retention is based on the primary insurer's financial needs and the types of insurance that the primary insurer sells, it is also negotiable by the primary insurer and the reinsurer. Cost is always a factor in selecting a retention, and the cost of a reinsurance treaty usually increases as the size of the retention decreases. In addition to cost, four factors are considered when selecting a retention:

1. Maximum amount the primary insurer can retain

This amount is a function of two aspects:

a. Regulatory requirements

- State insurance regulations effectively limit premium capacity to three dollars of net written premiums for each dollar of policyholders' surplus.

- Large-line capacity is limited by a statutory provision that an insurer cannot retain a net amount for a single loss exposure greater than 10 percent of its policyholders' surplus.

- Many conservative primary insurers retain significantly less than those limits.

b. The primary insurer's financial strength

- An insurer should not retain loss exposures so large that the losses under a worst-case scenario can threaten its solvency.

- The primary insurer must consider not only the losses within the retention of the possible reinsurance agreement, but also the retentions of closely related reinsurance agreements.

2. Maximum amount the primary insurer wants to retain

   Possible maximum retentions are rarely accepted. This may be partly because of the uncertainty of determining how much loss exposure can safely be assumed, and partly because of the conservatism of some managers.

3. Minimum retention sought by the reinsurer

   Reinsurers sometimes demand a minimum retention as a condition of providing reinsurance. This demand is especially likely for excess of loss treaties, particularly catastrophe treaties. The purpose of the minimum retention requirement is to encourage the primary insurer to implement sound risk control, underwriting, and loss adjustment practices.

4. Co-participation provision

   This provision requires the primary insurer to participate in losses beyond the retention for risk control, underwriting, and loss adjustment reasons previously described.

C. Factors Affecting Reinsurance Limit Selection

There are five factors to consider in selecting treaty limits, which vary depending on the kind of treaty involved:

1. Maximum policy limit

   a. The maximum policy limit sold by the primary insurer may not be as economical as relying on facultative reinsurance to provide full reinsurance coverage.

   b. The limit for a stop loss treaty is stated as a loss ratio. Ideally, the limit should be set at the highest loss ratio that the primary insurer is likely to reach.

2. Extra-contractual obligations

   a. If a reinsurance treaty is to provide protection against extra-contractual damages and excess of policy limit losses, the reinsurance treaty limit should be substantially higher than the primary insurer's highest policy limit.

   b. Damages resulting from extra-contractual obligations may be several multiples of the highest coverage limit offered.

3. Loss adjustment expenses

   Loss adjustment expenses can be a significant loss component in per risk and per occurrence excess of loss treaties, depending on the type of underlying policy. They should be considered when selecting retentions and reinsurance limits.

4. Clash cover
   a. Clash cover applies when claims from two or more policies arise as a result of the same occurrence.
   b. Clash cover limits should be set by considering the highest limits offered by the primary insurer and the perceived likelihood that multiple policies may be involved in a single occurrence.
5. Catastrophe exposure
   a. Selecting the limit for a catastrophe treaty is a more complex task than selecting limits for per risk excess of loss treaties because catastrophe losses involve an accumulation of losses arising from a single occurrence.
   b. The primary insurer's liability for such losses has no stated limit. The effective limit is set by the number and face amount of policies subject to losses by a single catastrophic occurrence that the primary insurer has in force in a geographic area.

Educational Objective 7

Given a case, identify the reinsurance needs of an insurer and recommend an appropriate reinsurance program to address those needs.

Key Points:

To successfully complete these case studies, students should first understand these concepts:

- Reinsurance and its functions
- Treaty reinsurance and facultative reinsurance
- Types of pro rata reinsurance and excess of loss reinsurance and their uses
- Factors that should be considered in the design of a reinsurance program

Students should then consider how reinsurance meets the objectives described in the case studies.

Educational Objective 8
Explain how reinsurance is regulated.

Key Points:

Reinsurers domiciled in the United States and alien reinsurers licensed in the U.S. are subject to the same solvency state regulations as primary insurers. Reinsurers are required to file financial statements with state regulatory authorities and to adhere to state insurance regulations regarding reserves, investments, and minimum capital and surplus requirements. They must also undergo periodic examination by the appropriate state authorities. Reinsurance rates are not regulated in the U.S.; however, the regulation of primary insurer rates could indirectly affect reinsurance rates to the extent that reinsurers receive a reinsurance premium based on the premiums of primary insurers. Reinsurance agreements are regulated to a slightly greater degree than reinsurance pricing.

A. Contract Certainty
1. Until recently, regulatory requirements were aimed at ensuring that reinsurance contracts were signed within a reasonable period of time (within nine months of the policy period's commencement).
2. Regulatory efforts now also focus on the concept of contract certainty, which generally requires the complete and final agreement of all terms between the insured and insurer by the time the contract is entered into, with contract documentation provided promptly thereafter.

B. Credit for Reinsurance Transactions
1. State insurance regulators have allowed primary insurers to take credit for a reinsurance transaction on their financial statements based on the reinsurer's authorization status and other conditions, rather than on the actual value of the economic benefit that the reinsurance transaction provides.
2. State insurance regulators have adopted requirements that must be met for a reinsurance agreement to be treated as a reinsurance transaction.
3. Regulators motivate primary insurers to require some desirable clauses in their reinsurance agreements by withholding permission to take reserve credit for the reinsurance transaction unless the reinsurance agreements contain the specified clauses.

4. The insolvency clause, which is required for the primary insurer to take credit for the reinsurance transaction, provides that the primary insurer's insolvency does not affect the reinsurer's liability for losses under the reinsurance agreement.

5. More recently, some states have required an intermediary clause in reinsurance agreements.

    a. The reinsurer assumes the credit risk that the reinsurance intermediary will be unable or unwilling to pay all of the premiums collected under its reinsurance agreements.

    b. The reinsurer also assumes the risk that the reinsurance intermediary will not transmit to the primary insurer all claim payments owed to the insurer.

Key Words and Phrases:

Reinsurance
The transfer of insurance risk from one insurer to another through a contractual agreement under which one insurer (the reinsurer) agrees, in return for a reinsurance premium, to indemnify another insurer (the primary insurer) for some or all of the financial consequences of certain loss exposures covered by the primary's insurance policies.

Primary insurer
In reinsurance, the insurer that transfers or cedes all or part of the insurance risk it has assumed to another insurer in a contractual arrangement.

Reinsurer
The insurer that assumes some or all of the potential costs of insured loss exposures of the primary insurer in a reinsurance contractual agreement.

Reinsurance agreement
Contract between the primary insurer and reinsurer that stipulates the form of reinsurance and the type of accounts to be reinsured.

Insurance risk
Uncertainty about the adequacy of insurance premiums to pay losses.

Retention
The amount retained by the primary insurer in the reinsurance transaction.

Reinsurance premium
The consideration paid by the primary insurer to the reinsurer for assuming some or all of the primary insurer's insurance risk.

Ceding commission
An amount paid by the reinsurer to the primary insurer to cover part or all of the primary insurer's policy acquisition expenses.

Retrocession
A reinsurance agreement whereby one reinsurer (the retrocedent) transfers all or part of the reinsurance risk it has assumed or will assume to another reinsurer (the retrocessionaire).

Retrocedent
The reinsurer that transfers or cedes all or part of the insurance risk it has assumed to another reinsurer.

Retrocessionaire
The reinsurer that assumes all or part of the reinsurance risk accepted by another reinsurer.

Large-line capacity
An insurer's ability to provide larger amounts of insurance for property loss exposures, or higher limits of liability for liability loss exposures, than it is otherwise willing to provide.

Line
The maximum amount of insurance or limit of liability that an insurer will accept on a single loss exposure.

Surplus relief
A replenishment of policyholders' surplus provided by the ceding commission paid to the primary insurer by the reinsurer.

Portfolio reinsurance
Reinsurance that transfers to the reinsurer liability for an entire type of insurance, territory, or book of business after the primary insurer has issued the policies.

Novation
An agreement under which one insurer or reinsurer is substituted for another.

Professional reinsurer
An insurer whose primary business purpose is serving other insurers' reinsurance needs.

Direct writing reinsurer
A professional reinsurer whose employees deal directly with primary insurers.

Reinsurance intermediary
An intermediary that works with primary insurers to develop reinsurance programs and that negotiates contracts of reinsurance between the primary insurer and reinsurer, receiving commission for placement and other services rendered.

Reinsurance pools, syndicates, and associations
Groups of insurers that share the loss exposures of the group, usually through reinsurance.

Reinsurance pool
A reinsurance association that consists of several unrelated insurers or reinsurers that have joined to insure risks the individual members are unwilling to individually insure.

Syndicate
A group of insurers or reinsurers involved in joint underwriting to insure major risks that are beyond the capacity of a single insurer or reinsurer; each syndicate member accepts predetermined shares of premiums, losses, expenses, and profits.

Association
An organization of member companies that reinsure by fixed percentage the total amount of insurance appearing on policies issued by the organization.

Adverse selection
The decision to reinsure those loss exposures that have an increased probability of loss because the retention of those loss exposures is undesirable.

Facultative certificate of reinsurance
An agreement that defines the terms of the facultative reinsurance coverage on a specific loss exposure.

Pro rata reinsurance
A type of reinsurance in which the primary insurer and reinsurer proportionately share the amounts of insurance, policy premiums, and losses (including loss adjustment expenses).

Flat commission
A ceding commission that is a fixed percentage of the ceded premiums.

Profit-sharing commission
A ceding commission that is contingent on the reinsurer realizing a predetermined percentage of excess profit on ceded loss exposures.

Sliding scale commission
A ceding commission based on a formula that adjusts the commission according to the profitability of the reinsurance agreement.

Quota share reinsurance
A type of pro rata reinsurance in which the primary insurer and the reinsurer share the amounts of insurance, policy premiums, and losses (including loss adjustment expenses) using a fixed percentage.

Catastrophe excess of loss reinsurance
A type of excess of loss reinsurance that protects the primary insurer from an accumulation of retained losses that arise from a single catastrophic event.

Surplus share reinsurance
A type of pro rata reinsurance in which the policies covered are those whose amount of insurance exceeds a stipulated dollar amount, or line.

Bordereau
A report the primary insurer provides periodically to the reinsurer that contains a history of all loss exposures reinsured under the treaty.

Line guide
A document that provides the minimum and maximum line a primary insurer can retain on a loss exposure.

Excess of loss reinsurance (nonproportional reinsurance)
A type of reinsurance in which the primary insurer is indemnified for losses that exceed a specified dollar amount.

Attachment point
The dollar amount above which the reinsurer responds to losses.

Subject premium
The premium the primary insurer charges on its underlying policies and to which a rate is applied to determine the reinsurance premium.

Working cover
An excess of loss reinsurance agreement with a low attachment point.

Co-participation provision
A provision in a reinsurance agreement that requires the primary insurer to retain a specified percentage of the losses that exceed its attachment point.

Per risk excess of loss reinsurance
A type of excess of loss reinsurance that covers property insurance and that applies separately to each loss occurring to each risk.

Loss occurrence clause
A reinsurance agreement clause that defines the scope of a catastrophic occurrence for the purposes of the agreement.

Per policy excess of loss reinsurance
A type of excess of loss reinsurance that applies the attachment point and the reinsurance limit separately to each insurance policy issued by the primary insurer regardless of the number of losses occurring under each policy.

Per occurrence excess of loss reinsurance
A type of excess of loss reinsurance that applies the attachment point and reinsurance limit to the total losses arising from a single event affecting one or more of the primary insurer's policies.

Clash cover
A type of per occurrence excess of loss reinsurance for liability loss exposures that protects the primary insurer against aggregations of losses from one occurrence that affects several insureds or several types of insurance.

Extracontractual damages
Damages awarded to the insured as a result of the insurer's improperly handling a claim.

Excess of policy limits loss
A loss that results when an insured sues an insurer for failing to settle a claim within the insured's policy limits when the insurer had the opportunity to do so.

Aggregate excess of loss reinsurance
A type of excess of loss reinsurance that covers aggregated losses that exceed the attachment point, stated as a dollar amount of loss or as a loss ratio, and that occur over a specified period, usually one year.

Finite risk reinsurance
A nontraditional type of reinsurance in which the reinsurer's liability is limited and anticipated investment income is expressly acknowledged as an underwriting component.

Capital market
A financial market in which long-term securities are traded.

Securitization of risk
The use of securities or financial instruments (i.e., stocks, bonds, commodities, financial futures) to finance an insurer's exposure to catastrophic loss.

Special purpose vehicle (SPV)
A facility established for the purpose of purchasing income-producing assets from an organization, holding title to them, and then using those assets to collateralize securities that will be sold to investors.

Insurance derivative
Financial contract whose value is based on the level of insurable losses that occur during a specific time period.

Contingent capital arrangement
An agreement, entered into before any losses occur, that enables an organization to raise cash by selling stock or issuing debt at prearranged terms after a loss occurs that exceeds a certain threshold.

Insurance-linked security
A financial instrument whose value is primarily driven by insurance and/or reinsurance loss events.

Surplus note
A type of unsecured debt instrument, issued only by insurers, that has characteristics of both conventional equity and debt securities and is classified as policyholders' surplus rather than as a liability on the insurer's statutory balance sheet.

Strike price
The price at which the stock or commodity underlying a call option (such as a warrant) or a put option can be purchased (called) or sold (put) during a specified period.

Reinsurance program
The combination of reinsurance agreements that a primary insurer purchases to meet its reinsurance needs.

Underwriting risk
A measure of the loss volatility of the types of insurance sold by an insurer.

Insolvency clause
A clause that is required in reinsurance agreements indicating that the primary insurer's bankruptcy does not affect the reinsurer's liability for losses under the reinsurance agreement.

Intermediary clause
A clause that is required in reinsurance agreements indicating that the reinsurance intermediary is the reinsurer's agent for collecting reinsurance premiums and paying reinsurance claims.

Insurer Strategic Management

11

Educational Objective 1
Describe the strategic management process.

Key Points:

The strategic management process is critical to any organization's success. However, effective strategic management is especially important for insurers because they must distinguish themselves in a highly regulated business where products may not widely vary. The strategic management process involves three interdependent stages:

A. Strategy Formulation

　1. Mission and vision statements

　　a. A mission statement is a broad expression of an entity's purpose or goals that reflects the entity's character and spirit. It specifies the products or services the organization provides, its stakeholders, and what is important to the organization.

　　b. Vision or value statements may be included in or accompany mission statements. They provide additional information about company values or principles important to the organization.

　2. Strategy formulation steps

　　a. Analysis of external and internal environments

　　　• This involves an internal analysis of the organization and an analysis of external factors including competitors, current and prospective customers' needs, the current and anticipated economy, and government regulations.

　　　• A strengths, weaknesses, opportunities, and threats (SWOT) analysis may enable executives to determine how receptive the market would be to its products and services and its competitive position within the market.

　　b. Development of long-term strategies and organizational goals

　　　• These goals will support the mission statement within the framework developed during the analysis step.

　　　• An organization's goals should reflect an understanding of its identity, customers, and purpose.

Study Tips

The Educational Objectives help you focus your studies. Consult the textbook or modules for a more detailed explanation of examples and/or concepts.

- Normally, the chief executive officer (CEO) and executive officers will develop these strategies and goals, often with input from the board and operational-level managers.
  c. Determination of strategy at different organizational levels
  - This involves agreement on more specific action and delegation of responsibilities to achieve long-term strategies and goals.
  - This step in the strategic management process involves formulating the "who," "what," and "when" responsibilities.

B. Strategy Implementation

Also called strategy execution, strategy implementation is the process of making strategies work.

1. The first consideration is designing the structure of the organization. The most appropriate structure will be determined by its strategic goals.
   a. In a single-business company, a functional structure might be most suitable, with departments defined by the operation they perform, for example.
   b. A diversified company is more likely to use a multidivisional structure to organize its operations and to segregate each division into separate profit centers.
   c. Other possible structures organize company operations by region or by type of product or customer.
2. Structure can also determine the reporting relationships or the company's level of vertical differentiation.
   a. Some companies are tall organizations, with many levels between functional-level positions and executive-level positions.
   b. A flat organization has fewer levels from the top of the organization to the bottom, which can help eliminate costs.
3. Companies should also decide what degree of centralization is needed to operate efficiently and meet organizational goals.
4. Organizational goals are communicated by top management. Often, managers at each successive level must "sell" organizational goals to their employees.

C. Strategy Evaluation

Strategy evaluation, also called strategic control, provides a method for measuring a strategy's success.

1. The control process has four steps:
   a. Establish standards
   b. Create and apply measurements

    c. Compare actual results to standards

    d. Evaluate and implement corrective actions if goals are not met

2. These are categories of organizational controls that may be used to monitor goals:

    a. Financial controls

    b. Operational or process controls

    c. Human or behavior controls

Educational Objective 2

Explain how the Five Forces and SWOT methods can be used to analyze the environment in which an insurer operates.

Key Points:

An insurer's success depends on its ability to analyze changing environmental factors and influences and to formulate sound business strategies based on its analysis. Many methods can be used to analyze the environment in which an organization operates. Two commonly used methods are the Five Forces Model and SWOT analysis.

A. The Five Forces Model

This widely used model deals with the external task, or competitive, environment and is often used to analyze customers, competitors and suppliers. Its creator, Michael E. Porter, describes five forces that drive competition:

1. Threat of new entrants

The strength of this force depends on how difficult it is for outsiders to enter the market.

    a. Barriers to entry include economies of scale, which contribute to lower overall costs by decreasing the unit cost of products as volume increases.

    b. Insurers can also raise barriers to entry by offering unique products or services through the establishment of leadership in certain distribution methods or by having established advertising or group marketing programs.

    c. State statute and regulatory policy can act as a barrier to entry if they deter potential entrants from considering the highly regulated insurance industry.

2. Threat of substitute products or services

    a. This threat arises when products that are capable of performing the same function as those from another industry become widely available.

    b. It makes it difficult for any one seller to substantially increase prices and tends to hold down profits for all participants in the original industry.

3. Bargaining power of buyers

When buyers have significant power, they can increase competition within an industry and demand lower prices.

       a. This force affects the insurance industry, principally in the personal insurance market, in which customers have exerted great pressure on insurers to lower prices and increase availability.

- The bargaining power of buyers is the reason that many government-sponsored or -mandated residual market plans were created.
- The bargaining power of buyers led to the explosive growth in a number of coastal property insurance plans and wind pools as property owners would not, or could not, pay rates sought by the private market.

       b. In a soft market, many insurers vie for business and provide undifferentiated products. Insurance consumers have greater bargaining power and can negotiate for broader coverages at lower premiums.

       c. In a hard market, limited capacity results in rising prices and makes it difficult for customers to bargain for broader coverage.

    4. Bargaining power of suppliers

       a. In some industries, suppliers can exert power over companies by increasing prices, restricting supply, or varying product quality.

       b. In the insurance industry, reinsurers are a supplier to primary insurers. Without access to reinsurance, many insurers would lack sufficient capacity to write certain types and amounts of insurance.

    5. Rivalry among existing firms

       a. Rivalry is reflected in pricing wars, aggressive advertising campaigns, and increased emphasis on customer service.

       b. A high level of competition can be expected in industries having many companies, little product differentiation, or high exit costs. All of these characteristics are present in the insurance industry.

B. SWOT Analysis

SWOT (Strengths, Weaknesses, Opportunities, and Threats) analysis allows organizations to consider both the general environment and the task environment. This method was devised by Albert S. Humphrey.

    1. Strengths and weaknesses

When identifying internal strengths and weaknesses, management considers these assets:

       a. Managerial expertise

       b. Available product lines

     c. Skill levels and competencies of staff

     d. Current strategies

     e. Customer loyalty

     f. Growth levels

     g. Organizational structure

     h. Distribution channels

2. Opportunities and threats

     a. Insurers might determine opportunities and threats through trend analysis, which identifies patterns related to specific factors in the past and then projects those patterns into the future to determine potential threats or opportunities.

       • Opportunities might be presented by new markets, possible acquisition targets, or a reduction in competition.

       • Threats might include new competitors, an increase in competition levels, economic downturns, or changes in customer preferences.

     b. Once the SWOT analysis has been completed, managers can develop strategies that position the company to gain a competitive advantage by leveraging organizational strengths and offsetting or reducing weaknesses.

Educational Objective 3

Explain how strategies are developed at the corporate, business, functional, and operational levels.

Key Points:

Strategic plans encompass a variety of organizational activities. Because organizations vary widely, every organization requires its own approach. Strategies can be categorized based on the levels at which they are carried out within an organization, how they relate to the development stage of the organization, and how they align with the organization's overall business approach.

A. Corporate-Level Strategy

1. At the corporate level, the chief executive officer (CEO) and the executive team determine the businesses in which the company will be involved, allocate organizational resources properly, and coordinate strategies at all company levels to maximize profits.

2. Competitive advantage is reinforced when each department or unit in an organization creates value for the customer.

3. Three generic corporate-level strategies are available for companies in a growth mode:

    a. Single business

    b. Vertical integration

    c. Diversification

4. Concentration on a single business

    a. By concentrating its efforts and resources on one industry, product, or market, a company can build distinctive competencies and gain a competitive advantage.

    b. Most disadvantages of concentration can be related to missing opportunities to build a competitive advantage through either vertical integration or diversification into related areas.

5. Vertical integration

    a. A vertical integration strategy can be either backward or forward.

    b. If an organization produces inputs for processing, it is backward integration.

    c. When an organization sells its product directly to the customer rather than through a wholesaler, it is called forward integration.

    d. Companies choose vertical integration to decrease expenses or increase efficiency.

6. Diversification

Because the industry is affected by the weather cycles, diversifying into lines of insurance or financial products that are unaffected by the weather can help smooth the demand for both financial and human resources. In pursuit of diversification, companies can pursue either related or unrelated diversification strategies.

    a. Related diversification allows companies to gain economies of scope by sharing resources, such as the same distribution system or research and development facilities.

    b. Another benefit of related diversification is the ability to leverage fixed expenses with additional revenues from diversified operations, resulting in a lower unit cost for each product or service offered.

    c. Unrelated diversification strategy (also referred to as conglomerate diversification strategy) involves acquiring companies that have no relationship to the existing business operations and is riskier than related diversification.

    d. The negative aspects of unrelated diversification include these:

- Additional costs of coordinating the divergent businesses
- A loss of synergy among business units
- Diminishing returns from any economies of scale or scope

7. Decline mode strategies

    a. When a company is operating in a market in which demand for its products or services is decreasing, it is in a decline mode and its strategic options are different than those of companies in a growth mode.

    b. In the worst-case scenario, the company might determine that the only option is bankruptcy or liquidation.

    c. There are other corporate-level strategies that can be used in a decline mode:

- Harvest strategy
- Turnaround strategy
- Divestiture strategy

B. Business-Level Strategy

Business-level strategies are developed at the business or division level by managers who are responsible for supporting the stated corporate-level strategy. There are three business-level strategies.

1. Cost leadership
   a. Cost leadership enables a company to charge a lower price for its products or services.
   b. It involves eliminating costs in every aspect of the operation, from product development and design to distribution and delivery.
   c. One requirement of a cost leadership strategy is that most products or services must be fairly standardized.
   d. For insurers, price cutting might be limited by regulatory constraints. Insurers must closely examine the three components of an insurance rate to determine where costs can be reduced:
      • Allowances for loss payments
      • Expenses
      • Profit
   e. When evaluating how to decrease costs, insurers can consider reducing acquisition expenses by lowering producers' commissions, using a direct writer system for some or all of their marketing, or exploring alternative distribution channels.
   f. Loss expenses can be reduced by streamlining claim adjusting processes, managing litigation expenses, or implementing cost containment practices, such as negotiation of repair or medical reimbursement rates with vendors.
   g. Underwriting expenses can be reduced by using expert computer systems or standardizing underwriting guidelines.
2. Differentiation
   a. A successful differentiation strategy requires products and services that customers perceive as distinctive and that are difficult for rivals to imitate.
   b. Insurers employing this strategy may choose to differentiate products or services to gain market share and to establish a competitive advantage.
   c. When an insurer writes only homeowners or personal auto insurance and targets multiple markets, it is following a differentiation strategy.
3. Focus
   a. A focus strategy involves concentrating on a group of customers, a geographic area, or a narrow line of products or services while using a low-cost approach or a differentiation strategy.
   b. The two types of this strategy are focused cost leadership strategy and focused differentiation strategy.

C. Functional-Level Strategy

    1. Functional-level strategies are the plans for managing a particular functional area, such as finance, marketing, underwriting, actuarial, risk control, premium audit, and claims.

    2. Companies build value and competitive advantage through efficiency, quality, customer responsiveness, and innovation.

    3. In insurance operations, functional-level strategies specify how the underwriting, claim, actuarial, and other departments advance business-level strategies.

    4. For an insurer to be successful at garnering market share using a cost leadership strategy, it must become a highly efficient organization.

D. Operational-Level Strategy

    1. Operational-level strategies involve daily business processes and workflows, and are implemented at the department level to support the strategies of the functional, business, and corporate levels.

    2. A premium auditing department, striving to achieve a functional-level budget strategy, might use pre-audit screening as an operational-level strategy to make the most effective use of resources to achieve its budget goals.

Educational Objective 4

Describe the strategic reasons, considerations, and approaches for insurers to expand their operations globally.

Key Points:

Insurers are increasingly expanding operations to foreign markets. These four topics provide a basic understanding of why and how insurers engage in global expansion.

A. Trends in Global Expansion

    1. Global commerce has been growing since the end of World War II. During the past two decades, this growth accelerated as a result of numerous trade agreements throughout the world, advances in transportation and communication, the influence of the Internet, and financial innovation.

    2. The insurance market has become a global market in which United States insurers compete in many other countries and in which insurers domiciled in other countries compete in the U.S.

    3. The U.S. experiences a trade deficit in global insurance trade that has increased steadily since 1995. While there is greater competition for U.S. insurers from foreign insurers within the U.S. market, growth of the U.S. market has been slowing.

B. Strategic Reasons for Global Expansion

Key strategic reasons why insurers pursue global expansion are revenue growth, financial stability, and building global competitiveness.

    1. Revenue growth and financial stability

    Revenue growth is the primary reason that insurers look to global expansion.

        a. Some insurance markets, including the U.S, are considered mature markets, meaning that there are few new potential customers.

         • In a mature market, competition for market share results in shrinking profit margins and companies will look for new opportunities for revenue growth.

         • Global markets, especially those in emerging economies (developing countries where the economy is growing rapidly) offer growth opportunities.

    b. Expanding into foreign markets has the benefit of allowing insurers to achieve these objectives:

- Greater stability during economic downturns—Spreading risks worldwide helps to counter the effects of economic downturn in a particular country.
- Diversification of risk—Spreading risk over a larger and more diverse base minimizes the impact of heavy losses in any one segment of the operation.

2. Global competitiveness

    a. Through the growth from global expansion, an insurer may achieve economies of scale and efficiencies that allow it to compete more effectively in its domestic market as well as in the global market.

    b. A global expansion strategy also provides an insurer with the technology and strategic resources to quickly expand into additional foreign markets or offer additional products when there is an opportunity.

C. Global Market Considerations

When deciding to operate globally, management needs to determine the global markets to target, what products could be sold in other countries, what distribution channels should be used, and how regulations and government restrictions might affect global operations. There are three key areas for an insurer to evaluate in making a strategic decision about expansion into a global market.

1. Market analysis

    a. When a company is considering global expansion, it must analyze the insurance market in the country it plans to enter.

    b. Financial requirements need to be evaluated. The company must also assess whether the potential return is worth the amount of capital that will need to be committed.

    c. The insurer will consider whether it has any competitive advantage that it can use to provide leverage in the country where it plans to expand.

    d. Distribution channels, the availability of producers, and underwriting practices are additional factors to analyze.

    e. Other factors include cultural and language differences, and whether the insurer has the staff or can hire and manage the appropriate staff to overcome any linguistic or cultural barriers.

2. Economic consideration

    a. Important considerations include the level of economic stability, monetary policies, the prevailing attitude toward foreign investors, and the potential for exchange-rate volatility.

    b. Other economic factors such as the country's gross domestic product or national income are also important, as is specific information including regulation, taxation, and premium tax requirements.

    c. Insurers need to have information regarding average personal income, disposable income, and the prevailing wages and economic growth risks in any country that is a potential market.

3. Political risks

Political risks are uncertainties faced by companies doing business in foreign countries that arise from the actions of host-country governments.

    a. Serious concerns include kidnap and ransom, terrorism, civil unrest, acts of war, revolution, and changes in government.

    b. Of greatest financial concern is the potential for the confiscation of business assets by a foreign government or other interference with the rights of ownership of corporate assets.

    c. Companies are also concerned when countries treat local businesses more favorably than foreign businesses regarding taxes, government contracts, or access to required financing.

D. Approaches to Global Expansion

    1. Strategic alliance—Strategic alliances have the advantages of bringing together separate areas of expertise and of gaining a host-country participant, who can access local markets and who is familiar with local laws, regulations, and customers.

    2. Joint venture—A joint venture is a specific type of strategic alliance that involves shared ownership, shared responsibilities, and often joint management of the foreign venture.

        a. A joint-venture agreement brings together two companies to form a new organization that is legally separate and distinct from the parent companies, with its own management and directors.

        b. Joint ventures with governments or state-owned industries are referred to as public-private ventures.

3. Merger—The advantage to a merger is the ability to combine resources and reduce overhead expenses, allowing the new company to be more successful than the sum of the parties to the merger.

4. Wholly owned subsidiary—Acquisition of, or formation of, a wholly owned subsidiary allows for direct ownership and control of assets in a foreign country. This presents the highest degree of business, political, and economic risk.

Educational Objective 5

Given information about an insurer's business strategies, conduct a SWOT analysis of its strategy.

Key Points:

To successfully complete this case study, students should follow these steps:

1. Conduct a current strengths, weaknesses, opportunities, and threats (SWOT) analysis of the organization's internal and external environments
2. Determine the business strategies relevant to the business issue that generated the need for evaluation
3. Evaluate the relevant business strategies using the SWOT analysis

Key Words and Phrases:

Key Words

Strategic management process
The process an organization uses to formulate and implement its business strategies.

Mission statement
A broad expression of an entity's goals.

SWOT analysis
A method of evaluating the internal and external environments by assessing an organization's internal strengths and weaknesses and its external opportunities and threats.

Functional structure
An organizational structure in which departments are defined by the operation they perform.

Multidivisional structure
An organizational structure in which divisions are organized into separate profit centers.

Cost leadership
A business-level strategy through which a company seeks cost efficiencies in all operational areas.

Five Forces Model
A method of evaluating the external environment in which a company operates. Involves assessing five forces that drive competition: threat of new entrants, threat of substitute products or services, bargaining power of buyers, bargaining power of suppliers, and rivalry among existing firms.

Trend analysis
An analysis that identifies patterns in past losses and then projects these patterns into the future.

Vertical integration strategy
A corporate-level strategy through which a company either produces its own inputs or disposes of its own outputs.

Related diversification strategy
A corporate-level strategy through which a company expands its operations into areas that are similar to its existing operations.

Unrelated diversification strategy
A corporate-level strategy through which a company expands its operations into areas that have no relation to its existing operations.

Harvest strategy
A corporate-level strategy through which a company seeks to gain short-term profits while phasing out a product line or exiting a market.

Turnaround strategy
A corporate-level strategy through which a company rebuilds organizational resources to return to profitable levels.

Divestiture strategy
A corporate-level strategy through which a company sells off a portion of an operation, usually a division or profit center that is not performing to expectations.

Differentiation strategy
A business-level strategy through which a company develops products or services that are distinct and for which customers will pay a higher price than that of the competition.

Focused cost leadership strategy
A business-level strategy through which a company focuses on one group of customers and offers a low-price product or service.

Focused differentiation strategy
A business-level strategy through which a company focuses on one group of customers and offers unique or customized products that permit it to charge a higher price than that of the competition.

Strategic alliance
An arrangement in which two companies work together to achieve a common goal.

Joint venture
A business association formed by an express or implied agreement of two or more persons (including corporations) to accomplish a particular project, such as the construction of a building.

Merger
A type of acquisition in which two or more business entities are combined into one.

Subsidiary
A company owned or controlled by another company.

Retention ratio
The percentage of insurance policies renewed.

Time to Take the Next Step....

Congratulations! You have finished the assignments for this course.

If you haven't registered for your exam, you should do so right away while your new knowledge is fresh in your mind.

As another "next step," most students take the SMART Online Practice Exams found on our Web site. The SMART Online Practice Exam not only gives you practice questions, but also helps you learn to manage your time during an exam.

Good luck on your exam! And congratulations on your decision to invest in yourself and your career.